The Refugee in International Society

With the unrelenting unrest in places such as Iraq, Afghanistan and the Sudan, the plight of refugees has become an increasingly discussed topic in international relations. Why do we have refugees? When did the refugee 'problem' emerge? How can the refugee ever be reconciled with an international system that rests on sovereignty? Looking at three key periods – the inter-war period, the Cold War and the present day – Emma Haddad demonstrates how a specific image has defined the refugee since the international states system arose in its modern form and that refugees have thus been qualitatively the same over the course of history. This historical and normative approach suggests new ways to understand refugees and to formulate responses to them. By examining the issue from an international society perspective, this book highlights how refugees are an inevitable, if unanticipated, result of erecting political borders.

EMMA HADDAD is a Research Associate of the Refugee Studies Centre, Queen Elizabeth House, University of Oxford. She has worked as a Policy Advisor on the external relations of immigration and asylum in DG Justice, Freedom and Security at the European Commission. She obtained her Ph.D. from the European Institute at the London School of Economics and Political Science, for which she was awarded the British International Studies Association prize for the best thesis in International Studies. She has published on the conceptualisation of the refugee figure in the modern international states system, the English School and EU external policy on migration and asylum.

The Refugee in International Society

Between Sovereigns

Emma Haddad

CAMBRIDGE
UNIVERSITY PRESS

CAMBRIDGE UNIVERSITY PRESS
Cambridge, New York, Melbourne, Madrid, Cape Town, Singapore, São Paulo, Delhi

Cambridge University Press
The Edinburgh Building, Cambridge CB2 8RU, UK

Published in the United States of America by Cambridge University Press, New York

www.cambridge.org
Information on this title: www.cambridge.org/9780521688956

First published 2008

Printed in the United Kingdom at the University Press, Cambridge

A catalogue record for this publication is available from the British Library

ISBN 978-0-521-86888-4 hardback
ISBN 978-0-521-68895-6 paperback

For Mum and Dad

Romeo: Ha, banishment? Be merciful, say 'death'.
For exile hath more terror in his look,
Much more than death. Do not say 'banishment'.

Romeo and Juliet, William Shakespeare

Contents

Preface

The inspiration for this book may have been derived, perhaps subconsciously, from the ebb and flow of my family history. At the end of the nineteenth century, my maternal grandfather's family were victims of the Russian pogroms. They left Vilna, now Vilnius in Lithuania, and arrived in London. My great-grandfather did not accompany the family to London, but went to find work in South Africa. There he was given a British passport, since these were the years of the British Empire, and, two years later, arrived in Britain a naturalised citizen. He opened a shop in London's Soho, where my grandfather was born in 1920. At a similar time, my maternal grandmother's family was leaving Poland. A little later, in 1955, my paternal grandfather moved the family from Tunisia to the young Israel. Jews were coming under increasing hostility from Arab neighbours as part of the violent resistance to French colonial rule that erupted in 1954. With the rise of Arab nationalism, the young Israel was the new enemy and with it the Jews. As Jews arrived to settle in Israel, the plight of Palestinian refugees was only just beginning. People frequently ask me where my interest in the refugee question comes from. Daniel Warner's phrase, 'we are all refugees', couldn't be a more appropriate answer.

This book builds on Ph.D research completed at the London School of Economics and Political Science in 2004. I am grateful to the European Institute, which provided an excellent research environment and generous financial support throughout my Ph.D, and to friends and colleagues in the department, who knew just when to criticise or encourage. The stimulating discussion on the text with Professor James Mayall and Dr Chaloka Beyani and their helpful reactions were highly appreciated. My greatest debt during my Ph.D years is owed to my supervisor, Dr Jennifer Jackson-Preece, without whose analytical insights and constant support this book would not have been born. Parts of the revised text were presented at the European University Institute, the BISA conference, the UACES Brussels Seminar and the Refugee Studies Centre, and thanks goes to all fellow participants who provided constructive feedback. During the publishing process, I am thankful to the two anonymous readers whose comments on the manuscript helped enormously in transforming the text into book format. I am also extremely grateful to my editor, John Haslam, and his colleagues at Cambridge University Press for all their assistance and support.

Writing a book is only partly about giving feedback on research methodology and international relations theory. The other half is about providing the encouragement to continue to see the project through. This has come, as always, from my mother, Andrea, and father, Motti, from my siblings, Orit, Jacob and Hannah, and my grandparents, Val and Ed, to mention only a few. My niece, Sophia, came along in the final stages of preparing this book, and one day I will tell her all about the refugee and the English School. Finally, Dermot provided academic insights, advice and critical engagement with a topic unfamiliar to him, as well as copious amounts of support and encouragement to get to the end via words, food and drink, and all his love. I can only say thank you and offer to return the favour when the opportunity arises.

1   The refugee 'problem'

> Unaccepted where they are, unable to return whence they came.
> Leon Gordenker[1]

The 'problem' of refugees in a world of states is important in the real world, consequential for our understanding of a current issue that significantly affects lives. Refugees are individuals fleeing their homes due to conditions that exceed those considered 'normal', and policies formulated in their regard and attitudes towards them will in some cases mean the difference between life and death. The evolving international legal regime that surrounds the refugee highlights the continued importance of the issue to the international community. And the study of refugee issues is essential to our understanding of the significant impact the 'problem' now has on aspects of international and national politics, policy-making processes, human rights and development.

This book examines the concept of the refugee and demonstrates how she is an inevitable if unintended consequence of the international states system. It begins from the hypothesis that there is a fundamental and mutually constitutive link between the refugee concept and international society and then seeks to unravel their relationship. Analysing the articulation mechanisms employed in regard to the refugee over three periods, the book looks at how such mechanisms impinge on national and international politics, the idea of refugee protection and the discourse itself that surrounds the refugee and 'refugee studies', and argues that this conceptual and historical elaboration has important implications for our understanding of responses to the refugee.

---

[1] Leon Gordenker, *Refugees in International Politics* (Beckenham: Croom Helm, 1987), p. 213.

Much of the growing field of refugee studies tends to see the existence of the refugee as a sign of the international system going wrong. She is portrayed as a given, known concept who is created by illiberal govern-ance in contrast to the 'normal', rooted citizen. The international context in which the refugee emerges as a 'problem' is not questioned. This book maintains, instead, that the existence of modern political borders will ensure the constant (re-)creation of refugees. Accordingly, it regards the refugee as a contemporary concept that was made a per-manent feature of the international landscape with the consolidation of the modern system of nation-states.[2] It therefore disputes the much-favoured assumption that there has only been a refugee 'problem' in the post-war years and, similarly, that an international protection regime was instituted only with the formulation of the Geneva Convention Relating to the Status of Refugees in 1951.[3]

The refugee domain is a highly politicised and internationalised area. Mass movements of refugees are the result of various political and social changes that affect the entire international states system and not just developments within individual countries. Since it emerged as a modern 'problem' it became clear that the refugee issue was beyond the capacity of any one government to deal with effectively. As such the discipline sits between domestic and international politics and brings to the fore the interdependence between the two. How one country deals with the problem will have consequences for others and influence future relations between states. The term 'refugee' itself acknowledges the fact that, due to some kind of adverse conditions, home is no longer a safe place. This in turn implicates the home government, which should be responsible

---

[2] At times this book refers to a 'states system', at other times a 'nation-state system'. Indeed, it is generally understood that the prevailing rule of legitimacy of European international society has been national self-determination. However, it is evident that there are some states, such as the United Kingdom, Belgium and Spain, that do not necessarily see their existence as being based on national self-determination. Further, the complexity of the composition of some of the successor states of Yugoslavia and the Soviet Union, for example, defy the simple label 'nation-state'. In other words, it is acknowledged that there are other possible origins of legitimacy and that the 'nation-state' idea is not always applicable as a descriptive tool. In this regard, this book tends to use 'nation-state system' when it aims to make a specific point about identity in relation to the 'national citizen', and 'states system' more generally. This is broadly in line with the shift from and distinction made between the inter-war ideal of 'national self-determination', based largely on an ethnic concept of the nation, to the post-1945 principle of 'self-determination of peoples' that rests on a more civic understanding of the nation.

[3] United Nations Convention Relating to the Status of Refugees, *done* at Geneva on 28 July 1951 (189 UNTS 137), hereinafter 'the 1951 Convention'.

for protecting those who fall under its jurisdiction. Refugee status shows that the government is no longer able or willing to provide such a safeguard and the refugee must find an alternative source of protection. Hence in granting refugee status a host state automatically makes a statement about the country of origin, recognising a failure that could have serious political or economic repercussions between states. Morally speaking, the humanitarian demands of offering international protection to the refugee should override any other concerns, but reality shows that it is impossible to divorce the ethical and the political in the modern world of inter-state relations. The failure to respond adequately to refugee movements is largely influenced by the political and international nature of the problem.

Refugees represent a permanent feature of the international landscape. They are the human reminder of the failings of modern international society. Much has been written about the domestic concerns refugees raise, the potential burden on national economies that they pose and the threat to national identity and security that they can invoke, but the international aspect is frequently overlooked. It is important to understand how the refugee is located at the intersection between the international and the domestic, since in this respect the refugee acts to challenge not only questions of belonging and identity, but also disciplinary distinctions. Within an international system made up of dichotomies and grey areas between the internal and the external, the refugee brings to the fore the clash between pluralism and solidarism, communitarianism and cosmopolitanism, sovereign rights and human rights. According to Dowty and Loescher, refugees illustrate the thin boundary between the national and the international: 'A large-scale movement of people across national borders, under duress, internationalizes what might otherwise be purely domestic issues related to the causes of that movement.'[4] Although evidence of something 'going wrong' internally, the refugee's situation is of great international concern. Conceptually the individual should belong to a state. Once she falls out of the state–citizen relationship, the individual becomes an international individual and ward of the international community:

> There is no way of isolating oneself from the effects of gross violations abroad: they breed refugees, exiles, and dissidents who come knocking at our doors – and we must choose between bolting the doors, thus

[4] Alan Dowty and Gil Loescher, 'Refugee Flows as Grounds for International Action', *International Security* 21, 1 (1996), 44.

increasing misery and violence outside, and opening them, at some cost to our own well being.[5]

Not only is the international flavour of the refugee often obscured, so too is the environment in which refugee flows take place. Many studies examine the causal factors that instigate displacement, but this is done without taking into consideration the very set-up and workings of the states system in which such factors operate. Refugee flows are too often seen as isolated events, removed from the context which gives rise to them. This gives the impression that refugees are only created when things go wrong. However, what in fact is 'going wrong' when refugees appear is that the theory and practice of the international states system and the concept of sovereignty on which it relies are failing to coincide. It is a fundamental assumption of international society that states possess positive sovereignty and are therefore good for their citizens, yet these obligations are far from always met. When a gap is created between the positive sovereignty of the individual state and the negative sovereignty of international society in which this state is situated, the discrepancy causes a failure both domestically and internationally, and this leads to the creation of refugees. In other words, much of the literature fails to examine the relationship of the refugee with the very workings of international society. But without an international states system there would be no refugees; thus the one cannot be divorced from the other.

Further, many books tend to portray the refugee issue as a purely recent, post-Cold War phenomenon, different and distinguished from previous refugee movements. Certainly the issue is topical and timely, but it is not new. Those authors who do take an historical approach tend to start from the 1951 Convention 'moment', as if this marked the beginning of both contemporary refugee flows and any kind of formal international protection regime. The fact that the way an issue is understood cannot be divorced from history or the political environment is frequently overlooked. When one takes a critical look at the dynamics of different refugee episodes over the years, one is faced with an overwhelming sense of history repeating itself. There is no conceptual difference between the Russian refugees of the 1920s, the Jewish refugees of the 1930s, the Hungarian refugees of the 1950s, the Vietnamese refugees of the 1970s, the Rwandan refugees of the 1990s and the

---

[5] Stanley Hoffmann, *Duties Beyond Borders: On the Limits and Possibilities of Ethical International Politics* (New York: Syracuse University Press, 1981), p. 111.

4

Zimbabwean refugees of the dawn of the twenty-first century. Of course, contemporary refugee movements do have certain unique characteristics. As Miller rightly points out, 'international migration has significantly affected international relations from time immemorial, but its saliency has increased in the post-Cold War period'.[6] In this vein Gordenker notes the unprecedented and unparalleled flows of refugees we now witness, both in aggregate and in number of occurrences, the fact that large-scale migration often takes the form of permanent immigration with fewer and fewer refugees able to return home, the growth of transnational networks and the elaborate international framework that has developed so as to deal with the issue, and the definitional insufficiencies that have come to be associated with the problem.[7] Yet this is not a contemporary 'problem' that has emerged from nowhere. Past refugee flows were not completely unrelated.

Nor have the actors involved in any refugee movement changed: each episode still needs a home country, a displaced individual and a host country. Other actors may come and go, such as non-state actors in the role of persecutor or non-governmental organisations in the role of protector, but the three core actors remain constant. Different refugee movements have, however, met with differing responses from the international community, and while certain refugee movements have made the headlines and attracted assistance from the international community, others have not – for every refugee there is always a non-refugee who could be a refugee were the political circumstances and priorities different. Thus what has evolved and continues to evolve would seem to be the normative understanding of refugees, as shaped in part by shifting realpolitik, in part by the transforming and constructed nature of international politics which affects states' interests and identities. There have been three main phases in dealing with the issue of refugees in the twentieth century – the inter-war, the Cold War and the post-Cold War. Each reveals different ways of coping with the contradictions inherent in the nation-state system. But if new groups of people from different regions are now becoming refugees, normative understandings of who the refugee is and how to deal with her have not developed in a vacuum. Rather, we can distinguish a continuum from

---

[6] Mark J. Miller, 'International Migration in Post-Cold War International Relations', in Bimal Ghosh (ed.), *Managing Migration: Time for a New International Regime?* (Oxford University Press, 2000), 27.

[7] Gordenker, *Refugees in International Politics*, pp. 49–59.

the early inter-war days. Comparing and contrasting state responses to the refugee in these periods allows for a better understanding of the refugee question.

Much research in the refugee studies field sets out, quite justifiably, to contribute to better policy. Indeed, where is the justification or purpose in pursuing academic work in refugee studies if the end result is not to offer something, sooner or later, for the benefit of those we are studying? Working towards 'solutions' to the refugee 'problem' would seem the obvious ultimate goal in a field that so directly impinges on people's lives. But research that proposes a fairer asylum determination procedure, a better aid distribution system or a fairer arrangement of responsibility-sharing is not the only valuable type of research. One cannot hope to improve protection mechanisms if the roots of the refugee 'problem' are not accurately grasped. As has been said, 'we cannot develop good policy without good theory and these are turbulent times for both'.[8] To adequately grasp these roots we must at times take a step back from what is generally taken for granted and considered normal, and question what it is we are really trying to study, how we perceive the object of study, and how exactly it has become an object of study. This means making room for research that both complements and challenges mainstream approaches. Attempting to provide a better grasp of some of the complexities behind the refugee label, to point at how it has been twisted, turned and shaped over the years and how the refugee identity has evolved accordingly, could be a step in the right direction to determining whether general understandings of how to 'deal' with current refugee movements are really the best ways of approaching the issue. Reconsidering the interplay between the refugee and her surroundings and how the two define and redefine one another is therefore crucial not only for academic research but also, hopefully, for future policy considerations. In particular, if by suggesting a mutually constitutive relationship between international society and the refugee we can begin to understand the inevitability of refugee flows, then the ad hoc nature of each experience could perhaps be avoided. Instead we could increase our understanding more generally regarding where and why refugee movements occur and, accordingly, be better prepared to deal with them.

---

[8] Jon Bennett, 'Internal Displacement in Context: The Emergence of a New Politics', in Wendy Davies (ed.), *Rights Have No Borders: Worldwide Internal Displacement* (Geneva and Oslo: Global IDP Survey/Norwegian Refugee Council, 1998), 15.

Refugees are not the consequence of a breakdown in the system of separate states, rather they are an inevitable if unanticipated part of international society. As long as there are political borders constructing separate states and creating clear definitions of insiders and outsiders, there will be refugees. Such individuals do not fit into the state–citizen–territory hierarchy, but are forced, instead, into the gaps *between* states. Indeed, it is the somewhat imperfect mixture of sovereignty, borders and territory that makes the state system responsible for the creation of refugees, rather than other systems generated by the complex interactions of human communities under the condition of late modernity. States can be differentiated from other forms of belonging by their attachment to sovereignty, borders and territory. Refugees therefore pose a problem for the international community quite different from that of other foreigners. National minority groups may strive to achieve their own state in accordance with the principle of national self-determination, thus challenging the territorial sovereignty of the state in which they find themselves. But they continue to belong to a political body and, accordingly, leave the states system itself untouched. Refugees, on the other hand, highlight that deviations from the 'normal' model of international society are in fact a possibility. They are misfits whose identity fails to correspond to that of any established nation-state,[9] having been pushed into the gaps in the system. The refugee's identity is forged precisely by her lack of belonging, her status as an 'outsider' and her position between, rather than within, sovereign states.

Other foreigners such as migrants and immigrants may of course present a challenge to the identity or ethnic make-up of a community. Yet their transnational movement has been one of choice and they remain rooted in the 'normal' state–citizen relationship. The refugee, in contrast, has had no choice in leaving her country of origin. She has been forced outside the domestic political community of her state of origin and arrives at the borders of a host state requesting entry. Thus there is an added moral obligation imposed on states by the existence of refugees – the humanitarian demand to admit outsiders into their territory and allow them to belong, at least in part, to their political community. Further, since the decision to leave her home has been taken for her, the refugee may wish to retain her original identity to a

---

[9] Aristide R. Zolberg, 'The Formation of New States as a Refugee-generating Process', *Annals of the American Academy of Political and Social Science* 467 (1983), 31.

greater degree than other 'outsiders'. She may have less of a desire to reinvent or reimagine a new identity or to adopt that of her host state; rather, she remembers her home with nostalgia and may try to act to ensure her ties with her native culture and identity survive. In this way the refugee lives between her country of origin and her host country, trapped by definition in a no man's land of hope and memory.

The refugee's marginal position also forces us to question ideas of identity and belonging in the international states system, and of the distinction between inside and outside. In her liminal position,[10] the refugee is part of the system yet excluded from it, an integral element of international society but denied full access to it. In this way she is both an insider and an outsider, existing at the borders and between sovereigns. She is a challenge to conventional conceptions of membership in political communities. As Rajaram has noted:

> Consideration of the way refugees are consigned to the margins, and the reasons for this, throws into stark relief notions of home, culture, identity, space and time that, in one way or another, are the raw material for outlining and reinforcing the theory and praxis of ethics and politics in international relations.[11]

Whereas traditional books in the 'refugee studies' field have overlooked this potentially illuminating nature of the refugee figure, recent work has begun to approach the field with a more critical eye, and it is in this vein that this book begins. Refusing to understand the concept of the refugee as a pure, given, uncontested figure, it maintains instead that the refugee is considered as such – a moving, exceptional figure – due to the way in which we imagine political life and our way of belonging to it. Indeed, there is a growing literature in the field covering a wide range of disciplines.[12] But it is really only when we start to

---

[10] Liisa H. Malkki, *Purity and Exile: Violence, Memory, and National Cosmology among Hutu Refugees in Tanzania* (University of Chicago Press, 1995), p. 1.

[11] Prem Kumar Rajaram, 'Exile and Desire: Refugees, Aesthetics and the Territorial Borders of International Relations', unpublished Ph.D thesis, London School of Economics (2002), p. 17.

[12] There are many different domains that fall into the 'refugee studies' category. For law, see for example Guy Goodwin-Gill, *The Refugee in International Law*, 2nd edn (Oxford: Clarendon Press, 1996); James C. Hathaway, *The Law of Refugee Status* (Toronto: Butterworths, 1991); Chaloka Beyani, *Human Rights Standards and the Free Movement of People Within States* (Oxford University Press, 2000); and Atle Grahl-Madsen, *The Status of Refugees in International Law*, volumes I and II (Leiden: Sijthoff, 1966 and 1972); for European asylum policy, see for example Sandra Lavenex, *The Europeanisation of Refugee Policies: Between Human Rights and Internal Security* (Aldershot: Ashgate, 2001);

venture out of the traditional refugee literature that we can begin to understand the inter-disciplinary nature of the subject and the complexity of the issues involved. Until recently there has been a bias towards the policy-analytic tradition and empirical case studies which, although interesting and important, fail to provide a theoretical background to the domain. Three key authors have attempted to cross bridges between the disciplines that impinge upon 'refugee studies', as well as to force an expansion of the field away from the case study bias, and this book takes their work as its starting point. It sets out to fill the gap between the main assumptions of Gil Loescher, Liisa Malkki and Nevzat Soguk, all of whom ask fascinating questions and bring to light many important issues and ways of understanding the refugee issue, but stop short of the line of this thesis: that the refugee is an inevitable if unanticipated part of international society, and that the conceptual elaboration of this idea is important for our understanding of the refugee and responses to her.

Malkki's work is highly constructive in opening the way for refugee studies that move beyond the one-dimensional acceptance of the dehistoricised, depoliticised, standard refugee figure. She notes:

> Nationalism and racism, xenophobia and immigration policies, state practices of violence and war, censorship and silencing, human rights and challenges to state sovereignty, 'development' discourse and humanitarian interventions, citizenship and cultural or religious identities, travel and diaspora, and memory and historicity are just some of the issues and practices that generate the inescapably relevant context of human displacement today.[13]

Malkki makes these kinds of 'background information' and 'root causes' her concern, showing the impossibility of discussing the

---

for anthropology, see especially the work of Liisa Malkki, in particular *Purity and Exile* and 'Refugees and Exile: From "Refugee Studies" to the National Order of Things', *Annual Review of Anthropology* 24 (1995), 495–523; for international security, see especially Gil Loescher, *Refugee Movements and International Security*, Adelphi Paper 268, International Institute for Strategic Studies (London: Brassey's, 1992); and Myron Weiner (ed.), *International Migration and Security* (Boulder, Colo.: Westview Press, 1993); and for historical overviews of the refugee in the twentieth century, see Michael R. Marrus, *The Unwanted: European Refugees in the Twentieth Century* (Oxford University Press, 1985); Gil Loescher, *Beyond Charity: International Cooperation and the Global Refugee Crisis* (Oxford University Press, 1993); Claudena Skran, *Refugees in Interwar Europe: The Emergence of a Regime* (Oxford: Clarendon Press, 1995); and Aristide R. Zolberg, Astri Suhrke and Sergio Aguayo, *Escape from Violence: Conflict and the Refugee Crisis in the Developing World* (Oxford University Press, 1989).

[13] Malkki, 'Refugees and Exile', 496.

refugee in isolation without taking into consideration surrounding, influencing factors. She notes how the refugee is outside the state–nation–territory trinity, an exception and anomaly in relation to the national citizen. Soguk's work follows a similar thinking. In analysing how the refugee has always been an expression of statist politics, he forces us to question the constructed nature of the discourse surrounding the refugee figure.[14] Meanwhile, Loescher's work, although more in line with that of the so-called 'conventional' refugee studies literature in providing somewhat factual, empirical accounts, opens up the third space for this study. Loescher has demonstrated the refugee's place in international relations, her link to international security issues and the need to understand the refugee as an issue of international politics 'beyond charity'.[15] That which all three authors point towards but fail to enunciate and take to its logical conclusion, however, is the fact that the refugee is tied up in and with international society and that the two cannot be separated. The refugee is the outsider in Malkki's 'national order of things',[16] constructed by Soguk's statist politics and needing Loescher's international and political response to even begin to be understood. But the authors fall short of demonstrating the consequences of their claims – that the refugee is an inevitable if unanticipated side-effect of the international states system at work, since there is a mutually constitutive relationship between the refugee's identity and the identity of international society.

With all this in mind, this book sets out to answer three interrelated questions – the why, the when and the how:

(i) *Why do we get refugees?* In a world of labels, where did the refugee label come from? What had to occur for the definition to be born? What are the conditions needed for the refugee to be created? Can these conditions be eliminated or is there some underlying factor that makes refugees a continual possibility? How does the refugee fit into an international system made up of paradoxes, contradictions and ambiguities?

(ii) *When did the refugee 'problem' emerge?* Is the contemporary refugee related to earlier exiles, migrants and other groups of displaced persons,

---

[14] Nevzat Soguk, *States and Strangers: Refugees and Displacements of Statecraft* (Minneapolis: University of Minnesota Press, 1999).

[15] See respectively Gil Loescher, 'Introduction: Refugee Issues in International Relations', in Gil Loescher and Laila Monahan (eds.), *Refugees and International Relations* (Oxford University Press, 1989); *Refugee Movements and International Security; Beyond Charity;* and *The UNHCR in World Politics: A Perilous Path* (Oxford University Press, 2001).

[16] Malkki, *Purity and Exile*, p. 2.

or is she a purely modern concept? Why did the refugee figure emerge when she did? What is the relation between refugee movements in the early part of the twentieth century and more recent ones of the end of the century? Are there similarities? If so, why the current portrayal of a new 'asylum crisis' in the West? What kind of image of the refugee was constructed with the formulation of the legal regime surrounding the refugee at the start of the Cold War era? And why the importance given to the '1951 moment'?

(iii) *How can the refugee ever be reconciled with an international system that rests on sovereignty?* If the refugee is a creation of a system of separate sovereign states, can the issue ever be ultimately resolved? If refugees were a sign of the system 'going wrong', would we not have found a definitive solution after all these years of experience if there was one? If the concept of asylum inherently clashes with the concept of sovereignty, what chance is there for refugee protection? Why did a humanitarian regime grow up in the first place? Why are states prepared or persuaded to concede parts of their sovereignty for the sake of other states' citizens?

This book views the refugee concept from an English School perspective following the work of scholars including Bull, Wight and Jackson, a perspective that regards the modern international system as an international society comprising a number of individual states.[17] International society is made up of values, rules and institutions, such as mutual recognition of sovereignty, the belief in the equality of all states, the principle of non-intervention and international law, that are commonly accepted by all states in the system. These make it possible for the international system to function and keep in check the potential for disorder and inter-state conflict, which could otherwise arise from the

---

[17] Bull and other English School proponents are keen to point out how international society is more than a group of states forming a 'system', in which the behaviour of one state affects the others. Rather, it is a 'society' in that states 'have established by dialogue and consent common rules and institutions for the conduct of their relations, and recognize their common interest in maintaining these arrangements' – Hedley Bull and Adam Watson, *The Expansion of International Society* (Oxford: Clarendon Press, 1984), p. 1. This book, however, uses the phrases 'international society' and 'international system' somewhat interchangeably. Whilst not denying the analytical specificity of the idea of an international 'society', it maintains that this society has elements of a system. For international society to function and keep some degree of order, institutions such as diplomacy and sovereignty must interact and further the existence of separate political entities. If we assume that international society is also a kind of system, we leave room for the conjecture that this system could go wrong.

inherently anarchical character of the system. Indeed, the international system knows order without government. In Bull's words:

> A society of states (or international society) exists when a group of states, conscious of certain common interests and common values, form a society in the sense that they conceive themselves to be bound by a common set of rules in their relations with one another, and share in the working of common institutions.[18]

Within the English School's conception of international society actors have ideas of right and wrong. In addition to the wish to survive as an independent political entity, the state also acts as a moral international agent, such that its moral consciousness may transcend its territorial borders. Humanitarian intervention and the use of force may well take place, therefore, and will not simply be a cloak for power politics. The English School does not deny, however, that national interest and power politics play a role in international society, nor that at the other end of the spectrum there are elements of idealist aspirations, as contained for example in the preamble of the United Nations Charter and its search for international justice. Indeed, the English School approach sees the foreign policies of state-leaders addressing realist concerns for their own state and citizens, Grotian concerns for international order and human justice and idealist hopes for humanity and the globe as a whole.[19] In other words, the morality of states means a certain responsibility for, in order of priority, the *raison d'état* or the national interest, the *raison de système* or the international interest, the *raison d'humanité* or the humanitarian interest and the *raison de justice* or the global interest.[20] It is when states try to combine these concerns that moral dilemmas or 'situational ethics' occur,[21] and hard choices have to be made – exactly the context in which refugee movements occur. And, as

---

[18] Hedley Bull, *The Anarchical Society: A Study of Order in World Politics*, 2nd edn (Basingstoke: Macmillan Press, 1995), p. 13.

[19] These are similar to Wight's three positions: the rationalist desire for international order is constantly being undermined by the realist pursuit of self-interest and the revolutionist quest for global justice. These positions, notes Wight, are intellectually distinct and internally coherent, but not mutually exclusive: they 'are streams, with eddies and cross-currents, sometimes interlacing and never long confined to their own river bed' – Martin Wight, *International Theory: The Three Traditions* (Leicester University Press, 1991), p. 260.

[20] Tonny Brems Knudsen, 'The English School of International Relations and the International Society Approach', in Kerstin Imbusch and Klaus Segbers (eds.), *International Relations Online* (Free University of Berlin, 2002), 5.

[21] Robert Jackson, *The Global Covenant: Human Conduct in a World of States* (Oxford University Press, 2000), pp. 143–8.

Mayall has noted, 'while the doctrine of sovereignty establishes ... the moral accountability of the state, it does not assume that the decisions of the sovereign are necessarily moral'.[22]

The English School perspective provides a convincing account of the historical origins of the international states system and the main institutional framework of international society, which is important for demonstrating the existence of the refugee as a concept.[23] It offers a useful analytical platform from which state action and interaction can be evaluated and future state action to some extent predicted. It shows how state behaviour is both enabled and constrained within international society via shared understandings of what is normal, rational, legitimate and just. Realist accounts of the international system would not recognise the standing of the individual in international relations; only states have rights, and the rights and duties of individuals are stipulated by state-leaders. The only duty of the state is to look after itself and its subjects in the interests of national security. Hence humanitarian intervention, which entails the use of force to defend non-nationals and the common good, is neither likely nor desirable. Within the English School international political and legal order based on the coexistence of sovereign states, there is room for other independent actors such as individuals. In this regard it is valuable for a study of the refugee's position vis-à-vis individual states and the international community as a whole. It allows us to understand the inherent contradictions states face in both understanding the refugee as a concept and offering protection to the refugee as an individual, drawing attention to the clash between the humanitarian needs of the refugee and the sovereign interests of the state.

Yet there are some weaknesses in adopting this approach. The English School perspective on the international system tends to overstate the assumption of a uniform, static international society, while

---

[22] James Mayall, *Nationalism and International Society* (Cambridge University Press, 1990), p. 5.

[23] It should be noted, however, that although the international society approach is a useful tool for understanding international relations, it should not be considered an impartial account of history. Rather, it makes certain statements about how contemporary practice has evolved 'under the guise of an objective neutrality' – Mayall, *Nationalism and International Society*, p. 16. To maintain that international society provides order in an otherwise anarchical environment, therefore, 'is not to prove that another structure would not be capable of doing likewise' – Jennifer Jackson-Preece, *National Minorities and the European Nation-States System* (Oxford: Clarendon Press, 1998), p. 9.

reality shows sovereignty and boundaries to be more blurred than such a perspective would suggest. It points to the refugee as an anomaly in an already constituted territorial system. This has a tendency to reify the concepts of sovereignty, the state and citizenship as natural pre-given features, and actors' identities and interests as fixed. However, the concept of sovereignty and the structure of an international system based on sovereign entities are not static, and 'sovereignty' and the 'state' are ambiguous and dynamic concepts. An analysis of contemporary world politics, of which refugees are such a fundamental part, indicates that the distinction between here and there is not all that clear. Indeed, as Walker notes, 'once upon a time, the world was not as it is [and] the patterns of inclusion and exclusion we now take for granted are historical innovations ... [The] fixing of unity and diversity, or inside and outside, or space and time is not natural ... nor is it inevitable'.[24] Shifts in statist conceptions of the refugee are important in highlighting how the concept changes over time and space, being influenced by the changing nature of sovereignty and continually evolving state interests. The refugee's identity is in constant flux, being transformed and reinterpreted according to decisions made about who constitutes the enemy at any one particular time.[25] Refugee-producing conditions may be formed in one area or at one time due to prevailing perceptions of 'self' and 'other', but may then shift to another area or disappear and then resurface at another time in line with different decisions states make about the enemy, the 'other'. As states 'are constantly maintained, defended, attacked, reproduced, undermined, and relegitimised on a daily basis',[26] so the refugee as a concept is continually remade and reinterpreted. Since the refugee relies on sovereignty and sovereignty relies on the refugee, it follows that both concepts will also move, ambiguously, between definitions. Thus the English School approach helps us understand the refugee as an outsider, an 'other', but it is not so helpful in telling us why the representation of this other is different at different times.

Although the international society approach emphasises a normative system, therefore, it offers little as regards how these norms actually shape actors' identities and actions within the system. It also ignores the

---

[24] R. B. J. Walker, *Inside / Outside: International Relations as Political Theory* (Cambridge University Press, 1993), p. 179.

[25] Mika Luoma-aho, 'Carl Schmitt and the Transformation of the Political Subject', *The European Legacy* 5, 5 (2002), 705.

[26] Walker, *Inside / Outside*, p. 168.

role of changing international norms on both state interests and refugee protection, such that it has arguably been less able to develop an explanatory model for norm creation and diffusion within international society. In an attempt to fill some of these gaps, the English School approach can be married with elements of the constructivist approach to international relations. Constructivism examines the social fabric of world politics.[27] It sees world politics as socially constructed, whereby agents or states, and structures or global norms, interact and are mutually constituted.[28] States' actions are seen to be 'reflective acts of social creation, not just enactment of pre-programmed scripts'.[29] The focus is on how international norms 'result in identities and interests being formed in the processes of interaction rather than being formed prior to interaction'.[30]

The constructivist approach is a useful and complementary tool that lends itself well to an examination of the role of norms and identity in refugee politics. It asks us to look at how identities and interests evolve and, accordingly, how and why statist perceptions of refugees and the refugee issue change over time and space. According to this approach state perceptions of the refugee 'problem' are influenced by 'inter-subjective practices',[31] which include norms and ideas, that socialise states and impact on states' interests and identities. Behaviour, interests and relationships are socially constructed; thus they can, and do, change. The norm of refugee protection acts to redefine state interests and identities towards refugees and forces a rethinking of concepts of the 'other' and of bounded political communities. If the refugee is seen as a threat, this threat is constructed according to social processes and the identities and interests within the states system at one particular time, rather than being natural or inevitable.[32] A global norm of refugee protection leads states to offer protection to non-citizens in spite of political or socio-economic factors that would suggest they act to the

[27] Jeffrey T. Checkel, 'The Constructivist Turn in International Relations Theory', *World Politics* 50, 2 (1998), 324.
[28] Checkel, 'The Constructivist Turn', 326.
[29] John Gerard Ruggie, *Constructing the World Polity: Essays on International Institutionalisation* (London and New York: Routledge, 1998), p. 4.
[30] Steve Smith, 'New Approaches to International Relations', in John Baylis and Steve Smith (eds.), *The Globalization of World Politics: An Introduction to International Relations* (Oxford University Press, 1997), 183.
[31] Smith, 'New Approaches', 183.
[32] Edward Newman, 'Human Security and Constructivism', *International Studies Perspectives* 2 (2001), 247–8.

contrary. States accept international norms and internalise them in domestic institutions, the constructivists tell us, because they are socialised to perceive such norms as legitimate. Accepting norms due to political pressure or for reasons of self-interest may well change state behaviour, but only when states begin to apprehend the norms as valid is their very identity changed.

The English School and the constructivist approaches to the study of the refugee are overlapping. Indeed Reus-Smit has suggested how constructivism can complement the English School by adding an important sociological dimension to the School's theory, and how, with their respective focus on norms and values, the two can learn much from each other.[33] There are three important similarities to be drawn out. First, both assume the state as the principal unit of study and the central actor, the identity of which, represented by the concept of sovereignty, 'has no meaning outside of the ideas and practices of the society of states where the rules of membership and succession are located'.[34] Both approaches show how states not only form a society through their interaction; moreover the identity of these states is shaped by the existence of this society. As Dunne notes, 'a central tenet of the English School is the belief that the agents are socialised by the structure'.[35] In the words of Wendt international society 'is what states make of it'.[36] The English School takes sovereignty and non-intervention as constitutive of international society, such that international society is sustained by the reproduction of these practices. In other words, the principles on which international society rests not only protect the independence of individual states, but also in observing them states reproduce both themselves and international society. Brown further notes that 'there is a sense in which the state and the society of states are seen as "co-constituted"'.[37] Actors who work in the state's name, for example in signing treaties, both affirm the state's sovereign identity and participate in the reproduction of international

---

[33] Christian Reus-Smit, 'Imagining Society: Constructivism and the English School', *British Journal of Politics and International Relations* 4, 3 (2002), 487–509.

[34] Timothy Dunne, *Inventing International Society: A History of the English School* (Basingstoke: Macmillan Press, 1998), p. 187.

[35] Dunne, *Inventing International Society*, p. 10.

[36] Alexander Wendt, 'Anarchy Is What States Make of It', *International Organisation* 46, 2 (1992).

[37] Chris Brown, 'World Society and the English School: An "International Society" Perspective on World Society', *European Journal of International Relations* 7, 4 (2001), 434.

society.[38] Wendt further points out that 'sovereignty norms are now so far taken for granted, so natural, that it is easy to overlook the extent to which they are both presupposed by an ongoing artifact of practice'.[39] But proclaiming the concept of sovereignty itself as a constitutive principle of international society means assuming a constructivist relationship between sovereignty and international society: without sovereignty and its corollary, the rule of non-intervention, there would be no society of states.[40]

The second similarity between the approaches is their focus on the normative context within which states operate. They interrogate the meaning of the international system according to the inter-subjective practices through which it is constituted. As Wight has observed, if there is an international society then 'there is an order of some kind to be maintained, or even developed',[41] thus the objective of English School theorists can be seen as a type of normative enquiry.[42] For the effective operation of common values, rules and institutions, and the operation of international society as a whole, norms such as international law and diplomacy are necessary, which in turn 'presuppose an international social consciousness'.[43] Moreover, according to international society theorists the society of states has a reason for its existence: the desirability of constituting a rational political order to allow for human flourishing. This may be according to the solidarist conception of the common good of humanity as a whole, or the requirement to allow for the pluralist flourishing of different conceptions of this good. The very fact, then, that the arrangement does not just happen to be the case, once again points to the social construction of the international system.[44]

Finally, English School and constructivist accounts both recognise the contingent nature of political and social 'reality', accepting that if reality is conditional it can change.[45] As an early English School thinker said in 1946, 'few things are permanent in history; and it would be rash

---

[38] Timothy Dunne, 'The Social Construction of International Society', *European Journal of International Relations* 1, 3 (1995), 379.

[39] Wendt, 'Anarchy', 412–13.   [40] Dunne, 'The Social Construction', 378.

[41] Martin Wight, 'Western Values in International Relations', in Butterfield, Herbert and Wight, Martin (eds.), *Diplomatic Investigations: Essays in the Theory of International Politics* (London: Allen & Unwin, 1966), 103.

[42] Dunne, *Inventing International Society*, p. 10.   [43] Wight, 'Western Values', 97.

[44] Brown, 'World Society', 428–9.   [45] Dunne, 'The Social Construction', 374.

to assume that the territorial unit of power is one of them'.[46] We can view the normative basis of international society as a human construct constantly being reshaped and recreated. This is a type of ongoing process or system, which has the potential to regress as well as to progress – a return to the Hobbesian state of nature is feasible if the recurrence and repetition of international life is disrupted. As Mayall has argued, 'the contemporary society of states … is an historical creation; its members share preoccupations, which is to say memories, that their predecessors did not entertain, [which is] to accept that the character of international society will change'.[47] Thus the English School and constructivist approaches work well together, addressing different aspects of the refugee issue and serving different purposes. The English School approach is fundamental for examining the refugee issue in terms of a territorial and international discourse. The constructivist approach can be better employed when we wish to move to the identity and domestic discourse that surrounds the refugee. The refugee draws on both approaches since she sits uncomfortably between domestic and international politics, at the point where inside and outside converge and become blurred. We need the international society perspective to explain the existence of the refugee as a construction of modern political borders. Yet she can also be imagined as a social threat, an outsider in that part of the international system which is made up of ideas, constructions and identities, and in this regard the constructivist approach is useful.

Among the literature written in the English School tradition, the concept of an international society has been applied to many different normative issues – Wheeler and humanitarian intervention, Jackson-Preece and minorities, Buzan and security, Vincent and human rights, and Jackson and failed states are just some examples. A specific study on the refugee written from an English School perspective is lacking. The refugee issue is of fundamental importance both to international relations and international politics, and the English School offers a good approach for research on such normative issues. Meanwhile, it has been noted that the current constructivist literature fails to 'give equal attention to the bad things in world politics that are socially constructed', with a tendency to consider only 'ethically good norms'.[48] Recent work

---

[46] E. H. Carr cited in Dunne, 'The Social Construction', 374.
[47] Mayall, *Nationalism and International Society*, p. 3.
[48] Checkel, 'The Constructivist Turn', 339.

is starting to take this into account – Rae's analysis on state formation and 'pathological homogenisation',[49] for example, gives attention to the role of social construction in ethnic conflict. An account of the 'refugee problem' using elements of the constructivist approach should accordingly help fill a gap in the literature further.

The remainder of this book is divided into three main sections, the first conceptual, the second historical and the third contemporary. In the conceptual analysis, chapter 2 first examines the definition of the refugee and the limitations of attempts at labelling, before suggesting a working definition suited to the aims of this book. Chapter 3 goes on to look at the refugee's position within the international states system, examining how the concept of this type of 'other' has developed alongside the evolution of the modern sovereign state. And chapter 4 places the refugee concept within a rights discourse, so as to ask what kind of international society the refugee inhabits and the motivations behind state action towards displaced persons. In the historical analysis, the book traces the shifts and continuities in the normative understanding of the refugee within international society in two key periods of refugee regimentation. Chapter 5 examines the inter-war period when the modern concept of the refugee was consolidated and a protection regime instigated, while chapter 6 then moves on to the Cold War era, during which changes in the structure of international society caused transformations in who was and was not imagined to be included in the refugee concept. In the contemporary analysis, chapter 7 brings together the normative understanding of the refugee concept set out in part I and the historical analysis of part II to look at the contemporary refugee discourse and examine the paradigm shifts in how international society now confronts the 'problem' of refugee protection. To illustrate how the theory fits with the contemporary reality, it analyses recent experiments with refugee policy at the European Union level. Finally, chapter 8 draws some conclusions, looking at how the refugee is finding a balance between security and humanitarian concerns in the twenty-first century and suggesting how the conceptual and historical analysis set out in the book can help find new directions for policy.

---

[49] Heather Rae, *State Identities and the Homogenisation of Peoples* (Cambridge University Press, 2002).

PART I

The refugee: a conceptual analysis

2   Who is (not) a refugee?

> Within the repertoire of humanitarian concern, refugee now constitutes one of the most powerful labels. From the first procedure of status determination – who is a refugee? – to the structural determinants of life chances which this identity then engenders, labels infuse the world of refugees.
>
> Roger Zetter[1]

In his provocatively entitled book, *Women, Fire and Dangerous Things*, Lakoff observes that 'categorization is not a matter to be taken lightly'.[2] The categorisation of concepts that are at once descriptive, normative and political is perhaps the most tricky. The refugee 'problem' is, first and foremost, one of categorisation, of making distinctions. None of the discussions in the field – among politicians, policy-makers or academics – can proceed without an idea of who exactly we are talking about when we apply the label 'refugee'. We use the term freely, with 'refugeehood' a seemingly popularly understood condition to the extent that it applies to around 8.4 million individuals across the world.[3] Of course, 'refugees' are forced migrants who have been granted an internationally recognised legal status. However, despite the use of the term 'refugee' in popular everyday speech, the actual meaning behind the concept remains unclear.

The issue is not helped by the fact that debates in the 'refugee studies' field span such a wealth of disciplines. This offers some explanation as

---

[1] Roger Zetter, 'Labelling Refugees: Forming and Transforming a Bureaucratic Identity', *Journal of Refugee Studies* 4, 1 (1991), 39.

[2] George Lakoff, *Women, Fire and Dangerous Things: What Categories Reveal about the Mind* (University of Chicago Press, 1987), p. 5.

[3] UNHCR, '2005 Global Refugee Trends: Statistical Overview of Populations of Refugees, Asylum-seekers, Internally Displaced Persons, Stateless Persons, and Other Persons of Concern to UNHCR' (Geneva: UNHCR, 2006), 3.

to why there should be so many definitions. But is the underlying reason in fact due to the impossibility of finding one essentialist definition? If so, can the operational definitions from across the disciplines differ without being in contradiction to each other, since they are trying to do different jobs? Or does the existence of a multitude of definitions indicate that they are all somewhat unsatisfactory? The problem in fact becomes one of how to define a concept that is labelled differently according to context and discipline. How to name a concept which defies definition, since it is impossible to make generalisations about the vast array of horrific events that force individuals to become refugees? Moreover, in a field linked to humans and human suffering, how can we avoid making the refugee simply an instrument of academic enquiry and instead ensure that the defining process serves the refugee herself?

This chapter begins with a look at the conceptual confusion surrounding the term 'refugee' by examining some of the many existing definitions. Next, it analyses the effects of the definition for both the refugee and the actor bestowing the label, before assessing some of the drawbacks of current approaches that attempt to define the refugee. It then briefly discusses the implications of the gender debate in the refugee field. Finally, it constructs a new definition of the 'refugee' which assumes that the fundamental criterion necessary for refugee status is a breakdown in the state–citizen relationship within a sustaining political community, an assumption which forms the main contention of this book.

Conceptual confusion

The 'impenetrable jungle' of semantics that surrounds the refugee, notes Tabori, includes a host of synonyms: 'displace, send out, exclude with dislodgement, eviction, ejectment, deportation, expatriation, relegation, extradition [and] excommunication'.[4] The domain is further complicated by the abundance of words and labels used in everyday parlance, and in the media in particular, to discuss 'refugees' and associated issues of 'asylum', words that have become so intertwined and conflated that it becomes continually harder to distinguish between them: economic migrants, illegal immigrants, asylum-seekers,

---

[4] Paul Tabori, *The Anatomy of Exile: A Semantic and Historical Study* (London: Harrap and Co., 1972), p. 23.

displaced persons, political refugees, bogus asylum-seekers, stateless persons, B-refugees, *de facto* refugees – the list goes on. Indeed, according to Shacknove, the current persistence of the 'refugee problem' in international politics and unsuccessful attempts to respond to it is only partly attributable to politics or questions of resources: 'conceptual confusion – about the meaning of refugeehood, its causes, and its management – also contributes to the misery of both refugee and host and to the inflammation of international tension'.[5] In talking of the 'refugee' we need an appreciation of the fact that the concept is both descriptive and normative. To employ the term 'refugee' is both to describe it and ascribe a value to it. It is a concept that has entered into both our explanations and valuations of political life. Yet to describe is not simply to name but to characterise, and this characterisation inevitably takes place from a certain perspective according to certain interests, objectives or criteria. The 'refugee' will always be shaped in part by the view from which she is being defined. A 'descriptive point of view', as Connolly observes, does not exist.[6]

As with any definition, contexts are crucial. But contexts, notes Mayall, are loaded: 'in human relations ... everything worth knowing is saturated with specific meanings and significances[:] there is no such thing as context-free knowledge'.[7] The politician, for example, would prefer a narrower definition and may act to limit the scope of any definition by tightening the procedural and substantive requirements necessary for the individual to satisfy the criteria for refugee status. A wide definition of who falls into the category 'refugee' may increase the potential burden on the host state, while accepting a greater failure on the part of the state of origin. A narrow definition, on the other hand, runs the risk of denying protection and assistance to individuals in need and thus not fulfilling basic moral and humanitarian obligations. The granting of refugee status has therefore come to mean that asylum is more an 'entitlement' than 'a discretionary bestowal of political grace'.[8] As Goodwin-Gill notes, 'in practice, satisfying the relevant criteria will indicate entitlement to the pertinent rights or benefits'.[9]

---

[5] Andrew E. Shacknove, 'Who Is a Refugee?', *Ethics* 95 (1985), 276.

[6] William E. Connolly, *The Terms of Political Discourse*, 2nd edn (Princeton University Press, 1983), pp. 22–5.

[7] Mayall, *Nationalism and International Society*, p. 6.

[8] D. Martin, 'The Refugee Concept: On Definitions, Politics, and the Careful Use of a Scarce Resource', in H. Adelman (ed.), *Refugee Policy: Canada and the United States* (Toronto: York Lanes Press, 1991), 35.

[9] Goodwin-Gill, *The Refugee in International Law*, p. 2.

Hence asylum and refugee status is now 'a scarce resource' the scarcity of which, however, is political and not physical.[10]

Following Connolly's useful discussion in *The Terms of Political Discourse*, the term 'refugee' can be described as an 'essentially contested concept'.[11] It causes disagreement, first because it is appraisive in character and involves value judgements; second, because it is internally complex, comprising a changing set of ingredients that are themselves relatively complex and open-ended – persecution, state, international, forced and protection, for example; and third, because the rules applying to the definition of the concept are relatively open, making a 'full and definitive resolution' hard to achieve.[12] Further, since refugees must cross an international border, they cannot flee their country of origin unless accepted in another state. Quite literally, in a world made up of a set of mutually exclusive states or 'membership communities', people cannot leave their country if they have nowhere to go. The refugee therefore emerges from a broader universe than solely the state in which the causal factor, such as persecution, occurs: 'This universe contains several interacting political entities ... controlling territories and the people they contain and varying significantly from one another with respect to some ideological elements.'[13] The result is that certain individuals become recognised as 'refugees' at certain times in certain places, others do not.

We must also consider the *point* of grouping certain criteria together to formulate a definition of the 'refugee' in the first place. The concept cannot be understood without a grasp of the very reason behind needing such a concept. In other words, we must go beyond the descriptive and look at the purpose of the term. But here again the purpose of the 'refugee' category will change according to the moral point of view from which it has been created. And it is an appreciation of the fact that such moral perspectives influence the definition, and therefore matter, that allows us to evaluate and predict how the concept 'refugee' can be applied to new situations. For example, if we maintain that the purpose of the 'refugee' category is to protect the unprotected, then it may seem sensible to extend the boundaries to include other groups of people in qualitatively the same position as 'refugees', such as 'internally

---

[10] Martin, 'The Refugee Concept', 36.
[11] Here Connolly's discussion of 'politics' is borrowed and applied to the 'refugee'. See Connolly, *The Terms*, p. 10.
[12] Connolly, *The Terms*, pp. 10–15.   [13] Zolberg *et al.*, *Escape from Violence*, pp. 6–7, 33.

displaced persons'. Indeed, the contemporary 'refugee problem' involves millions of individuals in similarly precarious conditions but who remain within the borders of their state. Accordingly, it could be opportune to revise or adapt the ingredients of the definition so as to grant international protection to a wider group of people, which can only be done by looking at the very purpose of the concept. In other words, 'attention to the point of the concept is in this way required if we are to apply it to new situations that deviate in some way from the case or cases that first occasioned its formulation'.[14] Of course, when the United Nations High Commissioner for Refugees (UNHCR) attempts to revise the defining elements of the 'refugee' concept, for example, states often protest that such revisions are unnecessary, ensuring that the 'refugee' remains a 'contested concept'. At this point we therefore face three options: to revise the criteria of the concept to preserve its point; to revise the point of the concept to preserve its criteria; or to 'leave the criteria, the point, and the theory within which the concept is embedded intact, but then to treat the whole complex as an anachronistic system irrelevant to the modern age'.[15] It is the third option which states continually seem prone to favour, ignoring the changing international structure within which the 'refugee' moves for the sake of keeping ideas of territorial sovereignty intact.

If the term 'refugee' at first glance defies definition, it might be easier to ask who a 'refugee' is not, and to distinguish the refugee from other 'moving' individuals. First, the refugee is not a simple migrant. Theoretically a migrant has chosen to move and has taken the decision to do so herself: 'it is the reluctance to uproot oneself, and the absence of positive original motivations to settle elsewhere which characterises all refugee decisions and distinguishes the refugee from the voluntary migrants'.[16] Migrants can also be distinguished by their having been influenced by the hope for a better life, while refugees are merely trying to rebuild the life they have lost.[17] Second, the refugee is not simply an individual from a minority group. Minorities may suffer oppression and persecution or may challenge the authority and legality of the state and strive, collectively, to disengage themselves from it. Both these

---

[14] Connolly, *The Terms*, p. 28.   [15] Connolly, *The Terms*, pp. 31–2.

[16] Egon F. Kunz, 'The Refugee in Flight: Kinetic Models and Forms of Displacement', *International Migration Review* 7, 2 (1973), 130.

[17] Danièle Joly, 'Odyssean and Rubicon Refugees: Toward a Typology of Refugees in the Land of Exile', *International Migration* 40, 6 (2002), 6.

scenarios may lead to refugee flows – refugees can of course be political dissidents as well as ethnic minorities or a whole range of other things. Yet until such disengagement occurs, the minority group will remain firmly attached to a state; refugees have no such relationship. Third, the refugee is not illegal. International legal instruments uphold the right to seek asylum. Being granted refugee status means being recognised legally as an individual in need of protection according to international law. Hence there is literally no way to be an 'illegal refugee': the term is a misnomer. Finally, the distinction economic migrant versus political refugee does not hold either. Vernant noted half a century ago that an individual's economic situation 'is no longer looked on as a "natural" phenomenon, but as a responsibility of the State ... In a great many States any measure, whatever its nature, is a political event'.[18] Politically conceived persecutory policies against certain sectors of the population, such as those directed against Russian Jews at the end of the nineteenth century, may undermine their economic position, which may then make survival impossible and flight the only alternative.[19] Similarly, it could be argued that even natural disasters such as drought or floods only instigate refugee flows if the state fails to respond adequately, thus the state's (political) response to events that cause economic failure is once again implicated in the creation of refugees.[20] Accordingly economic and political causes of flight are inextricably linked, and the separation of the two between (voluntary) migrants and (involuntary) refugees respectively is unsatisfactory.

In his search for a sociological definition, Kuhlman proposes labelling refugees as 'involuntary international migrants'. The spatial and temporal aspects of migration are less important in relation to the refugee, he maintains, than the classification or type of migration. After all, spatially the refugee is assumed to be 'international' and temporally refugee status is indefinite pending a change in circumstances 'back home'. Refugees therefore fall into the category of 'forced' or 'impelled' migration, with the underlying compulsion for flight coming from a breakdown in relations between the state and the individual. But, once again, the distinction between voluntary and involuntary migration can be blurred, with 'voluntary' migration sometimes so heavily influenced by external forces that the individual has been left with little choice but to move. Is the answer then, asks

---

[18] Jacques Vernant, *The Refugee in the Post-War World* (London: Allen & Unwin, 1953), p. 5.
[19] Zolberg *et al.*, *Escape from Violence*, p. 32.   [20] See Shacknove, 'Who Is a Refugee?', 279.

Kuhlman, to look at the push and pull factors involved in any move-ment? Migrants would perhaps take both into consideration, while refugees are influenced primarily by the push factors. As Kuhlman notes, 'it is not some paradise at the other end which they seek, but merely an escape from the hell in which they live'.[21] Yet here again the concepts are often blurred: push and pull factors cannot be observed in isolation; rather it is the perceived difference between the place of origin and the place of destination that counts. The only solution according to Kuhlman, therefore, is to view involuntary migrants in terms of 'distress': they are physically forced to leave their home or a serious crisis makes staying impossible, and it would be dangerous to return while these conditions persist. Thus prospective host govern-ments' attempts to make the destination seem less attractive – such as by the withdrawal of welfare benefits – are futile, since the attraction of the destination lies largely in the absence of the source of 'distress' present in the place of origin.[22]

Limitations of current approaches

The legal definition contained in the 1951 Convention forms the corner-stone to current refugee policy. According to the specialist in refugee law, Goodwin-Gill, 'the main purpose of any definition or description of the class of refugees is to facilitate, and to justify, aid and protec-tion'.[23] The 1951 Convention definition describes the 'refugee' as any person who:

> Owing to well-founded fear of being persecuted for reasons of race, religion, nationality, membership of a particular social group or poli-tical opinion, is outside the country of his nationality and is unable or, owing to such fear, unwilling to avail himself of the protection of that country; or who, not having a nationality and being outside the coun-try of his former habitual residence as a result of such events, is unable or, owing to such fear, is unwilling to return to it.[24]

Since the formulation of the 1951 definition, 'a considerable termino-logical, or conceptual, flora has grown up within which refugee realities

---

[21] Tom Kuhlman, 'Towards a Definition of Refugees', Refugee Studies Centre Docu-mentation Centre, University of Oxford (1991), 8.
[22] Kuhlman, 'Towards a Definition', 6–9.
[23] Goodwin-Gill, *The Refugee in International Law*, p. 2.
[24] Article 1(A)(2) 1951 Convention.

confront the language of the Convention'.[25] The array of terms that has been added to the legal literature acts to confuse the concept of the 'refugee' yet further. From the time of the Convention's inception, 'mandate refugees' were individuals fleeing generalised conflict and were agreed to fall under UNHCR's concern due to their need for international protection, despite the absence of a persecutor as such. Since 1957 the good offices of UNHCR have come to incorporate refugees not falling within the competence of the UN. In 1975 the UN also added 'displaced persons' to its list, although this was to be applied at the time to *externally* displaced persons who failed to qualify as Convention refugees.[26] By 1996 UNHCR claimed that the term 'refugee' included:

> (i) those recognised as such by states party to the Convention and/or Protocol; (ii) those recognised as such under the OAU Convention and the Cartagena Declaration; (iii) those recognised by UNHCR as 'mandate refugees'; (iv) those granted residence on humanitarian grounds; and (v) those granted temporary protection on a group basis.[27]

The road to the generalised definition contained in the 1951 Convention was a relatively short one. National legislation relating specifically to 'refugees' began to occur as early as the seventeenth century alongside the growing field of nationality laws.[28] International legal instruments defining refugees, however, only began to appear in the early twentieth century. The 1951 Convention definition is the culmination of a series of different attempts at defining and categorising various groups of specific 'refugees' in the inter-war period. Hathaway has divided the pre-1951 definitions into three groups, according to which he claims it is possible to identify three distinct approaches to defining 'refugees': the 'juridical' approach of 1920–35, whereby the international community recognised that membership of a certain group deprived the 'refugee' of governmental protection; the 'social' approach of 1935–9, which concentrated on providing international assistance to ensure the

---

[25] Jerzyv Sztucki, 'Who Is a Refugee? The Convention Definition: Universal or Obsolete?', in Francis Nicholson and Patrick M. Twomey (eds.), *Refugee Rights and Realities: Evolving International Concepts and Regimes* (Cambridge University Press, 1999), 64.

[26] Sztucki, 'Who Is a Refugee?', 64–5.

[27] United Nations, Office of the United Nations High Commissioner for Refugees, *The State of the World's Refugees, 1997–8: A Humanitarian Agenda* (Oxford University Press, 1997), p. 1.

[28] For a detailed account of the history of legislation concerning refugees, see Grahl-Madsen, *The Status of Refugees*.

safety of the 'refugee' – in the majority of cases, those fleeing Nazi persecution; and the 'individualist' approach of 1938–50, which abandoned a determination procedure based on political or social categories in favour of an examination of the merits of each applicant's case, on the basis of a perceived injustice or fundamental incompatibility with the home state.[29] It is of course the remnants of the individualist approach that provide the basis to the 1951 Convention definition, the definition that continues to dominate international refugee status determination procedures today.

Hathaway's three approaches reveal much about what the concept of the 'refugee' has meant to states and the international community as a whole at different times. The application of specific definitions relating to specific groups of refugees hints at the idea that states initially perceived the 'refugee problem' as one that affected very identifiable groups of people for particular reasons in certain places at certain times. Responding to such refugee flows on a case-by-case basis would, it was thought, resolve the problem. As numbers of refugees across Europe grew and the international community became more aware of the injustices that lay behind the creation of such vast flows of refugees, so the response became more humanitarian in flavour. Yet when numbers reached hitherto unimaginable heights, something had to change – one refugee is an individual in need who should be let in, a thousand refugees are a threat and a burden. Thus different approaches to defining the 'refugee' in different periods can be linked to prevailing debates relating to nation-states and their interests, concerns and identities. Underlying all three approaches, however, was the idea that the 'refugee' was a temporary problem, a concept brought about by specific transformations in international society which could be resolved as soon as international conditions were stabilised. Indeed, the constitutions of refugee agencies in this period, from the League of Nations High Commissioner for Refugees of 1921 to the International Refugee Organization of 1946, all set out specific life-spans for their respective organisations with the view that they would 'solve' the 'refugee problem' and then no longer be needed. UNHCR continues this tradition: it is a temporary agency of the United Nations the constitution of which has to be renewed every five years.

The practical importance of the legal definition contained in the 1951 Convention cannot be understated. As the cornerstone of the response

---

[29] Hathaway, *The Law of Refugee Status*, pp. 2–5.

of the international community to forced migration in the post-war era, the definition has saved millions of lives. But, as Zetter remarks, 'the interventionary and definitional practices of states, and their political interests, illustrate that the apparent simplicity of a *de minimis* legal label very quickly evaporates'.[30] Due precisely to the potential application of the legal definition to so many individuals, each of its words has at some point come under scrutiny and been subject to differences of interpretation. Yet a strictly textual approach obviously risks undermining the important normative concerns that the definition embodies, whilst ignoring the fact that the 1951 Convention is a product of history and context.[31] Thus, as is so often the case with international treaties, an interpretation of the 1951 Convention definition in light of its object and purpose, as upheld by the 1969 Vienna Convention on the Law of Treaties, would seem to be of substantially greater value.

The 1951 Convention definition is widely accused of being restrictive in citing individual persecution as the sole causal factor behind the acquisition of refugee status. Indeed, as Zolberg *et al.* have shown, the persecution criterion suggests that the causal factors behind any refugee movement are entirely internal to states, yet this overlooks the fact that 'persecution is related to broad historical processes in which complex internal and external forces interact'.[32] The main thesis of Zolberg *et al.* is that the common, defining element in every refugee movement, whether the refugee is viewed as an activist, a target or a mere victim, is 'a well-founded fear of violence'. Such violence may be direct or indirect, the consequence of external or internal conflict, or the imposition of conditions that make remaining impossible. Flight itself can be seen as a form of violence, if induced by the risk of harm or an expulsion order. Due to such violence refugees form 'a category of unfortunates' whose suffering can only be relieved in another state. In this regard, claim Zolberg *et al.*, refugees are a group with 'a strong claim to a very special form of assistance, including temporary or permanent asylum in the territory of states of which they are not members'.[33] Difficulties in defining refugees are inevitable since the very act of definition requires a combination of both a political choice and ethical motivation. Loescher's interpretation of legal definitions notes the border-crossing

---

[30] Zetter, 'Labelling Refugees', 40.
[31] Daniel J. Steinbock, 'The Refugee Definition as Law: Issues of Interpretation', in Nicholson and Twomey, *Refugee Rights and Realities*, 14, 19.
[32] Zolberg *et al.*, *Escape from Violence*, p. 25.   [33] Zolberg *et al.*, *Escape from Violence*, p. 33.

element and emphasises the specific rights received by the refugee, such as legal protection from deportation or forcible return to the country of origin. Yet he maintains that such a definition is inappropriate for today's refugee movements and hence offers a working definition of the 'refugee' that includes all persons who have been forcibly uprooted because of persecution or violence, regardless of whether they have left their country of origin or whether they are recognised by the governments of their host countries or by UNHCR.[34]

For an in-depth conceptual examination of the causal factors of refugee flows, Shacknove's work is illuminating. He identifies four implicit assumptions underlying the 1951 Convention definition: that a bond of trust, loyalty, protection and assistance between the citizen and the state constitutes the normal basis of society; that in the case of the refugee this bond has been severed; that persecution and alienage are always the physical manifestations of this severed bond; and that these manifestations are necessary and sufficient conditions for determining refugeehood. Yet both persecution and alienage are, according to Shacknove, assumptions that ought to be contested. Persecution is a sufficient condition for the severing of the normal bond between the state and citizen, but not a necessary one. It is just one manifestation of a broader phenomenon of the absence of state protection of the citizen's basic needs; other threats to physical security of the individual will come equally from other action, or inaction, of the state.[35] A state's response to a natural disaster, for example, or governmental control and allocation of economic resources in terms of the social policies and institutions put in place, will impact on the ability of an individual to be able to survive. But to distinguish between other persons deprived of their basic needs, the refugee must in addition be within reach of the international community. In other words, suggests Shacknove, alienage is also part of a broader category, namely the physical access of the international community to the unprotected person. The refugee need not necessarily cross an international frontier to gain such access, but must be in a situation that allows her to obtain international assistance: 'Whether a person travels ten miles across an international border or the same distance down the road into a neighboring province may be crucial for determining logistical and diplomatic action [but] conceptually ... refugeehood is unrelated to migration.'[36] Shacknove

[34] Loescher, *Refugee Movements and International Security*, pp. 6–8.
[35] Shacknove, 'Who Is a Refugee?', 275–7. [36] Shacknove, 'Who Is a Refugee?', 283.

concludes that the 'refugee' label should be reserved for individuals 'whose government fails to protect their basic needs, who have no remaining recourse other than to seek international restitution of these needs, and who are so situated that international assistance is possible'.[37]

Shacknove's analysis is important in extending the somewhat limited understanding of the 'refugee' concept in current legal usage. It forces us, for example, to examine causal factors behind the creation of refugees not usually considered state-induced, such as famine. Yet in terms of providing a better idea of who exactly is a 'refugee' it is problematic in several ways. First, in insisting on the ability of the so-called 'refugee' to be within reach of international assistance, Shacknove continues to limit the scope of who may or may not be eligible for protection as a 'refugee' in the same manner as the 1951 Convention. Second, Shacknove maintains that the actions of states and state-leaders are the causal factors behind every refugee flow. Yet by placing the importance on the behaviour of states, Shacknove fails to take into account the very structure of the international system within which states act. With its insistence on separate territorial states with clearly defined borders and populations, this structure is in large part responsible for the creation of refugees. War or persecution may be the factors that generate specific flows of refugees in specific places at specific times, but the creation of refugees would not be possible without the prior existence of political borders and separate states. Finally, Shacknove accepts the first assumption of the 1951 Convention definition, that a state–citizen bond constitutes the 'normal' basis of society. In so doing he confirms the widespread image of the citizen as the normal mode of belonging, the refugee as the exception. Thus he reifies the importance of state borders in a manner in which it would seem he has set out to avoid, indeed to correct.

Consequences of the refugee label

Besides the difficulties in finding a 'suitable' legal definition of the term 'refugee', any attempt to understand the concept as an all-encompassing category is problematic from the outset due to the images such a label tends to portray. Sociologists and anthropologists as well as non-governmental actors working in the field to protect refugees are

[37] Shacknove, 'Who Is a Refugee?', 284.

understandably critical of legal definitions and definitions per se in the 'refugee field'. Encoded in the definition 'refugee', they maintain, are 'images of dependency, helplessness and misery'.[38] This is clearly highlighted by Rajaram's analysis of the British charity Oxfam's project, 'Listening to the Displaced', which, he claims, resulted in a depoliticised, dehistoricised image of refugees:

> The bureaucratization of knowledge about refugees, the extrapolation of refugee experience from individual social and historical contexts and the creation of a veneer of objectivity and dislocation, occurs in a text designed to impart exhortatory information without problematizing – indeed, making invisible – the author's position.[39]

Accordingly, as Soguk argues, the paradox of the 'refugee discourse' is that it has no place for its very subject: 'When the refugee seemed to exhibit any sign of agency in the discourse, either as some kind of threat or as someone whose agency was manifested in her will to drag her body between distances, she hardly ever figured as a person but was part of an amorphous mass, faceless and speechless.'[40] But in the humanitarian regime the refugee is both the means and the end: it is the image of the refugee herself that will bring in the money for the relief programmes that will then assist and protect her.[41] Hence the victim-like definition is necessary for the survival of the concept in theory and the survival of the individual in practice. The definition of the refugee, therefore, frequently, but necessarily, becomes merely 'an abstraction, a category which qualifies a person ... to become eligible for UNHCR aid.'[42]

Having a 'refugee label' for such a diverse group of individuals can be difficult to justify. As Lammers notes, 'far too often the label of "refugee" artificially constructs and degrades people into a one-dimensional, homogeneous category [yet] except for their common experience of having felt forced to migrate, they are an extremely heterogeneous category of people'.[43] Without some care, any discussion of the 'refugee'

---

[38] B. E. Harrell-Bond and E. Voutira, 'Anthropology and the Study of Refugees', *Anthropology Today* 8, 4 (1992), 7.

[39] Prem Kumar Rajaram, 'Humanitarianism and Representations of the Refugee', *Journal of Refugee Studies* 15, 3 (2002), 248.

[40] Soguk, *States and Strangers*, p. 242.

[41] Barbara Harrell-Bond, Eftihia Voutira and Mark Leopold, 'Counting the Refugees: Gifts, Givers, Patrons and Clients', *Journal of Refugee Studies* 5, 3/4 (1992), 205.

[42] S. Waldron cited in Harrell-Bond *et al.*, 'Counting the Refugees', 209.

[43] Ellen Lammers, *Refugees, Gender and Human Security: A Theoretical Introduction and Annotated Bibliography* (Utrecht: International Books, 1999), p. 22.

risks relegating the individual behind the label 'to a floating world either beyond or above politics, and beyond or above history – a world in which they are simply "victims"'; and it is this 'floating world without the gravities of history and politics that can ultimately become a deeply dehumanizing environment for refugees, even as it shelters'.[44] Malkki, too, is keen to point out that the term 'refugee' does not constitute a naturally self-delimiting domain. It is impossible to use the term as a label for a generalised 'type' or 'kind' of person or situation, since the very idea behind the concept is that 'forced population movements have extraordinarily diverse historical and political causes and involve people who, while all displaced, find themselves in qualitatively different situations and predicaments'.[45] In other words, from an anthropological perspective it is impossible to squeeze diverse histories, experiences and people under one heading. Accordingly, the analytical usefulness of the term 'refugee' extends only insofar as it can be used as a 'broad legal or descriptive rubric'.[46]

Moreover, the different reasons for flight influence subsequent 'refugee life', further disrupting the quest for a unitary refugee identity. Joly has examined the standing of the refugee within her country of origin as a determining factor of how integrated she will allow herself to become in the host community, and this closes an important gap between the reasons for leaving and the conditions of arriving. 'Odyssean refugees', she claims, are individuals who were actively involved in a (political) struggle in their state of origin, and who bring their project with them into exile. Such refugees see their stay in the host state as temporary, with 'us' referring to all those involved in the same political struggle and 'them' meaning the regime and its supporters back home. 'Rubicon refugees', on the other hand, were not involved in any such struggle and hence retain little if any commitment to their state of origin. In this case life in the host state is seen as permanent, with 'us' generally referring to the more or less distinct community the refugees now constitute in the country of asylum, while 'them' becomes the rest of the host society.[47]

Although labels are familiar and ubiquitous and often go unnoticed in the world of bureaucracy, the 'refugee' label is much more than a simple, innocuous tool of language. Zetter has demonstrated how

---

[44] Malkki, 'Refugees and Exile', 518.   [45] Malkki, 'Refugees and Exile', 496.
[46] Malkki, 'Refugees and Exile', 496.
[47] Joly, 'Odyssean and Rubicon Refugees', 9–10, 16.

'refugees inhabit an institutionalized world of NGOs, intergovernmental agencies and governments, in which ... bureaucratic interests and procedures are themselves crucial determinants in the definition of labels like refugee'.[48] The imposition of the label makes the refugee 'vulnerable to institutionalized perceptions, an imposed crisis-based identity and a prescriptive programme of needs'.[49] The individual is designated a certain category of existence and becomes thus distinguished from other individuals. Conformity to the refugee category means inclusion, but in accepting refugee status, 'circumstances of "story" [have] to be relinquished to the bureaucratic dictates of "case"'.[50] This reveals, of course, the extent to which the refugee is a creature of states and state interests first and foremost, and only secondly a consequence of humanitarian concerns and cosmopolitanism.

The label connotes humanitarianism, yet it creates and imposes an institutionalised dependency; it assigns an identity, yet this identity is stereotyped; it is benevolent and apolitical, yet at the same time highly politicised; and it has the potential to threaten the sovereignty of states and the autonomy of the designated individuals, whilst simultaneously helping protect state sovereignty and granting the individual rights.[51] But perhaps most importantly, the term 'refugee' automatically conjures up an assumption of change in 'normal' and accepted global, national and regional structures. Since the application of the term 'refugee' is imposed on the forced migrant by bureaucratic activity, the concept can be seen as a form of control. The refugee 'client' is obliged to conform to the stereotype that the term conjures up, forgoing any distinctiveness or exclusivity.[52] A refugee can therefore be seen as an individual 'who conforms to institutional requirements', with the label acting merely as 'linguistic shorthand' for policies and bureaucratic requirements.[53] The 'client' must be loyal to the 'labeller', thus the 'labeller' is at liberty to impose, via the process of categorisation, those (political) values that are deemed important. Accordingly, a seemingly humanitarian refugee relief programme gives the appearance of neutrality in its use of the term 'refugee', yet hides 'the political in the apparently non-political'.[54] Food and aid programmes to refugee

---

[48] Zetter, 'Labelling Refugees', 40–1.   [49] Zetter, 'Labelling Refugees', 60.
[50] Zetter, 'Labelling Refugees', 47.
[51] Roger Zetter, 'Refugees and Refugee Studies – A Label and an Agenda', *Journal of Refugee Studies* 1, 1 (1988), 1.
[52] Zetter, 'Labelling Refugees', 44.   [53] Zetter, 'Labelling Refugees', 51.
[54] G. Wood cited in Zetter, 'Labelling Refugees', 45.

communities are a case in point. In the early 1980s various donor governments were keen to establish good working relations with the Obote regime in Uganda, and thus pushed UNHCR's official statistics to continuously underestimate the number of Ugandan refugees living in southern Sudan, so as to minimise the international criticism of a regime known to be causing its own citizens to flee the country.[55]

Via the 'refugee' label refugee communities acquire their own 'refugee consciousness' that can help form a particular identity. In time, this identity may create solidarity which can be used in the refugees' favour to apply pressure on the labellers – governments, refugee organisations and aid workers. For example, refugees hoping to repatriate will strive to keep their differentiation as 'refugees' and so avoid complete integration in the host society: 'were assimilation to be successfully achieved, a label would be blurred and pressure for repatriation would thus be lost'.[56] The label, therefore, allows refugees to pursue their own agendas and interests. The application of the label can empower, can enable the 'refugee' to participate in forging a political identity and thus give the individual some degree of control over her life.[57] Hence the ambiguous position of the refugee is further complicated by a definition which simultaneously integrates and seeks to create independence, yet excludes and perpetuates dependency and differentiation. In other words, the imposition of a label directly or indirectly affects the behaviour of the 'refugee community', constantly forming and transforming the identity of the individuals and thus giving a seemingly stable and apolitical refugee assistance programme its own momentum. The term 'refugee' is not static but forever evolving; labels are dynamic concepts. Indeed there are 'severe conceptual difficulties in establishing a normative meaning to a label which is as malleable and dynamic as refugee'.[58]

The term 'refugee' is far from just a bureaucratic description. It is intensely political and once employed will assume a distinctive yet transient politicised identity. The category therefore becomes a political instrument for both the categorised and the 'categorisers'. For the refugee and the host government, the 'refugee' label is a valuable 'political

---

[55] Harrell-Bond *et al.*, 'Counting the Refugees', 214–15.

[56] Zetter, 'Labelling Refugees', 53, 55.

[57] Zetter, 'Labelling Refugees', 49, 60. Of course, it is important to note that in some 'refugee situations' the constant risk of detection, detention and forced repatriation means the 'refugee' will choose to 'merge with the landscape and not to declare a political identity' – Zetter, 'Labelling Refugees', 58.

[58] Zetter, 'Labelling Refugees', 51, 55.

currency' that can be 'invested' to encourage assistance from donors and agencies.[59] In practice, however, conflicting interpretations of what the term 'refugee' actually encompasses will cause the value and exchange rate of the definition to fluctuate,[60] and competing interests in the underlying political objectives of employing the term 'refugee' may act to devalue the 'currency'.

Questions of gender

Some authors describe the refugee as 'she' with the justification that most refugees are women and children.[61] Despite the fact that women constitute an estimated two-thirds of the total victims of human rights abuses, they 'are rendered less mobile by structural conditions, cultural patterns and above all by a "broader universe" which privileges the public sphere over the private sphere in terms of the general recognition of, and thus by extension access to, human rights'.[62] Accordingly, notes Tuitt, since 'space is socially constructed in different ways for different groups or individuals ... Women are less able to conquer space to enable movement towards safety than their male counterparts'.[63] Works on women and gender in the 'refugee studies' field are now widespread, and have become intertwined in recent debates with both feminist and human rights discourses.[64] The issue of binary oppositions, for example, which are said to deny women their own identity by placing them constantly in opposition to men, strikes interesting parallels with the identity discourse surrounding the refugee that sees her constructed solely in opposition to the 'normal', sedentary citizen.

---

[59] Zetter, 'Labelling Refugees', 58.   [60] Zetter, 'Labelling Refugees', 40.

[61] See for example Hathaway, *The Law of Refugee Status*, p. v; Patricia Tuitt, 'Rethinking the Refugee Concept', in Nicholson and Twomey, *Refugee Rights and Realities*; B.S. Chimni, 'The Geopolitics of Refugee Studies: A View from the South', *Journal of Refugee Studies* 11, 4 (1998), 350–74; Rajaram, 'Humanitarianism'; and Daniel Warner, 'Voluntary Repatriation and the Meaning of Return to Home: A Critique of Liberal Mathematics', *Journal of Refugee Studies* 7, 2/3 (1994), 160–74.

[62] Tuitt, 'Rethinking the Refugee Concept', 113.

[63] Tuitt, 'Rethinking the Refugee Concept', 110.

[64] See for example Jacqueline R. Castel, 'Rape, Sexual Assault and the Meaning of Persecution', *International Journal of Refugee Law* 4 (1992), 39–56; Doreen M. Indra, 'Gender: A Key Dimension of the Refugee Experience', *Refuge* 6 (1987), 3–4; Jacqueline Greatbach, 'The Gender Difference: Feminist Critiques of Refugee Discourse', *International Journal of Refugee Law* 1 (1989), 518–27; Genevieve Camus-Jacques, 'Refugee Women: The Forgotten Majority', in Loescher and Monahan, *Refugees and International Relations*, 141–57; and Jacqueline Bhabha, 'Embodied Rights: Gender Persecution, State Sovereignty and Refugees', *Public Culture* 9, 1 (1996), 3–32.

Soguk has also employed the feminine pronoun in his discussion of the 'refugee discourse'. He stresses that an appreciation of the gender issues involved in the 'refugee problem' helps our understanding of the refugee event as a process. The threat of gender-specific violence and the power of male agency in defining and directing the contours of refugeehood provide particular difficulties for refugee women: 'Displaced female bodies are made to become specific sites of power where gendered, hierarchizing power relations privileging men over women ... are recuperated and stabilized precisely at a time (displacement) when those power relations are disrupted and most vulnerable to shifts and transformations.'[65] Accordingly, they experience a 'double displacement – a physical displacement from the so-called home community and a symbolic and at times violent displacement from agency'.[66]

However, acknowledgement of these particular difficulties on one hand extends the assistance available to refugee women as women, on the other promulgates certain representations of refugee women that can further discriminate against them. The dilemma is that depicting female refugees solely as victims acts to portray them as passive subjects, dependent on their male counterparts for survival and salvation.[67] At the same time we cannot overlook the fact that the male refugee experience can itself be a violent one and that refugee men also become tools of power networks: 'today murdered, tomorrow taken to concentration camps, and yet another day put to work to build more camps to concentrate refugees, both men and women'.[68] Hence it would seem of vital importance to focus attention not only on the specificities of the female refugee life, but on gendered differences as a whole.

This book does not look at the subject of gender in the refugee field per se. Rather, in employing the feminine pronoun throughout, it aims to draw attention to two things. First, like others, it acknowledges the high proportions of refugee women and girls in current refugee movements, along with the specific forms of persecution that may force them to move. UNHCR claims that women are sometimes now considered a specific social group under the wording of the 1951 Convention, since they may be subject to gender-based persecution, and hence should be eligible to claim refugee status for a subset of reasons. Sexual violence, genital mutilation and forced marriage, for example, have all come to be

[65] Soguk, *States and Strangers*, p. 248.   [66] Soguk, *States and Strangers*, p. 250.
[67] Helene Moussa cited in Soguk, *States and Strangers*, p. 249.
[68] Soguk, *States and Strangers*, pp. 250–1.

40

recognised as types of persecution.[69] Second, and perhaps more importantly for the purposes of this book, the feminine pronoun is used to make a point about identity. It questions the concept 'refugee' and exposes the ambiguities of identity in relation to the refugee category and in general. In our habitual use of the male pronoun the identity of the subject goes unnoticed. Referring to the refugee as 'she' arouses curiosity and provokes a response. It acts to deconstruct any spatial assumptions invoked by genderised language which can otherwise narrow the focus of discussions of the refugee concept. The preceding discussion in this chapter has highlighted the blurred and indistinct nature of the refugee's identity, the way in which the 'refugee' as a concept needs to be questioned and broken down from an apparently neutral and all-encompassing category, and the seemingly impossible task of ultimately defining the term 'refugee'. As Soguk intended in his *States and Strangers*, therefore, so it is the intention of this book 'to begin to question and disrupt the self-evidentiality of the refugee category . . . to suggest that the identity of the refugee, like that of the nonrefugee, is open-ended'.[70] Writing about the 'refugee' does not have to mean corroborating with the further silencing of refugees and of women refugees in particular. Rather, with some care it can force us to question our use of the refugee label and its costs and benefits for all actors involved in the defining process. This may lead to a more constructive way of understanding the refugee as a human category and the experience of displacement as one affecting very diverse individuals in a range of circumstances.

A new definition

Any definition risks coming under attack for being a restricting, generalising label that serves the purposes of certain actors at the expense

---

[69] UNHCR notes that 'In 1984, the European Parliament determined that women facing cruel or inhumane treatment because they seemed to transgress social mores should be considered a particular social group for the purposes of determining refugee status. The United States and Canada have exhaustive guidelines relating to gender-based persecution, and there has been similar progress in Germany, the Netherlands and Switzerland. In France, the Netherlands, Canada and the United States, it has been officially recognized that genital mutilation represents a form of persecution and that this can be a basis for refugee status. In one case, a woman who feared persecution in her country because of her refusal to inflict genital mutilation on her infant daughter was recognized as a refugee.' See UNHCR, 'Basic Facts: Who is a refugee?', www.unhcr.ch/cgi-bin/texis/vtx/basics.

[70] Soguk, *States and Strangers*, p. 259.

of those being labelled. However, without a clear understanding of who, broadly, we are talking about, however general we choose to keep this 'who', we cannot expect to further our grasp of how refugees emerge and how we should view the surrounding debate. Whilst agreeing that the 'refugee' is a complex concept and that no one definition is wholly satisfactory, it nevertheless makes sense for the advance of our understanding of the issue to formulate a definition for discussions to proceed. A definition that focuses on general commonalities of 'the refugee state' is possible without tying up every individual 'refugee' in one identical experience. And an analysis of the 'refugee' label itself and the way its margins are shaped and altered are just as interesting as that which it is employed to connote. In this regard, this book sets forth the following definition:

> A 'refugee' is an individual who has been forced, in significant degree, outside the domestic political community indefinitely.

This definition acknowledges code (international and legal), category (domestic and administrative) and identity (individual and subjective), and points to the interlocking relationship between each domain. It constitutes three assumptions about the 'refugee' concept: a degree of compulsion, an undetermined temporal element and an inherently political basis. Let us take each of these in turn:

(i) *A degree of compulsion will have been involved in creating the 'refugee'.* This rules out the possibility of an individual choosing to become a refugee. It insists, instead, on the element of compulsion in the process that leads an individual to become a refugee, yet it does not restrict variations in the degree of force. Whether, for example, the state issued a formal expulsion order, or whether conditions were made so extreme as to make remaining impossible – a kind of 'forced choice' – is irrelevant. If the relationship with the state of origin as a sustaining political community had been functioning correctly, the individual would not have been forced to move.

(ii) *There is a temporal element but this remains undetermined.* It is assumed that a migrant who is not a refugee would, in theory, be able to return to her place of origin whenever she so desires. On the other hand, for as long as the 'refugee' remains a 'refugee', conditions in the place of origin prevent her from returning. There is a certain period of time during which the individual cannot return from whence she came.

(iii) *The concept is inherently political.* From the point of view of 'politics' as an analytical domain, refugees are an enormously complex political issue on both national and international agendas, in the country of origin and the host country as well as in the international community as a whole. Whether or not intended, strategies of foreign policy are always involved in any decision regarding which refugees to help and when: 'In a world of competitive nation-states, the movement of people across an international border, in response to a conflict within, must to some degree affect the relations among nations', and as a result, even 'apolitical' refugees, if they can be said to exist, to a certain degree vote with their feet.[71] Accordingly, the refugee can be seen as the ultimate 'international outcast'; her status as a refugee is a result of political conditions directly or indirectly stemming from the state.[72]

Perhaps most importantly this definition contends that without political borders that act to delineate separate sovereign states and hence attempt to assign all individuals to one such state, the refugee as a concept would not exist; she is a political construction posited outside the state–citizen–territory trinity. The 'refugee' is created when norms of good governance within a state fail and she is forced to search for governmental protection in another state. Yet the individual may be physically unable to cross an international border to reach such protection in a host state, despite being to all intents and purposes in exactly the same situation as the individual who has crossed an international border. There is no conceptual difference between the 'refugee' and those individuals who have become known as 'internally displaced persons', yet the impenetrability of international, political boundaries further points to the arbitrariness of such borders. International borders generally symbolise the boundaries of the domestic political community, but the relationship between the state and the citizen may have broken down without a border crossing having taken place, hence the false dichotomy between 'refugee' and 'internally displaced person'. The idea of crossing an international border may therefore be both literal or fictitious.

International boundaries are the dividing line between the international and the domestic or the non-international. Accordingly, crossing the boundary means entering the realm of the international. Inside the boundary, in 'the inner sanctum of sovereign privilege', is the more tangible aspect of sentimental attachment to a political community. The border's 'conceptual abstraction is reified by such phenomena as

---

[71] Zolberg *et al.*, *Escape from Violence*, pp. 273–4.
[72] Zolberg *et al.*, *Escape from Violence*, p. 33.

border patrols and passports. Border patrols attempt to keep out the undesirables and passports help to regulate the temporarily desirables'.[73] Borders, of course, are fundamental to both the theory and practice of sovereignty, providing the focal point for absolutised territorial claims of sovereign states.[74] However, attachment to the political community can be lost without physically crossing an international border, such that the realm of the international begins to encroach on the national. The border becomes an ideal representation of the limits of both the national and the international, yet in practice the border becomes blurred when the state shows itself no longer to be a guarantor of the protection of its citizens, and the international community must step in to take responsibility. But while concept and practice do not always coincide at the border, the swapping of responsibility between the national and the international does not necessarily take place at the border either. The individual can lose her attachment to the domestic political community without moving across an international border that normally symbolises the extent of the national jurisdiction.

This definition provides an explanation of the 'refugee' concept that is sufficiently broad to appreciate the multiple histories behind the term, yet at the same time narrow enough to retain any practical value. The important common factors necessary to link one 'refugee' to another 'refugee' and so give the concept any analytical meaning are contained within the suggested definition, yet without denying the personal histories that accompany any 'refugee'. Indeed, by refusing to provide a finite list of the how, the why and the where, such a definition allows for the multitude of factors that can cause the individual to cross a political border and fall outside the state. Similarly, by employing the word 'individual', as indeed many international legal instruments dealing with refugees do, it hopes to maintain the sense of personal identity behind the label, which acts to remind us of the fact that the word is inevitably a generalisation and means something different to each person to whom it is applied. It should be noted here that this book focuses primarily on the individual who has crossed a border, since it is this understanding of the concept that has prevailed throughout the existence of the international refugee regime. Accordingly, any analysis of the regime and responses of states to the

[73] Kurt Mills, 'Permeable Borders: Human Migration and Sovereignty', *Global Society* 10, 2 (1996), 77.
[74] Mills, 'Permeable Borders', 91.

regime must take this understanding into account. The broader definition offered above, however, acknowledges the fact that there is scope for a widening of both the legal and normative understandings of the refugee within international society.

Conclusions

The 'refugee' defies universal definition. Just as each refugee has a different story to tell about her experience in becoming a refugee, so different contexts and perceptions involving the refugee cannot always be compatible: the refugee, 'while categorizable, nonetheless exceeds categorization'.[75] Thus the 'refugee' concept is bounded by normative considerations which shroud it in controversy. And this controversy is not, as Connolly notes, 'just *about* the concepts of politics but [is] *part of* politics itself ... for to get others to accept my account of an appraisive concept is to implicate them in *judgements* to which I am committed and to encourage political activity congruent with those commitments'.[76] Politics 'is the sphere of the unsettled', which causes an inevitable clash 'when appraisive concepts are shared widely but imperfectly, when mutual understanding and interpretation is possible but in a partial and limited way, when reasoned argument and coercive pressure commingle precariously in the endless process of defining and resolving issues'.[77] The implication of this understanding of politics in which the 'refugee' concept is situated is an awareness that different definitions are perhaps at once both necessary and desirable, and could open up a new and progressive way of looking at the 'refugee' and the 'refugee problem'. What is clear is that the definitional issue in the case of the refugee is more than just a question of semantics, and the issue of who is or is not included in the category may for some individuals be a matter of life and death.

The humanitarian community itself has participated in 'refugee studies' and thus in the creation of a label that now has a life of its own. Just as current legal, social and anthropological definitions have their limits, so it seems that an essentialist definition is not strictly possible, but varying definitions have different uses and can therefore coexist

---

[75] Michael Dillon, 'The Scandal of the Refugee: Some Reflections on the "Inter" of International Relations and Continental Thought', in David Campbell and Michael J. Shapiro (eds.), *Moral Spaces: Rethinking Ethics and World Politics* (Minneapolis: University of Minnesota Press, 1999), 106.

[76] Connolly, *The Terms*, p. 30 (Connolly's italics).   [77] Connolly, *The Terms*, pp. 40, 227.

and overlap. There need not, indeed there cannot, be one ultimate understanding of the refugee label. Differing definitions indicate both the malleability of the concept to suit different actors' purposes and the transforming, changing nature of the concept itself. The inherent clashes within the refugee definition will be brought further to light as we now look at the refugee's position in the international states system.

3   The refugee and the international states system

> Just beyond the frontier between 'us' and the 'outsider' is the perilous territory of not-belonging: this is to where in a primitive time peoples were banished, and where in the modern era immense aggregates of humanity loiter as refugees and displaced persons.   Edward Said[1]

The refugee is intricately tied up in the very workings of international society. Each concept relies on the other for its existence. They continuously create and re-create one another, inscribing identities onto each other and changing the normative course each takes. In this regard, the refugee can be understood as both an insider and outsider: pushed out of the normal state–citizen contract and forced to flee she is excluded; yet concepts of belonging and identity depend on differentiation from those who are different, thus she is also part of the system and included.

Starting with a look at the concept of sovereignty, this chapter asks how the refugee fits into an international society made up of separate sovereign states. It shows that as the state became nationalised, so the refugee became the vital 'other' necessary for national citizens to successfully forge their identity. With the rise of national identity as the new indicator of allegiance, the refugee became the imagined outsider who allowed the concept of the nation-state to take hold. By demonstrating how the refugee is defined in statist terms the chapter highlights her portrayal as an exception to the otherwise 'normal', sedentary state–citizen–territory trinity. Finally, it analyses the refugee as a truly modern figure, divorced from earlier exiles and other moving persons.

---

[1] Edward W. Said, *Reflections on Exile and Other Literary and Cultural Essays* (London: Granta, 2001), p. 177.

Sovereignty and the state

International society divides the world into sovereign states. Sovereignty means authority – external autonomy and internal control. A sovereign government is therefore Janus-faced: it simultaneously faces outwards at other states and inwards at its population.[2] External sovereignty concerns relations between states: a sovereign state is a political entity which is treated as a sovereign by other sovereign states.[3] Hence the principle of sovereignty demands that states must recognise one another as equally sovereign, that a sovereign state must refrain from interfering in the domestic affairs of other sovereigns, and that territory will be the ultimate object of political life. Internal sovereignty regards behaviour within states: a sovereign state may be described as 'a single governing authority which is acknowledged to be supreme over all authorities within a certain territorial jurisdiction and is independent of all foreign authorities'.[4] Thus statehood means territory. Accordingly, all individuals will be organised into populations and divided amongst this territory, divided amongst states. The international states system can therefore be described not just as a way of organising political power, but also as a means of organising people.

It is when the community responds to the state and the state responds to the community in which it rules 'that the discussion of political power can take place in terms of sovereignty'.[5] At this point there exists a final and absolute authority in the political community, and no final and absolute authority exists elsewhere to challenge such power. Collingwood discusses the distinction between community and society. If a community is a state of affairs, a *suum cuique*, in which something is shared by a group of human beings, then a society is a community whose members share a social consciousness. Any community, and therefore any society (which is a type of community), must have a home or place in which it lives, thus indicating the link between state, nation and territory which has come to dominate the make-up of the international states system.[6] If a community needs a territory,

---

[2] Robert Jackson, *Quasi-States: Sovereignty, International Relations and the Third World* (Cambridge University Press, 1990), p. 28.

[3] J. D. B. Miller, *The World of States: Connected Essays* (London: Croom Helm, 1981), p. 16.

[4] Jackson, *The Global Covenant*, pp. 156–7.

[5] F. H. Hinsley, *Sovereignty*, 2nd edn (Cambridge University Press, 1986), p. 21. Of course, authoritarian or totalitarian regimes are nevertheless also considered 'sovereign', albeit overbearingly so.

[6] R. G. Collingwood, *The New Leviathan or Man, Society, Civilization and Barbarism* (Oxford: Clarendon Press, 1947), pp. 138–9.

people outside the community may constitute a threat to its stability, 'thus, membership, territory and legitimacy become critical for security'.[7] And if questions of membership, territory and legitimacy become security issues, persons will accordingly be given 'insider' or 'outsider' status. Each individual will either add to the internal security of the community or threaten its cohesion by not belonging. An organised political entity is 'internally peaceful, territorially enclosed and impenetrable to aliens', preserving its identity in the face of threats from those who may want to destroy it.[8]

In the solidarist medieval world of Europe the international order was made up of dynasties based on ecclesiastical loyalties. The religious Peace of Augsburg of 1555 established the principle of *cuius regio eius religio* – like sovereign, like religion – whereby princes were given the right to rule local religious affairs. It was with the Treaty of Westphalia of 1648 that the legal and political relations between states were first established, and the horizontal feudal society of the medieval world was superseded by the modern vertical society of sovereign territorial states.[9] In time the principle of *cuius regio eius religio* developed into *cuius regio eius natio*, so that the secular concept of nationality became the defining factor of membership in a community. This marked the birth of very clear definitions of who belonged to a community and who did not.

When European politics were transformed from the solidarist norms of the *universitas* of Latin Christendom to the pluralist norms of the modern *societas*, and the principle of sovereignty passed from being the individual sovereignty of the prince to that of the nation he ruled, the internal–external dichotomy became evident.[10] Sovereignty was shown to be a principle that prevailed both within the majority of states that formed international society and in the relations between these states.

---

[7] Jennifer Jackson-Preece, 'Ethnocultural Diversity as a Security Dilemma', paper presented at the International Ethics of Security Conference, University of British Columbia, Vancouver, 5–7 April 2001, 5.

[8] Luoma-aho, 'Carl Schmitt and the Transformation', 704–5.

[9] Jackson-Preece, *National Minorities*, p. 6. The Treaty of Westphalia, which was signed on 24 October 1648 and brought an end to the Thirty Years War, is commonly taken as the albeit somewhat mythical beginning of the modern system of separate states. In fact, the transformation from solidarist to pluralist international relations was, of course, a gradual process that spanned several centuries, beginning at the time of the Council of Constance of 1414–17 and continuing until the Peace of Utrecht of 1715. Westphalia was important, however, as it instituted the belief in a Europe organised around the principle of a balance of power – a belief which was to provide the basis for many of the ideas that would later be developed by the League of Nations and United Nations.

[10] Martin Wight, *Systems of States* (Leicester University Press, 1977), p. 153.

Internally, 'territory was consolidated, unified, and centralized under a sovereign government [and] the population of the territory now owed final allegiance to the sovereign'.[11] The sovereign state could demand religious and sometimes linguistic conformity to ensure such allegiance. Externally, equal sovereignty, non-intervention and the balance of power developed into the basic norms of the system. Governance within a state's territory became a state's own jurisdiction, whilst the state's external behaviour became a concern of international relations between states.[12] Thus sovereignty as a concept highlights the 'region of approximation' between domestic and international politics.[13]

As the absolutist state gave way to the territorialised state and the territorialised state gave way to the nationalised state, so a specific concept of territory as a bounded, exclusionary space was articulated. As Walker notes, 'framed within a spatial metaphysics of same and other, citizens and enemy, identity and difference, the principle of state sovereignty expresses an ethics of absolute exclusion'.[14] The state became the uncontested political location for the realignment of power, place and population,[15] and the problem of how to make all individuals fit into such exclusionary spaces was born. Those individuals who crossed boundaries and thus in some sense transgressed upon states were accorded a separate normative status either as immigrants, migrants or refugees. And the latter is perhaps the most contentious because the very existence of refugees on the territory of another state is in some sense an infringement not only of the sovereignty of the host state, but that of their home state as well. Having left a political community and sought entry in another, refugees act to challenge the sacred sovereignty of the modern state.

The creation of clearly defined states therefore has the effect of simultaneously creating exclusionary identity practices based on dichotomies, which may be 'in terms of space (inside versus outside), membership in a specific community (citizen versus non-citizen) and agency (state versus individual)'.[16] It orders peoples on the basis of belonging and not belonging. Each of these dichotomies may be seen to reflect the contemporary distinction between the particular and the universal. The particularistic concept of the citizen with rights and membership in a state contrasts with the universal outsider who possesses rights only

---

[11] Jackson, *The Global Covenant*, p. 166.   [12] Jackson, *The Global Covenant*, p. 167.
[13] Wight, *Systems of States*, p. 153.   [14] Walker, *Inside / Outside*, p. 66.
[15] Soguk, *States and Strangers*, p. 72.   [16] Soguk, *States and Strangers*, p. 73.

in the abstract and has no state to uphold them. Thus sovereignty expresses the border between inside and outside, citizen and non-citizen, that frames the contemporary understanding of political space and the international states system as a whole.

Sovereignty and the refugee

If the end of the *respublica Christiana* signalled the beginning of a system of separate, sovereign states, so it is then that the ordering of Europe's population became an international question. The ordering of peoples is therefore a concern of the pluralist world of sovereign states. Accordingly, the refugee problem belongs to the pluralist world; there could be no such problem in the solidarist *universitas* since the refugee depends on exclusion from a political community which depends on well-defined borders. As a concept the refugee could not exist in the *universitas* because she is only created when boundaries are erected, thus the problem of potential refugees was avoided in the solidarist world. Groups and individuals were the subjects of their rulers who had a right to a particular territory, and there were no national minorities or putative refugees to question this with secessionist claims.[17] Questions of belonging and not belonging were not relevant. Jurisdictional boundaries in the medieval world were more porous and overlapping than the rigid, impenetrable borders of the modern world.

There were, nevertheless, movements of religious minorities in the solidarist world, and these can be seen to prefigure the modern concept of the refugee. Indeed, there have been expulsions and displacements of peoples throughout history. One of the largest movements of religious exiles was that of the French Huguenots who were forced to leave Catholic France after the revocation of the Edict of Nantes in 1685. This case hints at many of the characteristics common to the contemporary refugee phenomenon – indeed it was in regard to these French Protestants that the term 'refugee' was first coined. The expulsion constituted an example of a large mass of individuals fleeing the consequences of the actions of a government against its very own people, not in time of war or with any provocation on their part, and after almost a century of mutual accommodation. Such causal factors for flight are behind refugee movements today, refugees being produced, once boundaries are erected, by a dysfunction in governance designed to

[17] Jackson-Preece, *National Minorities*, pp. 31–2.

strengthen the state. Further, the expulsion of the French Huguenots represented a significant turning point in defining the state less in dynastic terms and more in modern territorial terms, and it is for this reason that the Huguenots can be categorised as the earliest example of a 'refugee' phenomenon in the modern sense of the term. The episode forewarned of the potential for creating refugees when attempts are made to attach certain people to a state on a given territory, and highlights the changing attitude of the state towards the individuals who found themselves within its territory. According to Zolberg, the expulsion was a 'state-building project manifesting the pursuit of ideological unity – here indicated by public adherence to the official religion'.[18] The expulsion was a result of and a response to certain practices performed by the state. The state attempted to define a political identity for itself via religious homogeneity, and identifying the 'other' was necessary to achieve this. Religion was used to mark out who the state considered inside and who outside, thus religious difference can be seen as an early ingredient in forging a French nationalism.

The revocation of the Edict of Nantes meant the end to the legal guarantees of the Protestant religion: ministers were exiled and the people were forced to convert. Calvinist churches were destroyed, Protestants were excluded from public office and restrictions were put in place on other professions. From the 1670s to the start of the eighteenth century it is estimated that between 200,000 and 500,000 French Protestants left France as refugees to seek protection abroad, despite the measures put in place by the French government to try to keep the Huguenots in the country and prevent their going to 'enemy territory'. The majority did remain in France, but became Catholics only nominally. Of those who left France, 40–50,000 came to settle in England. A minority of the refugees were wealthy, the majority were skilled artisans; all were generally highly literate. Thus the Huguenots brought resources, labour and new techniques to host countries, such that they made important contributions in many spheres of society. At times they were viewed as competition for scarce jobs, at times as anti-monarchical or a threat to the religion of the reigning monarch, such that violence and xenophobia were therefore not entirely absent. Yet the Huguenots were by and large welcomed and seen as an important resource in state- and economy-building. And we can therefore identify early examples of government initiatives to deal with these refugees.

---

[18] Zolberg, 'The formation of new states', 36.

First, the English government made mass grants of denisation so that the refugees were granted permanent residency rights and enjoyed certain citizenship rights. This predated the Act of Parliament for naturalising the Huguenots in England, passed in 1709, which allowed the refugees to become English. In this way the refugees actually contributed to the nationalisation of the state. Second, the government ordered parish collections for the refugees by way of emergency relief, as well as by allocating a significant amount of state money. This was assigned and administered by a body set up to cope with the new and growing problem of refugees, demonstrating that a shift was taking place: refugees were no longer an issue that could be dealt with solely by the action of the Protestant church of the Huguenots and local charities; rather a national strategy was now needed.

The French Revolution of 1789 finished what Westphalia had started. International legitimacy ceased to be based on the claims and status of rulers; the states system was built around the popular principle, deriving both its domestic and international legitimacy from the claims and consent of the governed. As the rights of man came to be superseded by the rights of nations, so a national consciousness began to emerge and take hold among the peoples of Europe. Dynastic principles of legitimacy gave way to nationalism and popular politics, which were accompanied by the concepts of democracy and citizenship. The actors in international society continued to be the territorially based political units known as sovereign states, but these now represented the political will of groups of people defined in national rather than dynastic terms.[19] The people were now the nation and the state existed as an expression of the national will. Accordingly, those expelled from France as exiles or 'émigrés' during the French Revolution are important in highlighting the beginning of the state being defined on national grounds, and the development of the formalised concepts of 'citizen' and 'foreigner'. Whereas the case of the Huguenots showed the emergence of a centralising modern territorialised state, exiles of the French Revolution marked the materialisation of the centralising nationalised state. Nationalism became an ideology of the state and people began to think of themselves as national citizens. France, for example, came to be imagined as a nation committed to the revolutionary ideals of *liberté*, *égalité* and *fraternité* such that aristocrats became the outsiders; more

---

[19] Jackson-Preece, *National Minorities*, p. 6.

recently, and in a similar way, Yugoslavia came to be imagined as the homeland of the Serbs such that Kosovars became the outsiders.[20]

Refugees, too, became defined in ideological terms, challenging the construct of the nation-state. The nation-state became an imagined and indeed ideological construct and thus, by extension, the refugee also became an imagined construct that acted to give meaning to the former. According to Anderson nations are imagined, existing in as much as the population believes them to do so. Members of even the smallest nations will never know or meet all their fellow members, 'yet in the minds of each lives the image of their communion'.[21] Fellow co-nationals are imagined to exist, and communities are distinguished not by their falsity or genuineness but by the style in which they are imagined. This is Collingwood's *suum cuique*; a community exists when it has a state of affairs shared by certain human beings, and the form this *suum cuique* takes affects the kind of community that it is.[22] Hence identities are always mythical, involving in significant measure an important element of wishing to think of oneself as forming a distinct community.[23] Further, they are imagined as limited because a nation will always have finite, if elastic, boundaries beyond which lie other nations – 'no nation imagines itself coterminous with mankind'.[24] Frontiers and borders are necessary for citizenship to have any meaning. The image of the 'other' or the 'outsider' contrasts with who we imagine to be the 'same', to be part of our 'nation'. This imagined 'other' is as necessary as the imagined 'self' in sustaining our idea of the 'nation' and hence our sense of identity. Political borders and those who do not belong, such as the refugee, designate 'a constitutive outside, a basis for identity formation against the identity or threat of something else'.[25] The 'we' is integrally related to and formed by its relationship with the alien.[26]

---

[20] For in-depth discussions on the rise of the ideology of nationalism and the concept of the nation, see for example Benedict Anderson, *Imagined Communities: Reflections on the Origin and Spread of Nationalism* (London and New York: Verso, 1983); Anthony D. Smith, *Theories of Nationalism* (New York: Holmes and Meier, 1983); Ernest Gellner, *Nations and Nationalism* (Oxford: Blackwell, 1983); and Eric J. Hobsbawm, *Nations and Nationalism since 1780: Programme, Myth, Reality*, 2nd edn (Cambridge University Press, 1992).

[21] Anderson, *Imagined Communities*, p. 15.   [22] Collingwood, *The New Leviathan*, p. 128.

[23] David Miller, *On Nationality* (Oxford University Press, 1995), p. 33.

[24] Anderson, *Imagined Communities*, p. 16.

[25] Jennifer Hyndman, *Managing Displacement: Refugees and the Politics of Humanitarianism* (Minneapolis: University of Minnesota Press, 2000), p. 1.

[26] Dillon, 'The Scandal of the Refugee', 107.

The French émigrés of the time of the French Revolution were also precursors to the modern refugee, they, like the Huguenots, a result of the process of state-building and the practice of statist governance. A mixture of terms was employed to refer to foreigners in this period– émigrés, exiles, refugees – and all such definitions helped to confirm the national citizen as the subject of membership in the nation-state. Host states generally exercised liberal policies towards the exiles and public opinion was by and large accepting. Even so, exiles continued to help construct an image of the external 'other', acting to establish the internal 'citizen' as the 'normal' subject of the state. And a look at the legal development of the concept of the refugee shows how definitions were being formalised and strengthened so as to assist in the consolidation of the state–citizen–territory hierarchy. Indeed, from the end of the eighteenth century a growing emphasis on belonging and not belonging meant that national legislation relating to aliens and 'refugees' was beginning to emerge. The British Alien Acts of 1793, 1796 and 1844 perhaps laid the foundations for the institutionalisation of the state as the final arbiter in deciding who could enter its territory and who would be granted membership in its nation and, conversely, who was denied access and membership. The preamble to the 1793 Alien Act, in large part a response to the albeit small number of refugees arriving from France, held that 'a great and unusual number of aliens have lately resorted to the kingdom'.[27] The Act's provisions included that all aliens arriving in the country were to give an account of their personal history and status to customs officers or risk deportation, and that the King had the power to refuse entry to any alien he so chose. Such Acts were, of course, to culminate in the Alien Act of 1905, which made sharp distinctions between refugees and immigrants. At this time refugees were still seen as the few hundred individually persecuted political activists; immigrants were the impoverished masses who had the potential to arrive in their thousands. New restrictions enforced by the state now demanded that refugees proved cases of individual persecution, creating clear restrictions on which outsiders would be allowed inside and foreshadowing the modern, legal criteria for refugee status.

As national citizens developed a sense of national identity and nationalist fever spread to the masses, large-scale displacements became more and more commonplace. The revolutions of the 1820s and 30s created

---

[27] Cited in Richard Plender, *International Migration Law* (Leiden: A. W. Sijthoff, 1972), p. 43.

new flows of refugees from Italy and Poland. Calls for the building of unified nation-states in 1848 then led to the (sometimes deliberate) creation of thousands of refugees from Italy, Germany and then France, as the state became linked to nationality. As a result of the wars of German unification, for example, France expelled 80,000 Germans in 1870 alone; when the region became annexed to the newly formed German empire in 1871, 130,000 refugees who considered themselves French left Alsace-Lorraine under the Treaty of Frankfurt. Increasingly large groups of civilians were engaged on behalf of the nation's cause as nationalistic sentiment swept the continent. With the newly perceived importance of citizenship, outsiders were a latent threat not just to the emerging national identity of the nation but to its security and welfare state as well. Refugees had the potential to bring alien doctrines that were seen as seditious and potentially rebellious towards local interests and identities. Further, the innocuous and affluent exiles of the early nineteenth century were being replaced by refugees from the impoverished working classes and a more violent type of Tsarist émigré than seen previously. Public opinion feared such anarchists, and this fear helped foster unease and mistrust towards refugees in general. At the same time the European welfare state was beginning to take shape, and in this new context outsiders started to be perceived as a burden on finite state resources.

The emerging 'other'

Nationality and citizenship could not have taken such a strong hold on members of each political space without the simultaneous invention of the foreigner: 'henceforth citizen and foreigner would be correlative, mutually exclusive, exhaustive categories. One would either be a citizen or a foreigner, there would be no third way'.[28] The 'citizen' could not have emerged without the surfacing of the 'foreigner' at the same time: the creation of the identity of the foreigner was vital in establishing the state–citizen–territory hierarchy. The refugee was to follow as one distinct category of the newly defined foreigner and would, of course, take centre stage in the twentieth century. Thus the mass displacements of individuals brought about by the French Revolution were all part of the processes by which the image of the 'other' was

[28] William Rogers Brubaker, *Citizenship and Nationhood in France and Germany* (Cambridge, Mass.: Harvard University Press, 1992), pp. 46–7.

constructed and used as a tool in the invention of the nation-state.[29] The refugee posed a potential threat to the process of inventing and imagining the nation-state and the national citizen. The relationship between state identity and the identity of the refugee has a normative quality that allows the refugee to be negatively constituted as a threat to the nation-state. Displacement was useful for the definition of certain individuals as outsiders, so that the process of consolidating identities within the nation-state could proceed. As Kristeva has pointed out, people need 'others' to be able to invent for themselves a 'we' as distinct from a 'they'.[30] Human displacement was a much-needed side-effect of the process of state-building; it acted to distinguish insiders from outsiders, which in turn operated to consolidate the concept of citizenship and the sovereign role of the state. In the words of Walker, 'knowing the other outside, it is possible to affirm identities inside. Knowing identities inside, it is possible to imagine the absences outside'.[31] This is not to say that, by extension, the modern nation-state in some sense requires refugees. Rather, the nation-state needs the 'other', the 'outsider', individuals who can quite feasibly be citizens of another state. In other words, the refugee is not an anomaly of the logic of the states system, but an inevitable part of this logic.

In France the Declaration of the Rights of Man and Citizen of 1789 granted natural and inalienable rights to those possessing citizenship of a nation and state. This was followed by the *Loi relative aux passeports* of 1797, and explicit definitions of the alien in the new constitution of 1799. The 1832 *Loi relative aux Etrangers réfugiés qui résideront en France* actually stated that foreigners without governmental protection should be called refugees, hence taking the sovereign state as given. Such legislation allowed the state to control the definition of its nation. The timing of this legislation and other similar pieces that were appearing across Europe in this period is noteworthy. Indeed, it challenges the idea that restrictive laws relating to aliens were a twentieth-century creation alone. Of course, totalitarian regimes brought such laws to drastic extremes in the case of Jewish refugees fleeing persecution from Nazi Germany, for example. But the fact that laws of some kind were being passed in this field as early as the eighteenth century, before mass

---

[29] Brubaker, *Citizenship and Nationhood*, p. 46.
[30] Julia Kristeva, *Strangers to Ourselves* (New York: Columbia University Press, 1991), p. 81.
[31] Walker, *Inside / Outside*, p. 174.

refugee movements took their place on the international landscape, is indicative once again of the changing relationship between the state and the constituents of its nation. As the international system was transformed from one with a universal, solidarist make-up to a more particular, pluralist one, so tighter controls would be needed with respect to who could be allowed into a state's territory.

In this regard the birth of European nationality laws at this time cannot be overlooked, 'a fateful development which has put its indelible mark on the law of refugees'.[32] Citing just a few examples shows the rapid development of such laws in a short time span: the French Civil Code of 1804, the Prussian Law of 1842, the Netherlands Aliens Act of 1848, the nationality laws of Austria, Italy and Russia in the 1860s, and the British Naturalisation Act of 1870. These covered provisions including the acquisition of original nationality and naturalisation. Nationality laws, of course, are closely related to states' laws regarding immigrants and aliens. Laying out the rights and privileges of national citizens by extension meant codifying who was not covered by such legislation and how such individuals should be treated. According to Soguk, European nationality laws were an historically unprecedented development, constituting 'yet another field of statist activity clearly linked to the name of the alien, whether a refugee-alien, an exile-alien, or an émigré-alien'.[33] Laws and acts all worked to inscribe meaning and identity onto such concepts, and so allowed the refugee to be constituted as the 'other' in the state-centric world of sovereign communities. The refugee, representing one form of human displacement, became a point of reference by which the state–citizen relationship, bounded by territory, could be privileged.

The modern emphasis placed on citizenship and nationality within territorially defined sovereign entities is therefore the natural extension of what was set in motion in 1648 and 1789, and it is precisely this thinking that acts to exclude the refugee. As Anderson notes, nation-statehood became central to the imagination of the future organisation of the polities across Europe,[34] and nation-statehood by definition involves a clear distinction of 'inside' and 'outside'. Brubaker further points out that politics of citizenship are also politics of identity, politics

---

[32] Grahl-Madsen, *The Status of Refugees*, p. 11.
[33] Soguk, *States and Strangers*, p. 98.   [34] Anderson, *Imagined Communities*, p. 114.

58

of nationhood, with the central question being not who gets what but who is what.[35] Conventional discourse on refugees therefore starts from the premise 'that the modern citizen, occupying a bounded territorial community of citizens, is the proper subject of political life: the principal agent of action, the source of all meaning of value'.[36] The citizen is unproblematic and rooted in her territorial space. The refugee constitutes a problem by lacking effective state representation and protection; she is uprooted, dislocated and displaced.[37]

The ordering of peoples, then, is a basic tenet of the pluralist world and places a sharp distinction on being inside or outside. But this ordering of peoples only takes place insofar as it relates to individual states. The refugee does not belong to any individual state, having been pushed outside the domestic political community; she exists by definition between states and thus falls outside the reach of international society. She is found in the gaps between states where individuals are not supposed to exist. Once borders are put up and territorial jurisdiction is defined, the refugee is forced between such borders by the very system that creates her. States exert their sovereign right to decide who they will represent and protect according to norms of good governance. In failing to fulfil their responsibilities of normal good governance, states fail to ensure respect for the state–citizen contract. When the individual loses her attachment to a particular territory, she ceases to behave according to the ordering of peoples that the international states system demands. Thus a breakdown domestically leads to a similar breakdown internationally; the refugee loses her relationship with the state both internally and externally. Refugees are an inevitable if unintended consequence of the nation-state system; they are the result of erecting boundaries, attempting to assign all individuals to a territory

---

[35] Brubaker, *Citizenship and Nationhood*, p. 182.   [36] Soguk, *States and Strangers*, p. 9.

[37] It is interesting to note the work of various authors who have looked at the idea of 'postnational' or cosmopolitan citizenship. This work draws a distinction between citizenship as a legal status, based on nationality, and citizenship as an identity, based on residence, such that the latter poses the possibility of affording the individual a position in the international system not linked to a particular political community. The situation of the refugee perhaps raises this opportunity. See for example Yasemin Soysal, *Limits of Citizenship: Migrants and Postnational Membership in Europe* (University of Chicago, 1994); Christian Joppke, *Immigration and the Nation-State: The United States, Germany and Great Britain* (Oxford University Press, 1999); and Pierre Hassner, 'Refugees: A Special Case for Cosmopolitan Citizenship?', in Danièle Archibugi, David Held and Martin Köhler (eds.), *Re-imagining Political Community: Studies in Cosmopolitan Democracy* (Cambridge: Polity Press, 1998), 273–86.

within such boundaries, and then failing to ensure universal representation and protection.

Since citizenship is seen as the correct mode of belonging in our
imagined territorially bound communities,[38] the refugee is an abnorm-
ality, not properly belonging anywhere: 'In a world that abhors the
presence of unadministered space or people, the presence of forced
migrants must be treated as abnormal.'[39] She disrupts the normal
conditions of international society imagined in terms of the state–
citizen–territory hierarchy. To restore order to international society,
the imagined state–citizen–territory hierarchy must be reaffirmed.
Repatriation, resettlement or naturalisation – all forms of reterritorialisation – are the solutions to redefining the refugee's relationship to a
space of sovereignty. The refugee is a 'morally demanding but not
intractable problem' within the otherwise 'unproblematic, stable, and
secure territorial bounds of the sovereign state'.[40] Until the problem is
solved she will be an individual operating internationally, without
direct ties to one particular state.[41] She is no longer territorially based,
as the states system dictates she should be; rather the refugee finds
herself in the 'no man's land' of the international landscape.

If the refugee's position in the states system is that of an anomaly, it is
because she is displaced, primarily, in the physical sense.[42] As such she
is associated with motion. Language employed in discourse on the
refugee mirrors this perception: we talk of flows and tides of refugees,
people who are running, escaping. They are victims of causal factors
that have an endemic mobilising force, be they war, persecution or
famine. And as Goodwin-Gill points out, flight then constitutes 'the
only way to escape danger to life or extensive restrictions on human
rights'.[43] Such liquid images associated with uprooting and displacement contrast with the territorialising metaphors of identity – 'roots,
soils, trees, seeds are washed away in human flood-tides, waves, flows,
streams, and rivers', underlining the 'sedentarist bias in dominant
modes of imagining homes and homelands, identities and nationalities'.[44] This imagery can be traced back to the early example of
Huguenot 'refugees', also seen to be moving and so disrupting territorialised notions of identity:

[38] Anderson, *Imagined Communities*, p. 15.
[39] Gordenker, *Refugees in International Politics*, p. 125.
[40] Soguk, *States and Strangers*, p. 13.   [41] Skran, *Refugees in Inter-war Europe*, p. 3.
[42] Tuitt, 'Rethinking the Refugee Concept', 106.
[43] Goodwin-Gill, *The Refugee in International Law*, p. 4.   [44] Malkki, *Purity and Exile*, p. 15.

> During the 1660s and 1670s there was a growing trickle of refugees;
> from 1679, as oppressive edicts increased sharply in number, a stream;
> in 1681, with the onset of the *dragonnades*, the stream became a river.
> After the Revocation of the Edict of Nantes ... the river turned into a
> torrent.[45]

In conceiving the refugee as a moving entity, we immediately construct her as different, an irregularity in the life of an otherwise stable,
sedentary society.[46] Displacement occurs within what Malkki
describes as the 'national order of things', in which having a fixed,
stationary existence is the norm. By virtue of her 'refugeeness' the
refugee occupies a 'problematic' and 'liminal' position in the national
order of things.[47] As the refugee cannot be fixed within one set of
borders, she acts to blur or 'haemorrhage'[48] national boundaries. The
national order of things is subverted, and the refugee becomes a
'problem' that requires 'specialised correctives and therapeutic interventions'.[49] If the nation classifies, orders and sorts people into
national kinds and types, 'refugeeness' can be seen as an aberration
of categories, a 'zone of pollution':[50]

> Transnational beings are particularly polluting, since they are neither
> one thing nor another; or may be both; or neither here nor there; or
> may even be nowhere (in terms of any recognized cultural topogra-
> phy), and are at the very least 'betwixt and between' all recognized
> fixed points in the space-time of cultural classification.[51]

Thus by imagining the refugee as fluid and between categories she can
be seen to constitute a threat to established boundaries. She challenges
the assumption that all individuals belong to a state and brings into
question the concepts of nation, state and national identity.

Just as sovereignty involves relations both within and between states,
so the refugee as a concept has an internal and external aspect. She faces
the duality of the international system by being shunned both domestically and internationally. The domestic reciprocal relationship
between the state and the individual has broken down, and the refugee
is forced out by her own government, yet externally there is nothing to
guarantee her acceptance internationally. The refugee is therefore an

---

[45] Robin D. Gwynn, *Huguenot Heritage: The History and Contribution of the Huguenots in Britain* (London: Routledge & Kegan Paul, 1985), p. 35.
[46] Malkki, 'Refugees and Exile', 508.   [47] Malkki, *Purity and Exile*, pp. 1–2.
[48] Mary Douglas cited in Malkki, *Purity and Exile*, p. 7.   [49] Malkki, *Purity and Exile*, p. 8.
[50] Malkki, *Purity and Exile*, pp. 4, 6.
[51] Victor Turner cited in Malkki, *Purity and Exile*, p. 7.

anomaly both within and between states: she is not supposed to exist internally or externally. The internal–external dichotomy is more than evident if we remind ourselves of the legal definition of a refugee. To qualify as a refugee an individual must have crossed an international border. In crossing such a frontier she becomes an international concern creating potential problems for other states, not just her state of origin. Mass movements of large numbers of refugees are often viewed as a threat to international order due to their destabilising effects on the states system. Thus the refugee becomes a problem to be put on the international agenda for discussion and resolution. However, the individual whose personal liberty and safety is in just as much danger but who has failed to cross an international border is differentiated from the refugee and labelled an 'internally displaced person'. She, in opposition to the refugee, generally remains an internal issue for her state of origin, be it for sovereign reasons of non-intervention or due to a realist lack of interest in humanitarian responsibility. As long as the individual remains within her country of origin, international order and stability are not threatened and so her situation need not be a cause for international concern.

The refugee is included in the states system by virtue of her exclusion; she is part of the system whilst not being part of it, both inside and outside at the same time. This ambiguous status defines the very concept of the refugee, brings the refugee into existence and guarantees the states system a reality and an identity. The refugee is at the threshold between inside and outside. She is an exception: 'The exception is what cannot be included in the whole of which it is a member and cannot be a member of the whole in which it is always already included.'[52] Thus the refugee blurs the dividing lines that the concept of sovereignty would like to draw between inside and outside. Just as sovereignty is a profoundly paradoxical concept, so the refugee is an ambiguous figure who exists by virtue of her in-between status.

The refugee as a modern phenomenon

There have been expulsions and displacements of peoples throughout history: the expulsion of the Jews from Spain in 1492, for example, will no doubt spring to mind. But there are clear distinctions between

---

[52] Giorgio Agamben, *Homo Sacer: Sovereign Power and Bare Life*, translation (Stanford University Press, 1998), p. 25.

today's refugees and forced migrants of the past. Pre-modern forced human migration lacked regulation and international cooperation, and involved relatively small numbers of individuals. Even with the case of the Huguenots, there are significant qualitative differences with refugees of the modern period: first, there was no international cooperation or agreement on how to cope jointly with the Huguenot displacement and no international aid schemes or camps, which would become commonplace three centuries later – rather states acted alone and could generally manage the problem in this way; second, numbers of refugees, although not insignificant, did not threaten to overwhelm host states and significantly affect their societies economically or socially; and third, Huguenot 'refugees' usually brought either money or skills and thus could be perceived as an asset rather than a burden as is often the case today. The fourth and crucial difference, however, is that the Huguenots were not refugees as they are now understood, since contemporary thinking defines the refugee in significant degree by the crossing of a well-defined jurisdictional boundary. Pre-modern exiles, émigrés, aliens and foreigners are important in pointing out the way early states had begun singling people out and excluding them from their territory, and in assessing early reactions of host states towards such 'refugees'. The Huguenots certainly had characteristics common to today's refugee, but it would take another couple of centuries for the contemporary refugee to be born. The (modern) refugee is only fully intelligible within the context of a pluralist system of states in which individual political communities fail to guarantee the content of substantive sovereignty.

Several authors agree on the refugee issue as being a particularly modern one. Nyers notes that 'while select groups of migrating people have been called "refugees" for almost as long as the Westphalian system of states ... most conventional accounts identify the refugee "problem" as a particularly twentieth century phenomenon'.[53] Marrus contrasts earlier exiles as individuals who had generally chosen their political path, whereas the forced movement is more 'imposed' on the modern refugee.[54] Further, it was only at the turn of the twentieth century that refugees began to be created on a staggering scale, that high levels of protection began to be offered by both governmental and

---

[53] Peter Nyers, 'Emergency or Emerging Identities? Refugees and Transformations in World Order', *Millennium: Journal of International Studies* 28, 1 (1999), 11.

[54] Marrus, *The Unwanted*, p. 15.

non-governmental organisations, that action was internationalised, that the paths of these forced migrants began to be highly regulated, and that refugees began to receive a different reception from earlier displaced persons. It is significant, also, that changes in violence and warfare in the twentieth century meant that conflict began to affect ever wider circles of persons who had to leave their home in search of refuge.[55]

In regard to the contemporary way of dealing with refugees, Malkki points to the fact that it was only post-1945 that 'standardizing, globalizing processes' occurred, allowing the refugee as 'a social category and legal problem of global dimensions' to take hold.[56] Here Malkki notes the leap in refugee camp administration and the institutionalisation of refugee settlement alongside the growing field of refugee law. The refugee camp became an essential empowering device:

> The segregation of nationalities; the orderly organization of repatriation or third-country resettlement; medical and hygienic programs and quarantining; ... the accumulation of documentation on the inhabitants of the camps; the control of movement and black-marketeering; law enforcement and public discipline; and schooling and rehabilitation were some of the operations that the spatial concentration and ordering of people enabled or facilitated. Through these processes, the modern, postwar refugee emerged as a knowable, nameable figure and as an object of social-scientific knowledge.[57]

In this regard it is useful, as Malkki notes, 'to resist positing an automatic evolution of the phenomenon or assuming that it has had a single recognizable germ or form growing out of the "beginning" of the phenomenon in Classical mists of time where banishment was a form of social death': of course, individuals have always sought refuge and sanctuary, but 'there is no "proto-refugee" of which the modern refugee is a direct descendant'.[58] Yet Malkki, like most of the other authors acknowledging the links between the refugee and modernity, fails to spell out the common element underlying all the factors that hint at the newness of the phenomenon – the influence of the consolidation of the state and the workings of the international states system. It is only modern international society that can produce the (modern) refugee, with its emphasis on parcels of territory divided by clearly defined political borders. The refugee is created by a breakdown in the state as a

---

[55] Dillon, 'The Scandal of the Refugee', 105. [56] Malkki, 'Refugees and Exile', 497–8.
[57] Malkki 'Refugees and Exile', 498. [58] Malkki, 'Refugees and Exile', 497.

sustaining political community, as symbolised by modern international political borders.

That the refugee is unique to and bound up with the modern international system of sovereign states is thus largely overlooked. It was in the twentieth century that the state was consolidated as the modern way of sorting peoples and the refugee emerged as a central figure of the international landscape. Nationalism and sovereignty can be seen as critical precursors to the modern refugee phenomenon. When the nation concept was attached to the state concept, the importance of borders was laid down and the fate of individuals forced to move as a consequence was sealed in the figure of the 'refugee'. More than just another migrant, the refugee is an inherent part of the development, reproduction and survival of the nation-state, itself a modern way of imagining international society: 'The modern era began with the creation of separate, independent sovereign states, each of them organized around a particular nation.'[59] As such a system spread across the globe, so the plight of the refugee became a global one. Modernity is this eclectic mixture of collectivities and individuals, where individuals do not always fit easily into collectivities. In Arendt's words, unlike their 'happy predecessors in the religious wars', these new refugees are 'welcomed nowhere and [can] be assimilated nowhere'.[60]

In other words, although the forced displacement of peoples is not new, it was only in the twentieth century that the refugee figure was invented as one particular sub-category due to the international system of separate sovereign states that creates her. Once the world became divided into such political units, being forced out of one unit meant finding another to enter. But since entering another state means obtaining the prior permission of that state, the refugee became a modern category of individual found *between* such sovereigns. Ironically, then, although the modern state is charged with defending both the integrity of its community and the rights of individual members within that community, the refugee emerges from between the gaps in the system. She represents the Achilles' heel of an arrangement that idolises the state–citizen–territory hierarchy. And in this respect the refugee harks back to a time of *pre*-modernity, the product of irrational, chaotic forces

---

[59] S. Toulmin cited in Howard Adelman, 'Modernity, Globalization, Refugees and Displacement', in Alastair Ager (ed.), *Refugees: Perspectives on the Experience of Forced Migration* (London and New York: Continuum, 1999), p. 85.

[60] Hannah Arendt, *The Origins of Totalitarianism* (New York: Harcourt, Brace and World, 1966), p. 267.

that could undo all that modernity stands for. Her salvation is her reinstallation in a modern, sovereign state, yet her very existence is, ironically, the result of the modern, sovereign state.

The refugee is therefore contrasted with different types of displaced persons that preceded her. In the words of Said:

> Although it is true that anyone prevented from returning home is an exile, some distinctions can be made between exiles, refugees, expatri-ates, and émigrés. Exile originated in the age-old practice of banish-ment. Once banished, the exile lives an anomalous and miserable life, with the stigma of being an outsider. Refugees, on the other hand, are a creation of the twentieth-century state. The word "refugee" has become a political one, suggesting large herds of innocent and bewil-dered people requiring urgent international assistance, whereas "exile" carries with it, I think, a touch of solitude and spirituality.[61]

Said's definition is important in characterising contemporary refugees as part of a mass phenomenon traditionally represented in starkly different ways to the individual figure of the exile. Exile has become the word favoured to characterise individuals fleeing their home before the twentieth century. Wrapped up in the refugee concept is a certain type of displaced person not applicable to all persons in the past who have sought asylum: '"Exile" connotes a readily aestheticizable realm, whereas the label "refugees" connotes a bureaucratic and international humanitarian realm.'[62] Indeed, the terms 'exile' and 'refugee' seem to denote different ideas. In religious imagery, exile from the Garden of Eden means that humans' stay on earth is automatically exile.[63] Greek mythology and poetry is full of examples of exile and ostracism: Oedipus, Orestes and Odysseus are well-known examples. Some of history's most famous literary figures, artists and political thinkers have been exiles, banished from their country of origin as a punishment or self-exiled as a way of avoiding penalty: Dante and Machiavelli from Renaissance Florence; Rousseau and Voltaire during the French Enlightenment; Marx, who left Germany and eventually settled in London; Garibaldi and Mazzini exiled during the road to Italian unity; and, of course, the Russians, Pushkin and Dostoyevsky – the list is a long one. But what is striking is the noble image such figures

---

[61] Said, *Reflections on Exile*, p. 181.   [62] Malkki, 'Refugees and Exile', 513.
[63] For a comprehensive history of religious exiles, see Frederick A. Norwood, *Strangers and Exiles: A History of Religious Refugees*, vol. I (Nashville and New York: Abingdon Press, 1969).

conjure up in contrast to the large groups of anonymous refugees that started to appear in the early twentieth century.

Russian exiles of the nineteenth and twentieth centuries have always been associated with the picturesque and the romantic. In the words of Tabori, 'exile and literature, Siberia and independent thought are inextricably linked in Russian history'.[64] Siberia, of course, represents the classic example of being in exile within one's native land, and personal testimonies underline the sense of being an outsider trapped inside, unable to escape. After two years in prison in Odessa as a 'political offender', Marie Sutkloff was taken into eastern Siberia in 1904 to be exiled alone in a small village for life. She was greeted with sympathy and seen as a victim, but her desire to escape remained high:

> As soon as I *felt* that I was free, the old wounds re-opened in my heart. Memories of the past, day after day and year after year, rose in my mind and whispered to me: 'There can be no freedom for you after all that you have gone through, after all that you *know*. There can be no freedom for you when all your best and dearest friends have remained in the world of shadows and stone walls, in the world of torture and humiliation.'[65]

It is as if the world takes notice when it is a case of individual demonstrations of dissent; the act of exile highlights the suppression of individual liberties by a state. While the individual seeks refuge abroad, the act is romanticised and poeticised. The Polish writer Joseph Wittlin called it 'the grandeur and sorrow of exile'.[66] Exile becomes something heroic, something noble, a punishment inflicted on an individual for the sake of his or her beliefs or opposition to the home government, or the only choice left to an individual who is being repressed. Once they have escaped they will be in a place where they will be free to express themselves and their opinions. The exiles that first started coming out of revolutionary France were even known as the 'joyous émigrés', hinting at their assumed bid for freedom and a celebrated status abroad.[67] Revolutionary activity by these and other political exiles was seen to have little relevance to western European politics and hence represented little cause for concern in liberal western

---

[64] Tabori, *The Anatomy of Exile*, p. 123.

[65] Marie Sutkloff, *The Life Story of a Russian Exile. The Remarkable Experience of a Young Girl: Being an Account of Her Peasant Childhood in Prison, Her Exile to Siberia and Escape from There*, translated by Gregory Yarros (London: William Heinemann, 1915), p. 250 (Sutkloff's italics).

[66] Tabori, *The Anatomy of Exile*, p. 32.   [67] Brubaker, *Citizenship and Nationhood*, p. 79.

states. And, of course, in the nineteenth century flows of exiles were still relatively small in number such that a relief problem just did not exist; rather, exiles were still thought to add to the general wealth of the host state via taxes and could boost military forces if necessary, meaning that such individuals were more an asset than a liability. Accordingly, they met with sympathy for their cause: exiles were seen to oppose autocratic rule and thereby emulate western standards. In this way the exile has usually been more self-defined than the refugee.[68] Exiles choose their path and seek refuge abroad in search of the freedom to continue that which was banned at home. Conceptually exile is thus made out to be something very different from the state of refugeehood: exile is poeticised, but as soon as individuals turn into destitute masses, all images of heroism are lost.

The (modern) refugee cannot be the same romanticised, idealised figure. She rarely arrives alone; hundreds of other refugees arrive at the same time, part of a perpetual movement of vast numbers of persons forced to move across the globe. With the twentieth and twenty-first centuries' predisposition to violence and the increased emphasis in the West on the welfare state and employment for national citizens first and foremost, the days of the (welcomed) political exile are over. The result is that the refugee is denied the possibility of establishing a home in a world in which home is the product and precondition of political life.[69] Once the international system became the modern method of organising peoples and territories, the (modern) refugee announced she was here to stay: 'Suddenly, there was no place on earth where migrants could go without the severest restrictions, no country where they would be assimilated, no territory where they could found a new community of their own.'[70]

Conclusions

Refugees are the side-effect of the creation of separate sovereign states, states that have failed to enforce a system of substantive sovereignty that would ensure the protection of all their citizens. Sovereignty is not merely a formal concept, but entails the duty to represent and protect

---

[68] Tabori, *The Anatomy of Exile*, p. 36.
[69] Nicholas Xenos, 'Refugees: The Modern Political Condition', in Michael J. Shapiro and Alker Hayward (eds.), *Challenging Boundaries: Global Flows, Territorial Identities* (Minneapolis: University of Minnesota Press, 1996), 243.
[70] Arendt, *The Origins*, p. 293.

all those who fall within the sovereign jurisdiction of the state: a failure of the sovereign to fulfil these duties has the potential to produce refugees. When the individual is forced outside the domestic political community, the refugee is pushed, whether literally or putatively, across political borders and into the gaps *between* sovereign states. They are anomalies in the international states system and challenge the assumption that all individuals belong to a territory. In other words, refugees are not a sign of the international system 'going wrong'. They are, in fact, an inherent if unanticipated part of the system. Without the modern state there could be no refugees. Sovereignty attempts to sort all individuals into homogeneous territorial spaces. In the process some are inevitably forced between the borders, between sovereigns. As such, refugees are victims of an international system that brings them into being, then fails to take responsibility for them. International protection relies on individual states, yet states retain the sovereign right to decide who may enter their territory and hence whom they will protect. Accordingly, the flight of the refugee highlights a failure both of individual governments to protect their citizens and of the international states system as a whole, the failure to assign every individual to a state and protect them as citizens.

The growth of the nation-state has implied the naming of certain peoples as outsiders, foreigners, unwanted. The designation of individuals as obstacles to the successful formation of the nation-state has become a fundamental aspect of nation-state creation, and refugee flows are a likely outcome.[71] They are a truly modern phenomenon that would not exist without international society. Refugees thus represent a quintessentially contemporary or 'modern' political identity crisis.[72] In her position as an 'outsider' the refugee is a threat to state sovereignty and it is to this threat, manifested in the clash between sovereign rights and human rights, that we now turn.

---

[71] Zolberg. 'The Formation of New States', 32.   [72] Xenos, 'Refugees', 243–4.

4 Sovereign rights, human rights and security

> Refugees serve as an index of internal disorder and as prima facie evidence of the violation of human rights and humanitarian standards. No other issue, perhaps, provides such a clear and unassailable link between humanitarian concerns and legitimate international security issues. Alan Dowty and Gil Loescher[1]

The international states system has long been the result of an uneasy relationship between communitarian and cosmopolitan values. The refugee brings to the fore the very tension between the state prerogative to exclude and the human rights imperative to include. How, therefore, can refugee protection be reconciled with state sovereignty if the two are logically in opposition? The fact that states do take action on behalf of refugees suggests a human rights thinking. But this is compromised since the refugee issue is an inherently political one, and humanitarian action cannot be divorced from national and international politics. If the refugee opposes the thinking that underlies the make-up of international society – that all individuals should belong to a state – the answer to why states act for refugees might rather be due to a securitarian logic, not a humanitarian one.

This chapter first looks at the idea of 'rights' in order to ask what rights the refugee may rely on and how her position between states limits her ability to enjoy supposedly universal human rights. Based on a natural law versus positive law dichotomy, the discussion leads on to an analysis of whether the refugee and refugee protection point to a solidarist or pluralist make-up of international society. It then builds on this thinking to examine the refugee's relationship with the concept of

---

[1] Dowty and Loescher, 'Refugee Flows', 70–1.

human rights. Finally, it asks whether the idea of refugee protection is better suited to a security paradigm.

Shifting conceptions of rights

Modern Europe speaks the language of rights. Rights have become part of our moral and political thinking. They are entrenched in constitutions and upheld in international declarations. A right is 'something which can be exercised, earned, enjoyed, or given, which can be claimed, demanded, asserted, insisted on, secured, waived, or surrendered'.[2] Whoever or whatever can possess an interest has the potential to possess a right, and to be capable of having rights a being must be conceived as a self-contained source of moral obligations.[3] Thus a right becomes characterised by a relation between two parties and, accordingly, will involve a correlative duty.

Vincent talks of a right as a moral possession, and defines it as consisting of five main elements: the *subject* of the right, for example an individual, a group or a state; the *object* of the right, that 'trumps'[4] ordinary interests; *exercising* the right, which connects the subject to the object either by claiming something concrete, enjoying something more abstract or seeking protection against some kind of infraction; the bearer of the correlative *duty*, against which the right is held; and the *justification* of the right, which entails the social acceptance of the right as being of importance via a custom, reason, statute or contract.[5] Rights can be negative, 'a claim to a secured *space* in which subjects might pursue their own concerns without interference',[6] or positive, 'a claim that the space be filled with something'.[7] A further categorisation of rights provided by Jones puts forward four types: claim-rights, liberty-rights, power and immunity. A claim-right is generated by a contract and accompanied by correlative duties; thus it is a claim that one party has upon another. Liberty-rights grant the right to do something, whilst there is no obligation not to do it: someone is 'at liberty' to dress as they please, for example, in that they have no obligation to dress or not to dress in any particular way. Immunity means a right to be free from,

---

[2] Alan R. White, *Rights* (Oxford: Clarendon Press, 1984), p. 90.
[3] Peter Jones, *Rights* (Basingstoke: Macmillan Press, 1994), p. 70.
[4] Ronald Dworkin cited in R. J. Vincent, *Human Rights and International Relations* (Cambridge University Press, 1986), p. 8.
[5] Vincent, *Human Rights*, pp. 8–9.   [6] K. R. Minogue cited in Vincent, *Human Rights*, p. 8.
[7] Vincent, *Human Rights*, p. 8.

immune from, another's authority. And the idea of rights as power clearly empowers the rights-holder to do something: an individual has the right to vote because she is legally empowered to do so.[8]

Until 1945 international law existed primarily to separate and confirm the separate jurisdictions of individual states and thus prevent conflicts, as it had done since 1648.[9] Rights of individuals were regarded as the subject of international law only in exceptional circumstances. Minority rights guarantees began to appear in the seventeenth century, first in relation to religious minorities and then, with transformations in the international order, to national minorities. As medieval society was replaced by the modern system of separate states, so arrangements began to be made to address the anomalies posed by those communities that did not fit the new spatial framework.[10] Indeed, minority rights agreements accompanied those settlements that brought about changes in the very organisation of international society, including the Treaty of Westphalia of 1648, the Congress of Vienna of 1815 and the Treaty of Berlin of 1878, when international recognition of newly independent states was contingent upon minority rights guarantees.[11] Such guarantees were given their final form in the inter-war period by way of the League of Nations minority treaties, which were an attempt to limit the potentially destabilising effects of the exceptions to the prevailing rule of state legitimacy.[12] With the collapse of empires and the subsequent redefinition of territorial boundaries, the League of Nations minority treaties were a response to the newly created insiders and outsiders, aiming to provide certain international rights to individuals of defeated states. There were some further developments in the rights of individuals from the mid-nineteenth century, when it was held that in times of war or armed conflict, nations at war had to allow medical assistance to the wounded under their control, and prisoners of war were to be guaranteed certain standards of treatment as of the 1920s; in times of peace, aliens residing legally in a foreign state had to be granted minimum civil rights; and from the 1920s, again, workers came to be protected legally by

[8] Jones, *Rights*, pp. 12–13.
[9] David P. Forsythe, *Human Rights in International Relations* (Cambridge University Press, 2000), p. 21.
[10] Jennifer Jackson-Preece, 'Minority Rights in Europe: From Westphalia to Helsinki', *Review of International Studies* 23 (1997), 76.
[11] For an in-depth discussion of the evolution of minority rights guarantees, see Jackson-Preece, *National Minorities*.
[12] Jackson-Preece, 'Minority Rights', 76.

agreements developed by the International Labor Organization.[13] In each of these examples, however, individuals were still taken as part of a group.

Unless states were under specific treaty obligations linked to their recognition or admission into international society, however, they had the sovereign right to treat their citizens as they so chose. In the absence of explicit treaty stipulations of this kind, one state attempting to address the treatment of another state's citizens was taken as illegitimate interference; and even where treaty provisions allowed for interference this remained deeply controversial and thus for the most part only sporadically enforced. In this context, therefore, individuals had rights but only insofar as they belonged to a state. Rights only became real when taken up and protected in the positive law of states. In other words rights were entitlements granted to individuals by the domestic law of states. This particularistic account of rights assumed a contract between the state and the individual; rights were granted in exchange for duties. Individuals possessed the rights they did because they were citizens of a particular state, and the law of that state endowed them with these rights in return for obligations such as exclusive loyalty to their state. Claiming one's rights was made possible by a judicial system that enforced and guaranteed them.

The American and French Revolutions of the eighteenth century brought about the first formal enunciations and definitions of the rights and freedoms of individuals within the state. It was acknowledged that the rights of man were possessed by all humans by virtue of their humanity alone, and 'inalienable' in that no one had the power to give these rights or take them away. But such rights were always bound up with membership in a particular community, and so remained a national matter to be accepted or denied by the state.[14] Rulers were now elected representatives of the people and constitutions set out their powers, but rights of individuals were only meaningful when granted by such constitutional governments. With the development of the nation-state in the nineteenth century and the simultaneous emergence of the doctrine of national sovereignty, it became clear that the subjects of international law would continue to be nation-states whilst individuals would remain in their role as subjects of the now popular sovereign: in other words, the 'rights revolution' did not extend beyond the borders of liberal states. It follows that as far as positive law is concerned, there is no guarantee of

---

[13] Forsythe, *Human Rights*, p. 21.   [14] Forsythe, *Human Rights*, p. 3.

genuine 'human rights' that an individual possesses simply on the basis of her humanity. Human rights do exist, but only in the abstract – people everywhere have rights, but these rights only have meaning within the legal systems of states. Thus at the domestic level human rights and positive rights can coexist and reinforce each other. The conceptual disjunction between the two is unimportant, although it is acknowledged that positive rights are the superior and 'real' rights.[15]

The foundation of the League of Nations, instigated by a desire and need for peace in the aftermath of the First World War, was based on the underlying assumption that member states would be governed by the rule of law and respect for individual rights. It attempted to guarantee the rights of minority groups and sought to offer protection to those who had been displaced by the War and border changes in the international system. It lacked, however, any explicit provisions relating to general human rights, and its failure may be evidenced in the atrocities of the Holocaust. Now it had been demonstrated that constitutional guarantees within individual states could fail drastically and leave individuals severely unprotected. Accordingly, it was only in the wake of the Second World War, with the realisation of the extremes to which national sovereignty could be taken, that the need to provide a universal position on respect for human rights within the modern states system was properly asserted. Hence the path was paved for a flourishing of human rights legislation in multilateral forums at both the regional and global levels.

For the first time how a state treated its own citizens became a matter of legitimate concern for all other states in the international system. International law laid down the rights of individuals against the states which exercised power over them, and a legally binding code of international human rights was born. The formation of the Universal Declaration of Human Rights in 1948 represented a major turning point: this was the first international document that sought to define a comprehensive code of conduct for the domestic government of sovereign members of the international community. In fact, contained within this post-war formulation of international human rights was the possibility of superseding the national order. The international system could potentially have formed some kind of global, cosmopolitan community

---

[15] Chris Brown, 'Human Rights and Human Dignity: An Analysis of the "Human-Rights Culture" and its Critics', paper presented at the Universal Human Rights Conference, University of Otago, 3–6 July 1998, 4.

beyond the sovereign state, where having rights did not depend on belonging to a state.[16] This has clearly not yet developed, but the possibilities it opens up are nothing short of revolution within the context of the Westphalian system of separate states.

The human rights regime that has matured since 1945 encompasses a universal, moral account of rights based on the requirements of human flourishing. Rights are said to rest on the general moral standards of natural law established by the use of human reasoning, and human reasoning suggests that moral standards can generate rights and duties. These are rights that we have by virtue of our being human, rights that are held equally by all human beings. Yet although natural law, as far as one believes it to exist, grants rights that do not rely on the individual being associated with any particular form of society or government, international human rights norms require enforcement if such rights are to be effectively upheld, and in reality this enforcement must usually take place at the national level. Thus what sets out to be universal in theory actually relies on a positivist system associated with individual states. In other words, the idea of human rights is offered to the international community in a form more appropriate to positive law. In the absence of any effective international enforcement machinery, individual states have nothing more than a personal, moral obligation to respect such norms. If successful in their crossing of an international frontier, refugees become wards of international society, in which protection relies on the endorsement, financial support and refugee-determination processes of individual sovereign states.[17] We see, therefore, an awkward rapprochement between the Westphalian system of sovereign states and the cosmopolitan order suggested by the idea of international human rights. Where respect for individual interests requires a compromise in state interests, compromise will be conditional, particularly where the requirement is not legally binding. Such a clash of interests unavoidably creates an international society coloured by inconsistencies, dichotomies and paradoxes.

Sceptics of the recent developments in human rights law insist that rights granted by membership in a particular state continue to be the only ones of any worth. As Walzer has pointed out, 'it is not the case that one can simply proclaim a list of rights and then look around for armed men to enforce it': rights are only enforceable within political communities where they have been collectively recognised via a

---

[16] Malkki, 'Refugees and Exile', 502.   [17] Hyndman, *Managing Displacement*, p. 7.

political process, and any such political process requires a political arena; 'The globe is not, or not yet, such an arena.'[18] While we continue to exist within a community of nations, not a community of humanity, we will continue to be granted a modicum of (largely negative) rights which are designed more to protect the integrity of nations than uphold any universal human rights which may or may not exist. 'Against foreigners,' continues Walzer, 'individuals have a right to a state of their own. Against state officials, they have a right to political and civil liberty. Without the first of these rights, the second is meaningless: as individuals need a home, so rights require a location.'[19] In other words, without membership of a political community our so-called human rights can be seen to have limited value.

How do positive law and natural law interact when we move to the international arena? We saw above that at the national level rights granted by states and rights that we possess *qua* human beings could coexist, even though rights granted by a political community were taken as superior. When we move out of the individual state to the international community, natural rights are assumed to be prior to positive law and the state. That is to say when the two meet in the international arena the idea of human rights should take the upper hand. It follows that the conceptual disjunction between positive law and human rights based on natural law thinking is wider at the universal level than at the national level.[20] The two coexist most uneasily since human rights aim to trump the authority of state sovereignty, the very foundation of positive law.

Solidarism within pluralism

There are two visions of international society that divide English School scholars. According to pluralists such as Jackson, members of the society of states can only be expected to be able to agree on the minimum requirements of international order – mutual respect for sovereignty, non-intervention and diplomacy, for example. Although these principles may be considered universal, states may not be able to agree and act in unison when it comes to actual enforcement of such principles. Consequently order, justice and the rule of law in international society all hang on the ability of states to first provide for these qualities

[18] M. Walzer, *Spheres of Justice* (New York: Basic Books, 1983), p. 234.
[19] Walzer, *Spheres of Justice*, pp. 234–6.   [20] Brown, 'Human Rights', 4.

in their own national societies in accordance with their own values. In other words, 'the good life' must be defined by the state, and there can be many different versions of it within international society at any one time – pluralism. International rules stipulate basic international agreement about the requirements of peaceful coexistence among different national societies but do not establish and enforce a particular global version of what this means within individual states. International order is first and foremost order among states, such that, by and large, only states have rights and duties under international law. Human rights, therefore, have the potential to become a source of international conflict as long as there is no international agreement about justice.

The solidarist conception of international society, as outlined by Wheeler and Vincent among others, is based on the assumption of solidarity among states with respect to the enforcement of law. The maintenance of the principles of international law is considered to be a common responsibility, and the international community has an obligation to offer support to any state whose rights have been violated. International solidarity is not confined to the relationship between states – individuals also have rights and duties under international law, and states have an obligation to defend the interests of all humanity. Thus solidarist thinkers support the idea of humanitarian intervention as part of the general belief that force may be used for the promotion of the common good, preventing crimes against humanity as a whole. This of course brings into question the meaning of sovereignty and the degree to which its power is absolute. Practices and institutions such as the collective defence of international peace and security, international peacekeeping, humanitarian assistance, development projects, international tribunals and systems of minority protection can all be seen as reflections of solidarist principles – as can the protection of refugees.

Pluralists therefore see international society as granter and guarantor of positive rights associated with the institution of citizenship, while solidarists underscore the natural rights of individuals *qua* human beings. Pluralists are inclined to focus on the good things that the Westphalian principles of state sovereignty, non-intervention, formal equality and diplomacy and the system of international law have done for international society and humanity. Solidarists focus on how international order could be improved, with respect to the protection of the individual and human security, the common enforcement of international law and platforms of global governance such as UN international peacekeeping. The mix of pluralist and solidarist principles

77

in international society brings issues such as human rights and humanitarian intervention to the very heart of international politics. In reality, however, it is difficult to make too great a distinction between the two conceptions. International society has always contained elements of both pluralism and solidarism, and it is precisely the dialectic between them that makes it a dynamic arrangement. Bull said as much when he noted that an international society of states implies some kind of latent global society of humankind, and when he described solidarism as being about 'the guardianship of human rights everywhere'.[21] Indeed, pluralism is not necessarily solely about collective enforcement of the rules, but may be about enforcement of a particular set of rules concerned with human rights and morality. Bull became increasingly disillusioned by the failure of the great powers to act as global guardians, and more and more convinced that both order and justice depended on developing more solidarist sentiments amongst states.[22] The 'problem' of refugees is a classic example of precisely this point – the limited efficacy of the pluralism versus solidarism schematic – since it seems to disclose the validity of both points of reference. The refugee would not exist were it not for the pluralist states system, but at the same time this pluralist system seems incapable of resolving this dilemma. Instead, a lasting response would seem to require a greater emphasis on precisely those sort of common (human) norms one tends to associate with solidarism. This is not to say that pluralist norms are irrelevant to contemporary issues, because that would be to miss the point that one cannot understand the refugee concept without reference to these pluralist norms.

The United Nations Charter signed on 26 June 1945 laid the basis for a rapid development in international law concerning the status of individuals including the refugee.[23] New refugee policy springing from the UN Charter was clearly located within or closely connected to the growing field of human rights legislation and the emerging principle of individual rights. Most multilateral instruments came to be based on the albeit non-binding 1948 Universal Declaration of Human Rights. The 1949 Geneva Convention Relating to the Protection of Individuals in Times of War included the provision that refugees shall not be

---

[21] Bull, *The Anarchical Society*, pp. 19–21; Hedley Bull, 'The Grotian Conception of International Society', in Butterfield and Wight, *Diplomatic Investigations*, 63.

[22] Dunne, *Inventing International Society*, pp. 147–9.

[23] Grahl-Madsen, *The Status of Refugees*, p. 17.

considered enemy aliens if they had formerly had the nationality of an enemy power. But the 'Magna Carta' for refugees was the Convention Relating to the Status of Refugees signed in Geneva on 28 July 1951.[24] This instrument marked 'a new level of world morality', comprising 'the most comprehensive charter' regarding refugee rights and an extensive international code of ethics for refugees.[25] Building on earlier Conventions, it covered an unprecedentedly large number of categories of refugees and established a broad base of minimal rights for such individuals.

Ever since the states system arose in its modern form, however, the state has retained the right to regulate entry to its territory as a funda-mental concomitant of sovereignty,[26] and that remains the case up to and including the present time. While the 1951 Convention accords the putative refugee the right to seek asylum, nowhere is the right to be granted asylum guaranteed. No international treaty, convention or other similar document of international law has managed to penetrate to any great degree the licence of sovereign states to determine who may enter their territory. Thus the right of states to grant asylum takes precedence over the right of individuals – would-be refugees – to receive it. Accordingly, the 1951 Convention and related human rights legislation that also acts to protect the refugee can be understood as a curious mix of the pluralist and the solidarist. The solidarist tries to move in the humanitarian direction, while the pluralist ensures the sovereign state retains the upper hand. This philosophical incongru-ence underscores the often contradictory policies of states and inter-governmental organisations dealing with refugees and refugee issues. Moreover, the fact that respect for the sovereignty of other states in the international system is equal to non-intervention in their domestic affairs means that states can use this principle as an excuse for denying responsibility regarding the humanitarian needs of the refugee. She may be forced to flee her country for fear of prosecution, yet any

---

[24] The 1951 Convention has since been followed by a stream of legislation specifically concerning refugees. A few examples are the 1954 Convention Relating to the Status of Stateless Persons; the 1957 European Convention on Extradition and the 1959 European Agreement on the Abolition of Visas for Refugees, both from the Council of Europe; the 1961 UN Convention on the Reduction of Statelessness; and the International Labour Organisation's Convention Concerning Equality of Treatment of Nationals and Non-Nationals in Social Security, also of 1961.

[25] United Nations Department of Public Information, *Magna Carta for Refugees* (New York: 1951).

[26] Zolberg cited in Skran, *Refugees in Inter-war Europe*, p. 68.

accusations of a sovereign government persecuting its own people are a breach of the non-intervention clause and may well jeopardise international relations between states. In other words, the non-intervention right of sovereign states may be used as a blanket for other sovereign states not wishing to take responsibility for non-citizens or 'others'. States can continue to be considered sovereign without being obliged to consider the situation of individuals who belong to other sovereign states, states that have failed to respect the no harm principle towards their citizens and who have therefore forced them out of their territory to become refugees. Once again we see that sovereignty is a reciprocal relationship between states as states, which does not have any explicit obligations for the treatment of the populations that make up such polities.

The prerogative of states to exclude is, of course, tempered to a certain degree by the principle of *non-refoulement*, as laid down in Article 33 of the 1951 Convention. This principle, described by many as the cornerstone of refugee protection, holds that 'no Contracting State shall expel or return ("*refouler*") a refugee in any manner whatsoever to the frontiers of territories where his life or freedom would be threatened on account of his race, religion, nationality, membership of a particular social group or political opinion'. Indeed, it acts as the key contemporary international legal obligation on states to refugees, prohibiting the return of a refugee to any country where she is likely to face persecution or torture.[27] It is important to note that the principle acts as a negative obligation rather than a positive obligation on states of admission to their territory, which can no doubt be traced back to the time of the drafting of the 1951 Convention: states were not willing to include any article that signed them up automatically to admission of refugees, and the principle of *non-refoulement* was consequently inserted instead.[28]

Although the applicability of the 1951 Convention has periodically been called into question in recent years, the continued relevance and importance of the principle of *non-refoulement* has regularly been underlined. It applies both to refugees, within the meaning of Article 1 of the 1951 Convention, as well as to asylum-seekers while their claim is being processed. Indeed, according to UNHCR's Executive Committee, the principle holds both at the border and within the territory of a state,

[27] Goodwin-Gill, *The Refugee in International Law*, p. 117.
[28] Goodwin-Gill, *The Refugee in International Law*, pp. 17, 122.

'irrespective of whether or not [the individuals] have been formally recognized as refugees'.[29] By and large states have recognised that the principle applies to the moment the individual presents herself for entry and claims asylum – in other words, it encompasses both non-return and non-rejection.[30] In its recent global consultations on international protection, UNHCR drew seven conclusions relating to the principle, among which: that *non-refoulement* is a principle of customary international law; that Article 33 applies to refugees irrespective of their formal recognition and to asylum-seekers; that the principle encompasses any measure attributable to the state which could have the effect of returning an asylum-seeker or refugee to the frontiers of territories where his or her life or freedom would be threatened, or where he or she is at risk of persecution, including interception, rejection at the frontier or indirect *refoulement*; that the principle applies in situations of mass influx; and that the attribution to the state of conduct amounting to *refoulement* is determined by the principles of the law on state responsibility.[31]

It is worth noting, however, that the principle of *non-refoulement* is not absolute. Derogations are permissible on the grounds of 'national security' and 'public order'. Article 33(2) expressly provides that the benefit of *non-refoulement* may not be claimed by a refugee 'whom there are reasonable grounds for regarding as a danger to the security of the country in which he is, or who, having been convicted by a final judgment of a particularly serious crime, constitutes a danger to the community of that country'. Of interest here, as Goodwin-Gill has pointed out, is that the exceptions to the principle are framed in terms of the individual, but the assessment of whether the individual constitutes a security risk or threat to public order is left to the judgement of the state.[32]

Admittedly the principle is not equivalent to the right to asylum, but it does take us beyond the simple dualism between the right to seek asylum and the right to be granted it. Although states have the right to determine who may and who may not enter their territory, the principle of *non-refoulement* appears to encroach on this right to a certain degree.

[29] UNHCR EXCOM, 'Non-refoulement', Conclusion No. 6 (XXVIII), 1977, paragraph (c).
[30] Goodwin-Gill, *The Refugee in International Law*, pp. 122–3.
[31] Erika Feller, Volker Türk and Frances Nicholson (eds.), *Refugee Protection in International Law: UNHCR's Global Consultations on International Protection* (Cambridge University Press, 2003), p. 178.
[32] Goodwin-Gill, *The Refugee in International Law*, p. 139.

Non-refoulement adds a degree of solidarist thinking into statist control over conditions of entry into sovereign territory. Indeed, the very fact that an international protection regime has grown up around the refugee points to the solidarist within the pluralist. In a strictly pluralist world only pluralist norms such as sovereignty, non-intervention and the rights of citizens would be recognised and would prevail. Yet the refugee regime introduces ideas of the equality of all human beings, human dignity and an end to human suffering. Such shared values are indicative of elements of solidarism, universal values that undermine the clearly-defined borders between sovereign states. The existence of the regime points to the interplay between solidarism and pluralism in international society. And it is this interplay that causes the paradoxes and contradictions that paint the international landscape. Of course, the refugee figure conjures up dilemmas regarding how far a state's duties extend beyond borders. And when states take decisions to act or not to act on behalf of other states' citizens, their motives may not be strictly or even predominantly humanitarian. But it is difficult to explain the status of refugees within international society without some reference to humanitarian ethics, even if in practice this is more muted than proponents of natural law would like.

What may we infer as the consequences of this clash of principles, this clash between sovereignty and humanitarianism, as far as the refugee is concerned? For Arendt, membership in a state is vital to existence itself. Forcing someone out of a political community, she says, results in their losing those parts of the world and those aspects of human existence which are the outcome of the human artifice. In refugee language, if the refugee suffers persecution and is forced to flee her state, she has lost her ties with a political community and now 'just exists because of birth', no longer allowed to partake in the human artifice.[33] In other words, relying on one's human rights, as opposed to the positive rights that come with membership in a state, is not enough to ensure a place within society, within the human artifice. Being rightless does not, she continues, entail the deprivation of the right of life or liberty, simply the fact that the person no longer belongs to any community whatsoever: 'The fundamental deprivation of human rights is manifested first and above all in the deprivation of a place in the world which makes opinions significant and actions effective'; it is not the loss of citizens' rights to freedom and justice that is at stake, but the fact that

[33] Arendt, *The Origins*, p. 301.

'belonging to the community into which one is born is no longer a matter of course and not belonging no longer a matter of choice'.[34] The importance of rights ensuing from belonging to a particular state is seemingly paramount.

Not only is the refugee at risk in this situation. From a communitarian point of view the existence of people outside the human artifice is a danger to our political life, and, as their numbers increase, so the risk to civilisation itself augments. The human artifice is threatened from within. When there is no longer any 'uncivilised' spot on earth, when the whole of humanity has become organised and, theoretically, 'civilised', the loss of home and political status, or the acquisition of refugee status, becomes identical with expulsion from humanity altogether. Thus Arendt advocates the view that refugee protection came onto the agenda just when the international community realised the importance of belonging to a state: 'We became aware of the existence of a right to have rights ... and a right to belong to some kind of organized community, only when millions of people emerged who had lost and could not regain these rights because of the new global political situation.'[35] In other words, in the post-war environment the importance of protecting the refugee as an individual in the in-between, outside the human artifice, was revealed just when the states system was being consolidated and the refugee problem announced it was here to stay.

We are left, then, with a dilemma. A state cannot now retreat behind the principle of national sovereignty if its violation of the rights of its own citizens results in mass flight, yet it can still retreat behind its sovereignty so as to avoid the moral question of protecting refugees. Emigration continues to be a matter of human rights, whilst immigration remains a matter of national sovereignty. Thus the refugee problem cannot be reduced to simple questions of morality, but neither is it solely a question of state sovereignty in which moral judgements play no role.[36] It is important to remember that actors in international relations are only humans, and humans are imperfect beings. As Isaiah Berlin's famous Kantian quote notes, 'out of the crooked timber of humanity no straight thing was ever made'.[37] In a similar vein Jackson points out that international relations is a human activity

---

[34] Arendt, *The Origins*, p. 296.   [35] Arendt, *The Origins*, p. 297.
[36] Jackson-Preece, 'Ethnocultural Diversity', 192, 195.
[37] Isaiah Berlin, *The Crooked Timber of Humanity: Chapters in the History of Ideas* (London: John Murray, 1990), p. 19.

and the society of states is a human arrangement, organised and operated by people. States do not exist apart from people, he says, thus international relations cannot be divorced from questions of human morality. The question of refugees might therefore be better discussed within the context of 'international human relations'.[38]

Refugee protection as a human rights issue

The international refugee and human rights regimes are closely linked. Refugees are the side-effect of the establishment of sovereign states which then fail to guarantee the protection of all their citizens. Human rights norms have evolved to limit the theoretically infinite and potentially destructive power of sovereignty. The origins of both the refugee as a concept and the idea of human rights are thus predicated on a system of separate states with sovereign status, territorial jurisdiction and clearly-defined borders. The refugee is a category of person with certain human rights that are under threat. It has been said that 'today's human rights abuses are tomorrow's refugee problems',[39] and it could be argued that in most situations of mass displacement the violation of human rights is involved. The fact that Article 14.1 of the Universal Declaration of Human Rights upholds that 'everyone has the right to seek and to enjoy in other countries asylum from persecution'[40] shows how refugee law is an inseparable part of the code of human rights. As Beyani points out, refugee protection has long 'suffered from the false dichotomy between "refugee specific" standards, and human rights standards', yet despite their distinct status in international law, restrictions that states put on the movement of refugees and their residence within states clearly fall within the realm of human rights standards.[41] The relationship is further underlined when noting that if an asylum claim fails the applicant will often seek to rely on other international human rights agreements for the protection of her rights,

---

[38] Jackson, *The Global Covenant*, pp. 29–30.

[39] Gil Loescher, 'Refugees: A Global Human Rights and Security Crisis', in Tim Dunne and Nicholas J. Wheeler (eds.), *Human Rights in Global Politics* (Cambridge University Press, 1999), 244.

[40] Universal Declaration of Human Rights, *adopted* 10 December 1948 (U.N. Doc. A/810). The right to seek asylum is also upheld in regional instruments, such as Article 12 of the Organisation on African Unity (OAU) Convention Governing the Specific Aspects of Refugee Problems in Africa, *adopted* 10 September 1969 (UNTS no.14691); and Article 22 of the Cartagena Declaration on Refugees, *adopted* 19–22 November 1984.

[41] Beyani, *Human Rights Standards*, pp. 110, 129.

such as the European Convention on Human Rights (ECHR).[42] Large groups of persons fleeing oppressive regimes, for example, can rarely demonstrate that each of them has been singled out for individual persecution, yet were such individuals to be forcibly repatriated, or *refouled*, they may be subjected to inhumane or degrading treatment or death, all of which are expressly forbidden by the ECHR. In such cases many would-be refugees may be granted other types of permission to stay in the host country, such as the United Kingdom's system of 'Humanitarian Protection'. Thus the link between human rights and refugee protection is again evident.

But human rights are inherently cosmopolitan whereas the refugee is an expression of positive law in a pluralist world: her existence relies on separate sovereign states founded on positive law, sovereign states that fail to fulfil the requirements of substantive sovereignty that would ensure the protection of the refugee's basic rights within the domestic political community. Sovereignty after all implies not only power but also the responsibility to ensure the well-being of all citizens living within a sovereign territory and respect for their human rights.[43] A refugee protection regime started to be formulated in the inter-war period and was then consolidated post-1945 alongside the field of international human rights. In the wake of the Second World War international society saw that human rights violations and the creation of refugees were inextricably linked and hence both issues had to be addressed. It is important to remember, however, that while natural rights would still exist in a world without states, the refugee would not. Hence if natural law fails to stop the denial of the basic rights that it claims all persons possess, and allows the concept of the refugee to come into being, then basic human rights would appear to be of little use to the refugee who lacks a state to enforce them.

Under the 1951 Convention the refugee can rely on international law to uphold specific individual rights. Once the refugee arrives in a host state the very rights regime that expresses the essence of modernity is extended via the 1951 Convention to ensure a set of rights for the refugee.[44] She is afforded claim-rights, since in return for protection she has duties to the host country in terms of respecting its laws and

---

[42] European Convention for the Protection of Human Rights and Fundamental Freedoms, *opened for signature* 4 November 1950 (213 UNTS 221).

[43] Catherine Phuong, 'Internally Displaced Persons and Refugees: Conceptual Differences and Similarities', *Netherlands Quarterly of Human Rights* 18, 2 (2000), 221.

[44] Adelman, 'Modernity, Globalization', 95.

maintaining public order (Article 2); certain liberty-rights, such as the right to freedom of religion (Article 4); as well as guarantees of specific immunity rights, including the right to *non-refoulement* (Article 33). It is important to keep in mind that almost all the rights set out in the 1951 Convention are only granted once refugee status has been determined. The 'asylum-seeker' whose application is being processed is not protected by the 1951 Convention save for the important right to *non-refoulement*, which it is generally agreed applies to those claiming asylum as well as those who have been formally granted it. Moreover, if we take into consideration the enforceability and practical value of lists of what can be seen as somewhat abstract human rights, the status of the refugee may not be as secure as the 1951 Convention would maintain. It is based on the positivist notion that rights necessitate enforcement, but it is up to individual states within the international community to carry out such enforcement. And since states strive to protect their sovereignty it seems clear that they would often wish refugees to remain refugees – non-rights bearers – unless they decide it is in their sovereign interest to offer them some rights.

We must accept, of course, that the refugee is endowed with natural rights in her status first and foremost as a human being. If fundamental human rights are rights that all humans have by virtue of our being human, then all humans must hold them whatever our sub-category. But if a functioning state is essential for the protection of people's pre-existing rights,[45] the refugee has no means of using her rights. She is caught by the so-called 'possession-paradox' of human rights – the implication that everyone has the right to fundamental human rights, but we are not always able to enjoy them due to the problem of enforcement.[46] Instead, the refugee is served only by the specific set of rights associated with being granted refugee status in a host state as laid out in the 1951 Convention, since she will only need protection as a refugee whilst the concept and importance of the state as a sustaining political community continues to exist. She would not exist if natural law rights were respected. In her position outside and between sovereign states the refugee does not belong to a particular state and thus does not have the means of claiming the rights associated with

---

[45] Mervyn Frost, 'Migrants, Civil Society and Sovereign States: Investigating an Ethical Hierarchy', *Political Studies* 46 (1998), 871.

[46] Jack Donnelly cited in Vincent, *Human Rights*, p. 10.

membership of a political community. She has been forced out of her relationship with a political community into the refugee category.

It should also be noted that the refugee protection regime offers a set of rights that only persons who have left the territory of their state may claim. Accordingly, individuals with a well-founded fear of persecution are defined only as those who are no longer within the borders of their country of origin. In the inter-war period a displaced person was someone who found herself outside the borders of her home state but who could be, and perhaps should be, sent home. In the attempt to create homogeneous national entities, population exchange and transfer and forced repatriation were seen as legitimate means of solving any potential refugee or displacement crisis. In the post-1945 era, however, displacement has come to be associated with those persons uprooted from their homes but remaining within their home states, individuals who are left outside the protection of the international refugee regime. This again points to the refugee regime being inherently communitarian: states will act to control refugee flows as and when they become a risk to international stability and threaten states other than their country of origin. The international border can be seen to symbolise the extent of the domestic political community, beyond which the international community cannot pass. However, that is not to say that all individuals within the territorial borders of the state remain members of the political community, pointing once again to the false dichotomy between granting refugee status to individuals who cross borders and not to those who for whatever reasons do not.

It would seem, therefore, that refugee protection and refugee rights cause a blurring of communitarian and cosmopolitan values. Since a refugee is agreed to be fleeing some kind of governmental failure, protection of her fundamental human rights is paramount: her citizenship rights have clearly failed and, accordingly, her right to leave the source of persecution is not contested. But what she should do once she has fled and where she should go is a matter for states to decide in line with communitarian thinking. The cosmopolitan approach grants the refugee the right to leave the source of persecution, but the right of entry into a state remains the domain of state sovereignty. In other words emigration may be a matter of human rights, but immigration remains a concern of national sovereignty,[47] since nowhere is the right

---

[47] Myron Weiner, 'Ethics, National Sovereignty and the Control of Immigration', *International Migration Review* 30, 1 (1996), 171.

to obtain asylum guaranteed. And the disjunction between emigration and immigration gains more weight when we differentiate (voluntary) immigrants from (forced) migrants: the immigrant undertaking an economic form of migration is a potential threat to the nation-state's resources and well-being; refugee movements, on the other hand, could entail considerably greater risks to the stability of the sovereign state due to the political and security issues they encompass. As Loescher highlights, 'refugee problems are in fact intensely political: mass migrations create domestic instability, generate interstate tension and threaten international security'.[48]

If we assume that the international system asks that all individuals belong to a state, the refugee regime can be seen as an attempt to make refugees into 'quasi-citizens'. The specific body of refugee rights contained in the 1951 Convention was created as a substitute for those citizenship rights available to individuals who follow the rules of international society and belong, as they should, to a specific state. It is a corrective mechanism set up by states to prevent further disturbance of the internationally accepted model of belonging to a political community. Based on a positive international law foundation, there is little in the internationally agreed list of refugee rights that suggests natural law thinking. Rather, the idea of refugee protection is tied up with statist definitions of the refugee – that all individuals must fit into the state–citizen–territory trinity. Granting refugees a special status has the aim of overcoming the anomalous and threatening position of 'not belonging' that refugees pose. The irony is that in granting refugee status and its associated rights, no state is actually offering membership within their domestic political jurisdiction which would act to correct the situation completely. The right to asylum is not guaranteed and the most states will offer is the half-way house of the right to seek it. The refugee is destined, therefore, to stay categorised as the refugee, equipped with a modicum of rights that form a sub-category of the rights generally available to individuals via the institution of citizenship. She may never reach citizen status but will remain a 'quasi-citizen'. This at least partly redefines her ties with a particular territory.

Thus, whereas the human rights regime aspires to a solidarist world beyond the nation-state, the refugee regime rethinks the state as the 'solution' to the 'problem'. Refugee rights are an interim measure for those cases of disruption to the states system throughout which the

[48] Loescher, *Refugee Movements and International Security*, pp. 4–5.

state remains the ultimate goal and reference. Refugee protection is therefore more of a pluralist idea designed to fit into the international states system based on positive international law rather than a universal and solidarist conception brought about by human rights norms. The refugee can only exist as long as there are separate sovereign states, states that fail in their role as protectors of individual rights. Whilst these states acknowledge that some regulation of the refugee problem is necessary if it is not to totally destabilise the international system, any regime set up will logically be largely communitarian in thinking and value, and any cosmopolitan or humanitarian effects simply an added extra.

The refugee regime and security

A convention is an international agreement to which states adhere voluntarily. Since they are voluntary, conventions do not violate the basic principles of international legal sovereignty or positive law. They can and do mean the concession of a degree of sovereignty, but this is a prior condition of belonging to international society with or without the signing of conventions. As Roth points out, states cannot claim, in the name of sovereignty, 'the freedom to behave in ways that contradict the very purposes for which the international community respects and protects sovereignty'.[49] State sovereignty only has meaning within the context of international society whereby states recognise each other as equal players and respect the principle of non-interference in one another's internal affairs. This by definition means adhering to certain rules and behaving according to certain standards. Sovereignty has never been absolute, and international society could not exist without an element of concession on the part of individual states. It has frequently been compromised by contracts, imposition or interventions and infringement of domestic autonomy via agreements such as conventions. Accordingly, it is possible to view the human rights regime of the twentieth century as 'but the latest example of a long-standing tension between autonomy and international attempts to regulate relations between rulers and ruled'.[50]

[49] Brad R. Roth, *Governmental Illegitimacy in International Law* (Oxford University Press, 2000), p. 10.
[50] Stephen D. Krasner, *Sovereignty: Organized Hypocrisy* (Princeton University Press, 1999), p. 126.

However, becoming party to norms such as the 1951 Convention means conceding more sovereignty than the minimum required for states to coexist. Article 38 even allows for referrals to be made to the International Court of Justice by one of the signatories. Were such a referral to take place, judicial review could signal the growth of a more cosmopolitan order in this policy area. The potential contradiction is evident in that the 1951 Convention was created by states to form part of the international system that assumes the sovereign state as the basic political unit, yet external monitoring of how a state adheres to the principles it has signed up to could represent a threat to the principle of non-intervention in a state's internal jurisdiction. It would seem appropriate to ask, then, why a state would decide voluntarily to sign up to the refugee protection regime that puts its internal affairs under scrutiny and limits its scope of action unduly.

It is, it seems, in the interests of national and international security that states will cooperate with one another in signing up to human rights norms. Refugees are a creation of states that fail to ensure the normal standards of protection towards all individuals within their jurisdiction. They are consequently seen as an exception to the normal state–citizen–territory trinity and hence a source of instability. Instability is a security risk and needs to be corrected. It follows that the refugee regime was set up in large part to restore normal state–citizen relations. The solution to the refugee problem is seen as the reterritorialisation of those individuals acting between states, so as to put an end to disorderly movement of this kind. Refugee protection is an attempt to correct the deviation from the normal model of international society in which all individuals belong to a state. Any humanitarian effects of such protection may accordingly be seen as secondary to the primary objective of restoring the refugee to a sovereign territory. While the refugee wanders the international community as an individual without ties to any state, she presents a security risk and threatens to destabilise the states system. Of course, refugee protection combines both pluralist and solidarist norms and granting protection is not solely for reasons of security, but in practice national and international security interests may play a disproportionately large part.

As the human rights regime has grown since 1945, so the protection of the rights of refugees has gained greater importance. Thus, although population transfer and exchange were once seen as a legitimate means of making people and geography fit neat boundaries, they are no longer accepted on humanitarian grounds. Similarly the system of minority rights guarantees was discredited by the Second World War and became subsumed within the international human rights regime. But the refugee protection regime continues to operate in the same form as that in which it developed in the League of Nations era. As Aleinikoff notes, 'the situation of hundreds of thousands of displaced persons after both world wars, coupled with a new emphasis on human rights protection, supplied a humanitarian basis for emerging international refugee law norms, but the legal thinking remained state centered'.[51] We saw earlier that refugee law was instigated by a need to prevent the destabilising effects of the creation of new states and changes in borders, coupled with the desire to prevent nationalism being taken to devastating extremes. In other words, the refugee regime has been linked since its outset to questions of political identity and security. Indeed, refugees are created following a fundamental breakdown in the political community as a sustaining entity. As the underlying thinking behind refugee protection has not changed since the refugee became an international concern, it follows that the regime is still bound up with concerns for national security and the desire to make all individuals belong to a state. Hence even if the nature of refugee protection has changed since it first became an item on the international agenda, the underlying premise has not.

If we accept that refugee protection is more a communitarian security issue than a cosmopolitan humanitarian concern, it follows that refugees are perceived and controlled more as a matter of national and international security than a matter of human security. The security paradigm sees the state as the legitimate basis for sovereign authority in the international system, necessary for peace, order and good governance.[52] At the international level the states system can be viewed as a society without a government, in which states agree to conduct their affairs in accordance with specified international standards. The common objective among states is the preservation of international order, which is taken as the continued existence of international society as a whole. The idea of national security adds assumptions about the composition of states. When states began to be imagined on national rather than religious terms, so it became easier to imagine outsiders as a threat

---

[51] T. A. Aleinikoff, 'State-centred Refugee Law: From Resettlement to Containment', in E. V. Daniel and J. R. Knudsen (eds.), *Mistrusting Refugees* (Berkeley: University of California Press, 1995), 259.

[52] Jackson-Preece, 'Ethnocultural Diversity', 7.

to national identity and security. Indeed it was with the nationalisation of the state that sharp distinctions between insiders and outsiders began to be formulated and the concept of the refugee as one such outsider started to be consolidated. Accordingly, the refugee came to be perceived as a threat to the homogeneous nation-state and peace and stability both within and between states.

Where the nation-state is based on civic ideas of national identity, the refugee is imagined as a threat to the security of its institutions, welfare system or resources. Where the nation-state is built on ethnic grounds, the refugee is imagined as a threat to its dominant ethnicity, language or culture. Civic nations may wish to control refugee flows for fear of a burden on resources, whereas ethnic nations would regard the control of refugees necessary for guaranteeing the security of the dominant ethnicity of its population. The answer to ensuring national security would be the assimilation or elimination of the outsider, while international security would be guaranteed by population transfer and exchange or minority rights legislation. It can be seen, therefore, that although the refugee regime is intricately linked to the human rights regime, the underlying thinking of the two is fundamentally different. States may sign up voluntarily to human rights norms which allow them to participate fully in international society and to take advantage of the benefits, such as respect and recognition, that participation brings. Yet signing up to the 1951 Convention and other norms of protection related explicitly to refugees is in large part due to reasons of national and international security. At the national level states realise that their national identity and community are at risk if the destabilising effects of refugees are not controlled. At the international level the society of states sees that the continued existence of international society as a whole is at risk without some attempt to reterritorialise refugees to a state.

In this respect it follows that the framework of international order is inhospitable to demands for respect for human rights and human justice.[53] Giving precedence to human rights, as opposed to peace, security and the coexistence of sovereign states, would seriously undermine the pluralist international order. In a pluralist context, therefore, international security is prior to human security. A full commitment to cosmopolitan justice and human rights would only be realisable in the framework of a world or cosmopolitan society, and such a global community is not reconcilable with current systems of world order.

---

[53] Bull, *The Anarchical Society*, p. 85.

The discussion of human rights in international society could be seen more as a symptom of disorder than order.[54] Within an international system based on separate sovereign states, the need for consensus on both national and international security is paramount for the system to function. Disorder is a possibility when we start to place issues of human security above concerns for national and international security. Thus, following Bull's thesis, the idea of rights and duties of individuals, as opposed to those of states, has the potential to destabilise international society itself.[55] Accordingly, refugee protection will be instigated more by issues of state security than humanitarian concerns.

If international society rests on a presupposed consensus among states, a certain code of behaviour among states is ensured. Adherence to the code acts to maintain stability in the international system. When a state is seen to be abiding by the rules of international society it gains respect and recognition from the other actors in the states system. Thus there is an unspoken consensus on non-disruptive behaviour between states that ensures the continuation of international society.[56] Yet such behaviour is only required of states towards other states, not towards individuals within states. Accordingly, unstable conditions within a state's sovereign jurisdiction do not upset normal conditions of international society. Hence where states fail to fulfil their duties of representation and protection towards citizens *within* their territory, the international community has less of an incentive to intervene than if the same state was threatening to disrupt relations *between* states. We see once again, therefore, the same motives behind keeping a distinction between 'refugees' and 'internally displaced persons'. Refugees threaten instability in the international community; internally displaced persons only threaten one state as long as they are kept within its borders. Of course refugees and internally displaced persons are often qualitatively part of the same group yet have been divided artificially by a political border, and insisting that the individual must cross a border in order to claim refugee status effectively reinforces the border's legitimacy.[57]

Refugees may therefore be created whilst states are respecting the unspoken code of non-disruptive behaviour externally with other international sovereigns, fulfilling their external role while failing to meet

---

[54] Bull, *The Anarchical Society*, p. 147.   [55] Bull, *The Anarchical Society*, p. 80.
[56] Andreas Osiander, *The States System of Europe, 1640–1990* (Oxford University Press, 1994), pp. 6–8.
[57] Hyndman, *Managing Displacement*, pp. 5, 164.

their responsibilities of good governance internally. In this sense, refugee movements are a consequence of international *stability*. As long as the presupposed consensus to a code of behaviour between states has not been compromised, international stability will be maintained. Movements of refugees created under conditions of international stability may well go on to cause instability in the international arena due to the tensions and burdens such flows are capable of creating. And of course this is not to deny that refugee movements are also brought on by war or other types of violence, hence flows may also be initiated under conditions of international instability as would be expected. But this does highlight that the conditions for the creation of refugees are present when the international climate is stable. Accordingly, refugee movements can be understood as a characteristic of the very nature of the international states system. They are created while international society is functioning according to its normal rules. Whether accepted definitions of stability and instability are now beginning to change, however, such that international society believes it necessary to intervene in a state's internal affairs when refugees are being created, is now a question of some debate.

In the context of an international system resting on the norm of sovereignty, the tension between communitarian interests and humanitarian concerns is unavoidable. But this is perhaps just another illustration of the fact that sovereignty has never been a foregone conclusion. The clash between human rights and sovereign rights in the international arena serves as one more example of the fact that sovereignty is, from a humanitarian perspective, simply 'organized hypocrisy'.[58] And it is 'organized hypocrisy' that states create refugees, then fail to take responsibility for them. A system of separate sovereign entities with distinct borders creates clear definitions of insiders and outsiders: if a state fails to respect the norms of good governance to ensure normal standards of protection and representation of its citizens, refugees are the likely outcome – and repetitive failures in good governance remain almost inevitable. But nowhere is protection by a host state guaranteed: 'Although refugee status is grounded in the idea of loss of membership,' points out Aleinikoff, 'refugee law does not guarantee attainment of membership elsewhere.'[59] To ensure the refugee is protected once again she must be restored to a state–citizen relationship. In other words, states are both the source of the 'problem'

---

[58] Krasner, *Sovereignty*, p. 125.   [59] Aleinikoff, 'State-centred Refugee Law', 259–60.

and the location of the 'solution'. Finding an external solution would be inconceivable, since outside the world of states there would be no refugees. As Buzan notes, 'the security of individuals is locked into an unbreakable paradigm in which it is partly dependent on, and partly threatened by, the state'.[60] There is little choice, perhaps, but to accept the hypocritical international arrangement and take action within it.

Conclusions

The refugee has the right to leave her state to seek protection, yet nowhere is the right to enter another state and be granted such protection entirely guaranteed. Accordingly, it would seem that any attempts to offer refugee protection are made in the interests of national and international security. Since the solution to the refugee problem is seen as reinstalling the refugee within a state, it follows that the underlying thinking behind the international refugee regime is based on concerns for stability and restoring the normal order of international society, rather than on ideas of human rights. In this respect the international refugee regime may be understood as an attempt to bring such 'transnational' individuals back within the state–citizen–territory hierarchy, thus making the refugee a 'quasi-citizen'. Hence a pragmatic approach to ensuring the human rights of refugees are protected needs to acknowledge the workings of the international system and attempt to formulate a feasible refugee policy within it.

Of course, the fact that states have signed up to the 1951 Convention means that they have certain obligations towards refugees. In this regard states have perhaps imposed an element of institutional constraint on themselves. But this constraint is minimal: the 1951 Convention grants the refugee the right to seek asylum, but nowhere is the right to obtain it guaranteed. The right to flee the source of persecution is acknowledged, while the right to offer protection from the persecution remains a state prerogative. In other words, the most important right the refugee needs – one that would reinstall the refugee in the state–citizen–territory hierarchy – is not included. Thus the 1951 Convention is just one more example of the way in which the refugee brings to the fore the clash between sovereign rights and human rights.

---

[60] Barry Buzan, *People, States and Fear: An Agenda for International Security Studies in the Post-Cold War Era*, 2nd edn (Hemel Hempstead: Harvester Wheatsheaf, 1991), pp. 363–4.

Having established the normative basis for the existence of the refugee in international society, we now have an understanding of how she is wrapped up in the very workings of the states system. Refugee movements can be seen as an inevitable if unanticipated reality, as long as there are clearly defined political borders attempting to separate peoples and failings in sustaining political communities within such borders. This study now moves to an historical analysis of this normative understanding of the refugee to highlight how she has always been a fundamental part of the modern states system. By tracing the continuities and contradictions in the refugee concept and the international protection regime over the next three chapters, the similarities between early and more recent refugee movements come to light, and the artificiality of assuming the 1951 Convention as marking the beginning of international attention towards the refugee issue is highlighted.

PART II

The refugee: an historical analysis

5   The inter-war perspective

> It became a common experience for a refugee to find himself on a frontier, trapped between a country that had spat him out and a country that would not let him in.   Dorothy Thompson[1]

Several events between the end of the nineteenth and beginning of the twentieth centuries led to the creation of refugees hitherto unknown. When pogroms were unleashed against Jews in Tsarist Russia in 1880, millions fled in search of refuge. The wars in the Balkans of 1912–13 caused the displacement of millions more as did, of course, the First World War. By 1926 the refugee population in Europe was estimated at 9.5 million, while more than twenty million individuals were displaced within states.[2] International society had never had to deal with a mass refugee 'problem' prior to this period, and the way the international community responded to the ethical dilemma posed by the emergence of the modern refugee was based on underlying normative assumptions about both international society and, by extension, the individuals within it. Experiments in regimenting the phenomenon led to a formalised regime.

This chapter discusses the specific way the refugee developed as a concept in international society in the inter-war period and how the international community dealt with her. It first looks at the construction of the refugee in relation to particular understandings of sovereignty prevailing at the time. Next it analyses what this meant in terms of defining the refugee and establishing her as an individual of specific international concern. It then examines how the interaction of the international community with the refugee not only helped define and consolidate the concept of

---

[1] Dorothy Thompson, *Refugees: Anarchy or Organization?* (New York: Random House, 1938), p. 39.
[2] Marrus, *The Unwanted*, p. 52.

the refugee but also influenced state behaviour and identity. Finally, it examines the particular solutions tried in response to refugee movements in this period, in light of the underlying suppositions of the refugee figure as she was beginning to be constructed.

Positive sovereignty and the refugee

Internal and systemic forces interact to produce refugee movements, and these forces are significantly high during the process of nation-state formation.[3] Where nation-states emerge within already defined jurisdictions, such as France, or where smaller jurisdictions are united to create nation-states, as was the case with Germany and Italy, the defence of national territory and institutions will much less frequently invoke calls for a homogeneous ethnic make-up of the nation. Accordingly, indiscriminate targeting of ethnic minorities will generally be avoided,[4] as will, therefore, mass flows of refugees. In contrast, creating homogeneous ethnic nations out of multilingual and multicultural empires with far-flung and scattered territories, in which the ethnicity of the people determines the jurisdictional boundaries, means that territory and peoples are more likely to overlap and intermingle and limitations will be blurred and contested in the absence of any ready-made civic basis. As Jackson-Preece points out, 'once the ethnic bond is accepted as the *raison d'être* or *suum cuique* of the state ... ethnocultural diversity tends to be viewed as a threat'.[5] Those anomalous populations not possessing the dominant ethnic characteristics will need to be eradicated from the territory and, whatever the means used – wars of secession and irredentism, forced assimilation, ethnic cleansing or genocide – refugees may result on a mass scale.

The inherent turmoil of ending empires therefore unavoidably creates refugees.[6] Refugee flows may be seen as a concomitant of the secular transformation of empires into national states, particularly where states strive to achieve homogeneity among their people. It was when multinational empires collapsed in the early twentieth century and the nation-state formula was adopted to organise political life in regions of ethnically mixed populations that peoples were uprooted and forced to leave their homes in search of fellow co-nationals and governmental

---

[3] Skran, *Refugees in Inter-war Europe*, p. 20.
[4] Jackson-Preece, 'Ethnocultural Diversity, 9.
[5] Jackson-Preece, 'Ethnocultural Diversity', 9–10.
[6] For a demonstration of this in the context of decolonisation and the ending of European empires in the developing world in the 1960s, see Zolberg *et al.*, *Escape from Violence*.

protection.[7] The old European empires collapsed to give way to the formation, consolidation and expansion of the states system, and these transformations from imperial social and political orders to successor nation-states were accompanied by conflict, persecution and massacre in the search for homogeneity. With the gradual decline of the Ottoman Empire, eastern Europe was the main focus of such pre- and post-war political transformations. The polyglot nature of the region meant that national identities had long been denied or left unrealised by imperial domination. With the prospect of autonomy, groups separated along linguistic, ethnic and religious lines and were thus brought into conflict. Widespread violence and massacres compelled thousands of individuals to leave their homes and wander the changing international landscape as refugees. Ethnic groups fought for independence, national cohesion and territory. The result was new, weak and unstable successor states – and refugees.[8] Attempts to make nationality and territorial boundaries coincide left millions of individuals unaccounted for, from the 100,000 Turks fleeing Bulgarian forces and the 177,000 Muslim refugees entering Turkey in 1912, to the two million Poles, five million Russians and one million Germans by the early 1920s.[9]

The number of refugees generated by the collapse of the Tsarist Empire is also staggering. Between 1880 and the outbreak of the First World War, 2.5 million Jews left eastern Europe for the West. These refugees faced pogroms and systematic persecution in Poland, the Ukraine, Russia and Hungary, and deportations began in 1914. An estimated 211,000 Jews were in exile in Russia alone by 1918, and of those who managed to flee abroad most went to Poland, which was by no means a safe alternative.[10] When transatlantic migration ceased to be an option following the 1924 Johnson Act, refugees were forced to remain in Europe, where they faced further oppression and forcible expulsion from state to state. The 120,000 Jewish refugees who managed to enter Britain between 1880 and 1914 helped bring about the introduction of the British Aliens Act of 1905. The Act placed a limit on the number of 'unwanted immigrants' entering Britain, marking the first big break with the liberal attitude of the nineteenth

[7] Zolberg, 'The formation of new states', 30.

[8] From the Hapsburg and Ottoman Empires the states of Poland, Czechoslovakia, Hungary, Yugoslavia, Austria, Romania, Bulgaria and Albania emerged, while the Tsarist Empire gave birth to Finland, Estonia, Latvia and Lithuania.

[9] Marrus, *The Unwanted*, pp. 45–9; Soguk, *States and Strangers*, p. 103.

[10] Marrus, *The Unwanted*, p. 62.

century: refugees now had to prove their case to qualify as such, and legal legitimisation of the ideology of immigration controls was born.

The greatest numbers of refugees of any one national group in the 1920s were found among the Armenians. These peoples had long represented a Christian minority of around two million in the Ottoman Empire but became increasingly repressed with the consolidation of the Turkish nation-state. When the Empire was defeated in 1877–8 their fate was sealed, and the massacres of 1894–6 by the Turks forced many to flee as refugees. The violence reached genocidal proportions during the First World War, and two-thirds of the total Ottoman Armenian population – at least one million persons – are thought to have died.[11] The flight of the Armenian refugees represents a clear example of ethnicity and territory coming into conflict; as territory and boundaries changed hands, individuals became the victims of statist attempts to create homogeneous territories with 'insiders' identified by nationality. Whether refugees had fled direct persecution as in the case of the Jews, civil war in the case of the Russians, or like the Armenians had been forced out by the dominant national group, these outsiders had begun to assume immense proportions on a truly international scale. And changes in international warfare meant that entire populations were affected by the First World War and millions of individuals displaced as a result. Numerous other instances of international unrest also acted to generate refugee flows: the Balkans Wars, the Greco–Turkish War of 1922, the Russian Civil War, the Russo–Polish war. The cumulative result of all these events was perhaps 'the largest displacement of peoples in Europe in modern times'.[12]

The extent of the problem was achieved precisely by the creation of separate, independent states in which the state–citizen–territory hierarchy was seen as supreme. The League of Nations gave the state-building process a new impetus and a new role and importance, and so acted to give final form to legitimacy based on popular rather than dynastic politics. With the consolidation of the principle of sovereignty, the state now had the power and institutional authority to exclude refugees from civil society.[13] The 1919 peace treaties legitimised the belief that each nation had a right to an independent state. Giving scope to national aspirations through the right to national independence or national self-determination was seen as a condition for instilling peace. Thus the principle of nationality was one of the main considerations in the

[11] Soguk, *States and Strangers*, p. 76.   [12] Loescher, *Beyond Charity*, pp. 34–5.
[13] Arendt, *The Origins*, p. 272.

territorial arrangements undertaken by the League of Nations in the immediate post-war climate. Making frontiers run along lines of nationality would, it was thought, avoid the flights of refugees and subsequent international instability that had occurred when territory had hitherto changed hands. The added security of the Minority Treaties would eliminate the risk of any further persecution of these groups of people that had continually led to refugee movements. But practical difficulties in the application of the principle were rife: it was to prove impossible to avoid creating new minorities when frontiers were moved and new states created. Furthermore, it was not clear what conditions an applicant nation had to fulfil so as to legitimately claim the right to self-determination.[14] Such were the problems that self-determination came to be substituted for a different albeit related set of ideals: the belief in small states as a justifiable part of the international system; the belief in the equality of states whatever their size; and the belief in the right to absolute national sovereignty. Here the apparently blunt opposition and incompatibility of a peace system in the form of the League of Nations and its constituent parts in the form of individual sovereign or aspiring-to-be sovereign states based on the principle of national sovereignty were supposedly reconciled on the basis of 'self-constraint'. But whether conscious of it or not, notes Cobban, 'by wrapping up national sovereignty in the idealistic language of self-determination the peacemakers concealed from themselves the flaw in the system they had created'.[15]

The concept of sovereign states postulates a neat fit between boundaries and politically significant identities, yet, as Jackson-Preece points out, in practice ethnicity and geography rarely coincide.[16] Thus out of the gap between the formula and social realities emerged the refugee, whose situation meant that she had 'lost those rights which had been thought of and even defined as inalienable, namely the Rights of Man'.[17] The emergence of the nation-state coincided with the development of constitutional government and the formation of mutual recognition and respect between nations that constrained the full exercise of sovereign power by governments. The inherent danger of linking rights with nationality was not therefore immediately evident. Some years later the Minority Treaties revealed 'that only nationals could be citizens,

---

[14] Alfred Cobban, *The Nation State and National Self-Determination* (London: Collins, 1969), pp. 66–8.
[15] Cobban, *The Nation State*, pp. 82–3.   [16] Jackson-Preece, *National Minorities*.
[17] Arendt, *The Origins*, p. 268.

only people of the same national origin could enjoy the full protection of legal institutions, that persons of different nationality needed some law of exception'.[18] In other words, they indicated that rights had become tied up with nationality, but this reality was concealed from view until the First World War, and its aftermath 'sufficiently shattered the façade of Europe's political system to lay bare its hidden frame'.[19]

With the insistence on a positivist view of sovereignty during this period, and the reliance on the constitutional provisions of inter-state treaties, the international community looked to solve the problem within the state. States would now guarantee protection for their citizens, and so avoid the potential for refugee creation. Its domestic affairs were a product of its action, resources and self-dependence. Yet mass displacement of refugees was an illustration that the state could fail as a sustaining political community and thus fail to protect all individuals within its territory as citizens. It was precisely the Jews fleeing persecution, the Russians fleeing civil war and the Armenians stripped of their nationality for whom the peace settlements of 1919 did not cater. Organising the ethnically mixed peoples of the disintegrating empires into homogeneous political entities of viable size was difficult if not impossible, and national minorities and the stateless were the result.[20] Minorities have the potential to become refugees if forced out by the dominant nationality, while 'all refugees are for practical purposes stateless'.[21] If

---

[18] Arendt, *The Origins*, p. 275.   [19] Arendt, *The Origins*, p. 267.

[20] It is important to note the difference between these two sets of people. The minorities were created due to the practical impossibility of every putative nation achieving supreme control over a specified territory. They had existed before this point, but had now become 'political misfits'. It was when the doctrine of nationally guaranteed rights came to be equated with the notion of rights guaranteed only to nationals that it was recognised that certain groups of people would live permanently outside normal legal protection. The Minority Treaties were to provide for this exception to the norm, as well as to ensure international security – granting special concessions to the minority groups would, it was assumed, make them less likely to challenge the existing territorial status quo. Indeed it is for this reason, according to Jackson-Preece, that minority status issues have historically come to the fore in European international relations just when a new international order is being established: in the years following 1648, 1815, 1878, 1919, 1945 and 1989 – see Jackson-Preece, *National Minorities*. The minorities therefore still belonged to a political body but needed additional protection, thus leaving the states system itself untouched. The stateless, on the other hand, highlighted that deviations from the system were in fact a possibility and a reality. The stateless would exist no matter how boundaries and categories might be organised. They were misfits whose identity failed to correspond to that of any established nation-state or recognised national minority – see Zolberg, 'The Formation of New States', 31.

[21] Sir John Hope Simpson, *The Refugee Problem: Report of a Survey* (Oxford University Press and the Royal Institute of International Affairs, 1939), p. 4.

no other state accepted such peoples they became the *apatrides*, the *Heimatlosen*, falling into the gaps between states – 'born in the wrong village, speaking the wrong language, naturalized at the wrong date, finishing the war in the wrong part of Europe'.[22]

Although numbers of refugees in the 1920s were high, refugees in the 1930s had to face problems quite unlike their predecessors. In the wake of the First World War the boom of post-war reconstruction encouraged foreign labour. A decade later, western European states found themselves in severe economic depression. And as waves of thousands of eastern European Jews began to move westwards, fears of exacerbating the situation stopped states from offering asylum. As Loescher notes, 'potential host governments feared that welcoming Jewish fugitives from Nazism might open the floodgates and provoke the flight of hundreds of thousands more Jews from Eastern Europe'.[23] Eastern Europe was home to more Jews than Germany: over three million in Poland, almost 757,000 in Romania and 445,000 in Hungary. Added to the 525,000 Jews in the Reich, this put the potential Jewish refugee population that could arrive in the West at 4.3 million.[24] Such figures were a frightening prospect. The potential influx of vast numbers of Jewish refugees constructed a threat to states previously unknown: 'While in normal times an exodus of some fifty thousand persons, nearly all of them of energy and intelligence, might have been readily absorbed in the European countries, the abnormal economic circumstances of the time rendered absorption extremely difficult.'[25] Europe had never before coped with refugees spilling across borders on such a scale.

Jewish refugees faced obstacles specific to their case. First, they had no nation of their own; in effect, Jews were outside the state–citizen–territory hierarchy even before they became refugees, with no state or nation into which to fit naturally. Russian, Armenian and Saar refugees in the 1920s had been able to find temporary asylum relatively easily, such that the role of the international refugee regime was one of attempting to improve and regularise the refugees' legal status within their host states; with the Jewish refugees from Germany and eastern Europe, however, the main problem was one of actually finding states that were willing to allow the refugees to enter their territory in the first place.[26] Indeed, the absence of

---

[22] Marrus, *The Unwanted*, p. 74.   [23] Loescher, *Beyond Charity*, p. 42.
[24] Marrus, *The Unwanted*, pp. 141–2.
[25] Norman Bentwich, *The Refugees from Germany: April 1933 to December 1935* (London: Allen & Unwin, 1936), p. 38.
[26] Skran, *Refugees in Inter-war Europe*, p. 121.

an obvious place of refuge coupled with the difficulty of securing a new permanent home for the refugees distinguished the experience of Jewish refugees from refugees of earlier years.[27] Second, Jewish refugees faced rising anti-Semitism in many states from both governments and majority populations. State-leaders feared large influxes of Jewish refugees could worsen this situation and cause public unrest, thus exclusion was justified in the interests of public order.[28] Governments talked of their fears of 'importing a racial problem', once again highlighting that it was not just the numbers of refugees worrying states but also the types of refugees.[29] A third obstacle to their case was that Jewish refugees were often also stripped of their financial resources before being forced out of their country. This meant arriving in a host state destitute and entirely dependent on public funds or charity: 'nobody's responsibility but potentially everybody's burden'.[30] Finally, the plight of Jewish refugees was strongly worsened by the standing of their persecuting country in international relations: they 'had the misfortune to be from a Great Power on the rise in world politics'.[31] Germany was increasing its influence across Europe and, as long as she remained a member of the League of Nations, could exercise a veto over any policies on refugees. Even when Germany left the League there was a continuing desire on the part of some states, Britain and France in particular, to try to appease the very state that was responsible for the creation of increasing numbers of refugees. And of course, whatever Nazi Germany was doing was occurring within the confines of a sovereign state. In 1933 the German delegate to the League of Nations

---

[27] Loescher, *Beyond Charity*, p. 41.

[28] Note that Article 3(2) of the 1933 Convention Relating to the International Status of Refugees contained exclusion clauses justified on grounds of national security or public order, as did Article 5(2) of the 1938 Convention Concerning the Status of Refugees Coming from Germany, which held that 'refugees who have been authorized to reside in a country may not be subjected by the authorities of that country to measures of expulsion or be sent back across the frontier unless such measures are dictated by reasons of national security or public order'. These exclusion clauses were later translated into Article 32(1) of the 1951 Convention, which also allows for expulsion of refugees on grounds of national security or public order, and Article 33(1) which provides for a derogation from the principle of *non-refoulement* on the same grounds.

[29] John P. Fox, 'German and European Jewish Refugees, 1933–45: Reflections on the Jewish Condition under Hitler and the Western World's Response to Their Expulsion and Flight', in Anna Bramwell (ed.), *Refugees in the Age of Total War* (London: Unwin Hyman, 1988), 70, 75.

[30] Fox, 'German and European Jewish Refugees', 76.

[31] Skran, *Refugees in Inter-war Europe*, p. 195.

stressed that 'a State retained the sovereign right to settle a special problem of this kind as an internal question'.[32] This was reiterated by the League Assembly in 1936, announcing that 'a refugee only became a refugee on leaving his country of origin, and that the High Commissioner could, therefore, only enter into negotiations with the Governments of the countries of refuge'.[33]

When the Nazi regime took control in 1933, 65,000 refugees left Germany that year, of whom about 80 per cent were Jews.[34] The first flows sought refuge in neighbouring countries for reasons of proximity and cultural affinity, as well as in the belief that they would shortly be able to return home. The majority went to France, while many also arrived in Belgium, Holland, Switzerland, Czechoslovakia and Austria, as well as the Saar Valley, Yugoslavia and Hungary. By December 1937, 135,000 Jewish refugees had been forced out of Germany, representing 90 per cent of the total number of refugees leaving the Reich.[35] Between January 1933 and September 1939 an estimated 1.2 million persons were made refugees, of whom 420,000 were Jewish refugees from Germany and areas subsequently annexed, occupied or allied with it. Numbers of Jewish refugees seeking protection increased substantially following the instigation of the Nuremberg Laws of 1935, which effectively deprived Jews of German citizenship, and increased five times after the intensification of the anti-Jewish laws and the annexation of Austria in 1938.[36]

Such movements of people highlighted that the sovereign territorial state had failed to guarantee the protection of those it considered its citizens, leading to the mass displacement of refugees. A positivist view of sovereignty emphasised that conditions within states were a matter solely for the state's jurisdiction within its defined territory. Yet the inter-war period showed that a sovereign power with sole jurisdiction over its community could not be relied upon to guarantee the protection of its citizens. According to the principles of sovereignty and non-intervention, the state could admit and expel at its discretion, and the creation of refugees was allowed to continue. The greater the emphasis put on all individuals belonging to a state, and the greater the

---

[32] League of Nations, *Monthly Summary* vol. XIII No. 12 (December 1933), 273.
[33] League of Nations, 'International Assistance to Refugees: Report Submitted by the Sixth Committee to the Assembly', 1936 [LN.1936.XII.B.12], 3.
[34] Marrus, *The Unwanted*, p. 129.   [35] Simpson, *The Refugee Problem*, pp. 140–1.
[36] Malcolm J. Proudfoot, *European Refugees 1939–1952: A Study in Forced Population Movement* (London: Faber, 1957), pp. 25–7.

importance given to boundaries and national identity, the greater were the chances of exclusion of unwanted individuals who threatened the identity of the nation-state. With the rise of national identity and nationalism as the new indicators of national allegiance to a community, only the national citizen had to be protected by a state. Where the state refused to protect it could merely force out. The refugee was the imagined outsider who could be passed from state to state to fall between sovereigns. In other words, when the nation was 'hyphenated' with the state,[37] the exclusion of certain individuals was inevitable. The creation of refugees was simply the natural extension of the bounding of individuals within sovereign territorial entities under the jurisdiction of states which then failed to represent and protect those individuals within its domestic political community according to the responsibilities of substantive sovereignty. The international states system showed it had failed to see the dangers of arranging populations within the sovereign territorial jurisdictions of nation-states according to national identity. The state had failed both internally towards its citizens and externally as a member of international society.

Intergovernmental regimentation

In the inter-war period the League of Nations High Commissioner for Refugees (LNHCR) was the most active intergovernmental organisation addressing the refugee issue and acting on behalf of such individuals. Faced with the millions displaced by the years of fighting before and during the First World War and a further 800,000 Russian refugees fleeing revolution and civil war post-1918, the first High Commissioner for Refugees, Fridtjof Nansen, was appointed in 1921. Under Nansen's leadership the LNHCR was instrumental in promoting intergovernmental cooperation in dealing with the refugee crisis by way of conventions, conferences, arrangements, resolutions and agreements. Most accounts of refugee regimentation in this period view the role of the LNHCR as a relatively minor development in the history of the refugee 'problem', one that failed to come up with an effective refugee regime. However, intergovernmental regimentation under the leadership of the LNHCR can be seen to have problematised human displacement in state-oriented terms, allowing a refugee problem to come into being

---

[37] Nicholas Xenos cited in Daniel Warner, 'The Refugee State and State Protection', in Nicholson and Twomey, *Refugee Rights and Realities*, 257–8.

that was characterised by identities and subjectivities strongly supporting the sovereign state. According to Soguk, the LNHCR was a fundamental practice of statecraft, during whose tenure 'the ontology of the
refugee was fully determined and thoroughly formalized, thus
enabling the subsequent regime activities'.[38] Its creation and action
helped establish the refugee as the focus of displacement, while affirm-
ing intergovernmental action as the norm for confronting the phenomenon. Thus the international refugee regime that took shape during the
inter-war period was important in providing the foundations and
legacy for the contemporary regime.[39] By casting the refugee issue as
one 'of interest to the entire world',[40] the LNHCR was important in
'intergovernmentalising' the refugee problem.

The persecution of Jews was first discussed in the Council of the
League of Nations in May 1933. The League had received a petition
from a Jewish individual who had been dismissed from his employment
in Upper Silesia, allegedly due to discrimination on grounds of race.
Minority rights guarantees were in force in this region following the 1922
Geneva Convention between Germany and Poland. However, according
to Bentwich the Council, 'apart from expressions of opinion in the discussion, was not in a position to tackle the broader question of Jewish
persecution in Germany'.[41] Clearly this would have seemed to encroach
on domestic German policy and so constitute an infringement of sovereignty. Hence from the very start, states under the guise of the League of
Nations Council were wary of being seen to criticise one particular state's
internal affairs when debating the issue of Jewish persecution, even
when this was resulting in large flows of refugees. This is neatly summed
up in the statement of the Dutch foreign minister who introduced the
topic when it was brought before the League Assembly, who claimed,
'We have no wish to examine the reasons why these people have left
their country; but we are faced with the fact that thousands of German
subjects have crossed the frontiers of the neighbouring countries and
refused to return to their homes for reasons which we are not called upon
to judge.'[42]

With the dissolution of the LNHCR in 1930, other international refugee
organisations sprang up in its place, including the Nansen International

[38] Soguk, *States and Strangers*, pp. 111, 119.   [39] Skran, *Refugees in Inter-war Europe*.
[40] League of Nations, 'Conference on the Question of Russian Refugees: Resolutions
Adopted by the Conference on August 24th, 1921', 1921 [L.N.1921.7], 902.
[41] Bentwich, *The Refugees from Germany*, p. 56.
[42] Bentwich, *The Refugees from Germany*, p. 58.

Office for Refugees (NIOFR) in 1928, under whose auspices the first international convention on refugees was adopted in 1933; the High Commissioner for Refugees from Germany (HCRFG) in 1933, which tended to opt for a general policy of appeasement towards Germany that somewhat impeded progress towards refugee protection; and the Office of the High Commissioner responsible for All Refugees under the League of Nations' Protection (OHCAR) in 1938, formed when its two predecessors were merged. All the organisations that followed the LNHCR acted to formalise and normalise the refugee as an international concept. Since one gave way to the other, the refugee space was maintained as a continuous site of intergovernmental activity. They allowed the specific figure of the refugee to be brought to the fore so that the refugee was firmly established as the 'problem-figure' of state-centric governance in the twentieth century.[43] Yet it is important to stress that such intergovernmental action was, of course, dependent on the agreement and cooperation of member states, and by the time of the League of Nations a shift had taken place in statist conceptions of the refugee. In the nineteenth century refugees were few in number and hence presented little threat to national security or resources. Refugees were noticeable by their differences but were by and large an object of charity. Moreover, they were thought to offer potential wealth and knowledge to the state, thus they were generally welcomed. By the inter-war period humanitarian objectives were lower on the list of a state's priorities. The main concern of the modern state was now the building of a strong national identity within a given territorial jurisdiction; mass refugee movements, with their potential for racial tensions and insecurity, were not conducive to such a project. In other words, a transformation in state interests brought about a correlative change in the international response now given to the refugee. Accordingly, anything the LNHCR proposed had to take the states system as the given, normal order of international society, the refugee as the anomaly. Indeed, during the 1921 Conference the LNHCR concluded that 'each government must solve [refugees'] difficulties by adapting its own legal regulations to prevent abnormal conditions',[44] therefore indicating that a refugee 'problem' existed and the 'solution' was to be found within the system of separate sovereign states.

The LNHCR further institutionalised the refugee in statist terms by introducing refugee identity papers as an alternative to the national

---

[43] Soguk, *States and Strangers*, p. 121.
[44] League of Nations, 'Conference on the Question of Russian Refugees', 901.

citizen's passport. The League saw that a lack of official identification was equal to a lack of state protection and representation. Further, without papers refugees were restricted in their movement across international boundaries just when European states were erecting stricter border controls after the First World War. Accordingly, substitute national passports in the form of identity certificates were agreed upon by European states under the guise of the LNHCR, first for Russian refugees in 1922, then Armenians in 1924, Assyrian, Assyro–Chaldean and Turk refugees in 1928, and Saar refugees in 1935. These intergovernmental arrangements identified certain individuals as refugees and so further consolidated the image of the state as the agent representing and protecting already established 'normal' state–citizen relations. Refugees were not to be granted national passports; rather, they would be kept in check by states via specific identity certificates. Although the certificates became known as the 'Nansen passports', the word 'certificate' was strictly adhered to in official use so as to distinguish between the privileges offered the citizen and those offered the refugee. Once again, therefore, the refugee, forced outside the domestic political community, was the exception to the state–citizen–territory hierarchy, whose position was to be corrected via institutions similar to but not the same as those in place for national citizens.

The inter-war refugee regime has been criticised for inventing limited legal definitions that only dealt with specific groups of refugees.[45] Yet the main purpose of such legal definitions was 'to formalize the political consensus which had already been reached within the Council or Assembly of the League of Nations about the groups that should be given refugee status', as well as to assist governments and international organisations in defining who qualified as which type of refugee.[46] In other words, the formulation of international definitions relating to refugees acted to change the way states viewed certain groups of refugees, who they should include in definitions and hence to whom they should offer assistance. This highlights once again the influence of international norms on the construction of state identity, which in turn swayed statist responses towards the refugee. The various definitions subtly alerted states to the idea of a link between human rights abuses and refugee flows, which in turn affected states' ideas about their role as moral international actors. Similarly, certain international legal

---

[45] See for example Loescher, *Beyond Charity*, p. 40.
[46] Skran, *Refugees in Inter-war Europe*, p. 111.

agreements promulgated by the League of Nations and its associated refugee agencies acted to set specific standards by which governments then judged their action with regard to the refugee question. The 1933 Convention Relating to the International Status of Refugees contained provisions to be granted refugees in host states ranging from labour conditions to welfare and education. Its overall principle was that refugees should be accorded the same treatment as that given to other foreigners within a host state. Although only eight countries ratified it and eight others adhered to it in practice without ever ratifying it, the standards contained within the Convention certainly impacted on states that were members of the refugee regime. In the sphere of social welfare, for example, the French government upgraded certain benefits available to refugees and extended special benefits to some categories of refugees, such as children and pregnant women. At the same time it proceeded to loosen labour restrictions on refugees obtaining work permits and thus led to an improvement in conditions for such individuals.[47] In other words, the emergence of new international norms aimed at protecting and assisting refugees brought about a change in national norms by causing a shift in the interests and identities of states in regard to refugees.

Finally, on the question of expulsion of refugees, the impact of international norms on individual states was also impressive. Here, soft legislation in the form of opinions, propositions and recommendations issued by international refugee organisations often had the same effect on individual states as legal instruments. The Intergovernmental Advisory Commission for Refugees, a body that acted under the auspices of the League of Nations but which included both state officials and representatives of private organisations, focused its efforts on attempting to put a stop to arbitrary expulsions of refugees from host states. In a statement issued in 1935 the Commission recommended that expulsions should be carried out through specific national authorities created for the purpose of deciding whether such an expulsion was legitimate, rather than allowing the practice to continue unofficially and in secret. In numerous countries expulsion procedures were subsequently altered. Belgium, for example, established a commission before which refugees could present their cases, while France changed its regulations so that an

---

[47] Skran, *Refugees in Inter-war Europe*, pp. 125, 129–30.

expulsion order had to go through the higher echelons of the Ministry of the Interior.[48] The 1933 and 1938 Conventions also contained prohibitions on expulsion, leading numerous states to transpose the principle into national law. International and national provisions of this sort were, of course, a prelude to the principle of *non-refoulement* contained in Article 33 of the 1951 Convention, a fact that once again points to a continuum running through different periods of refugee regimentation. States therefore adjusted aspects of their national policies, which forced a redefinition of their interests in line with international ethical standards, norms that at times may have impinged upon national laws and practices. In this way national and international boundaries were blurred. International actors provided governments with policy options that then became the subject of debate at the national level, such that 'they harnessed national interests for the achievement of their own humanitarian goals and convinced the Great Powers to do something that otherwise they would not have done'.[49]

Mutually constituted identities

The 'refugee' as a socially constructed category was constituted in the inter-war years through the discourse generated by the international refugee regime. The boundaries of those included in the category 'refugee' evolved during this period. It was first someone from Russia, could then also be an Armenian, and later anyone fleeing Germany and Austria. Shifts were a reflection of the changing international climate as well as the result of state action that altered the definitional circle and so defined the number of individuals eligible for protection. Boundaries can thus be seen as ideological constructs, but the effects of where these boundaries are placed determine the placing of people within or, in the case of the refugee, between state territories. Boundaries were placed in such a way that certain individuals became refugees, others did not. Further, the word 'refugee' came to be associated with a 'problem' that demanded a 'solution'. It invoked images of destitute masses pouring over sovereign borders and creating problems for the receiving state. The 'normal' citizen could maintain her identity as a British national, a French national, a German national: the Polish refugee became merely a 'refugee', the Russian refugee just a 'refugee'. The refugee was an

---

[48] Skran, *Refugees in Inter-war Europe*, pp. 134–6.
[49] Skran, *Refugees in Inter-war Europe*, p. 183.

individual forced to claim a specific status and accept the definition so as to have access to the rights and protection the category offered, albeit in the knowledge that 'quasi-citizen' status was better than no status at all. Seeking international protection as a refugee was the only short-term option available, even though this meant that in the long term the individual was pursuing a morally difficult course. By implicitly recognising the state–citizen relationship as the norm, the refugee in essence accepted her out-of-the-ordinary status and her between-sovereigns position.

In early discussions of the refugee issue in the League Assembly there was no definition of the 'refugee' as such, nor did reports even refer specifically to the question as a 'political' one. Already sensitive to the infringement on sovereignty the refugee issue could pose, the League referred instead to potential 'economic problems' or 'social problems', thus avoiding an overtly threatening tone. For example, in the League's Monthly Summary of October 1933 concerning 'Assistance for Refugees (Jewish and Other) Coming from Germany', it is reported that the Assembly 'considered the economic, financial and social problems arising from the fact that a large number of German nationals (Jewish and other) had, during recent months, taken refuge in several countries'.[50] In fact, deliberations on the refugee question did not even take place under the 'political' section of the Assembly's agenda until May 1933, being considered a 'Social and Humanitarian Question' prior to this date. In this way discussions and ensuing legislation neatly side-stepped any need to actually define the refugee for some years. It was not until the formulation of the 1938 Convention Concerning the Status of Refugees Coming from Germany that a definition was laid down, albeit of one particular group of refugees. It viewed a refugee as 'any person who was settled in that country, who does not possess any nationality other than German nationality, and in respect of whom it is established that, in law or in fact, he or she does not enjoy the protection of the Government of the Reich'.[51] The international community recognised that there was a flow of refugees coming from one particular place that posed a particular problem, thus the response was to define that problem and attempt to deal with it in isolation. As a result, one particular group of refugees – Jewish refugees – became the problem, not the factors causing the individuals to try to leave their country in the first place.

---

[50] League of Nations, *Monthly Summary* vol. XIII No. 10 (October 1933), 222.
[51] League of Nations, *Monthly Summary* vol. XVI No. 7 (July 1936), 225.

This construction of the refugee problem was in large part created and maintained by the 'symbolic manipulation' of the 'myth' of the refugee.[52] 'They', the refugees, posed a threat, and this threat had the potential to undermine the existence of 'us'. For Germany the threat of Jewish refugees was controlled by means of expulsion and eventually extermination, while potential host states used processes of border control and visa restrictions to keep the refugees out of their territory. In the eyes of European governments and publics, refugees were the 'alien from the enemy country'.[53] Such statist conceptions of the refugee through the inter-war years are important in highlighting how the concept changed over time and space, being influenced by the changing nature of sovereignty and continually evolving state interests. The identity of international society was in part formulated by the refugee issue, and the refugee question itself in part constructed by the evolving identity of international society and its constituent parts, sovereign states.

Although no formal legal documentation existed along the lines of the 1951 Convention that would later be established, and the experience of helping such huge masses of refugees was new, refugees were nonetheless offered some protection and assistance by western states. Further examination of the intergovernmental activity undertaken on behalf of refugees shows that the LNHCR and organisations that were created alongside it actually had an internal dynamic of their own and, using this dynamic, they were able to influence state behaviour and change state perceptions of the refugee question as a whole. There was no real history of international cooperation on humanitarian issues before this time; rather, Europe had a list of failed attempts at international humanitarian projects in the 1920s, including disaster aid, unemployment support and the elimination of statelessness. In 1921 the League even decided not to assist the thirty million individuals threatened with starvation in Russia and the Ukraine, with League members agreeing that nothing should be done that may in any way help bolster Bolshevism.[54] In any case, there was the commonly held assumption that 'charity' should be the exclusive domain of private agencies and national governments, as reflected

---

[52] See Rae, *State Identities*, chapter 5 '"Ethnic cleansing" and the breakup of Yugoslavia', for a discussion of the 'symbolic manipulation' of the 'myth of Kosovo' that took place in Serbia 'to draw a sharp moral boundary between Serbs and the Muslim ethnic Albanians of Kosovo, and, by implication, all Muslims in Yugoslavia' (p. 186).

[53] Yvonne Kapp and Margaret Mynatt, *British Policy and the Refugees, 1933–1941* (London: Frank Cass, 1997), p. 7.

[54] Skran, *Refugees in Inter-war Europe*, p. 86.

in the preamble to the Covenant of the League of Nations. In the goal of achieving international peace and security, it held that the League was only 'to promote international co-operation'.[55] Consequently, any progress that was eventually made in the way of assisting and protecting European refugees in the inter-war period can be seen to reflect changing international norms and the way these altered state identities and interests.

Of course, changes in the international context over time affected normative understandings of the refugee issue, which in turn modified state interests and helped determine what type of international response the issue would receive. In this respect international politics were very conducive to the important work that the League of Nations did on behalf of refugees in the 1920s. It dealt with Russian refugees at a time when the Soviet Union was not a member of the League, which made its job politically easier, and assisted refugees from the Balkans when the new states in the region were still weak and vulnerable and therefore held no important weight in the international arena.[56] Thus there was no danger of upsetting a League member or of one member state disturbing relations with another. Further, the United States and western Europe were generally open to asylum-seekers and willing to let refugees resettle within their states. This allowed the League to successfully assist thousands of refugees from Russia and Armenia, as well as Greece, Turkey and the Balkans. And the Greek Refugee Commission had already settled thousands of displaced Greeks over a ten-year period when the Nansen International Office for Refugees was established in 1922. According to Bentwich, therefore, the precedent for action faced with more refugees in the 1930s was there: 'The League had already proved that international collaboration was an effective means of dealing with urgent humanitarian problems.'[57] But this successful international collaboration broke down in the following decade, which can in part be attributed to the decreased ability of the international refugee regime to construct international norms of protection as compatible with state interests.

Nansen had been appointed the first High Commissioner for Refugees in 1921. When he died in 1930, the regime was left without the vision and leadership of someone described as the 'the greatest

---

[55] Covenant of the League of Nations cited in Skran, *Refugees in Inter-war Europe*, p. 86.
[56] Marrus, *The Unwanted*, p. 158.   [57] Bentwich, *The Refugees from Germany*, p. 58.

humanitarian of the era', in dealing with the ensuing 'Jewish refugee problem'.[58] Nansen had greatly influenced the development of the international refugee protection regime, having acted as 'moral entrepreneur' and therefore helped ensure the development of certain norms at certain times.[59] With the LNHCR Nansen put in place a global norm of protection that led states to redefine their normative interests, even when it was not always in their material interest to do so. Nansen's achievements are indeed remarkable: in setting up the office of the High Commissioner he established the basic institutions of the refugee regime that continue to provide the basis to the current system of refugee protection. He also appointed delegates, who became accepted by host governments without any precedent for such a set-up in international relations, and he helped loose norms become fixed rules, for example when his guidance brought states together to institute the 'Nansen passport', the first internationally recognised identity document for refugees.[60] Here, Nansen was keen to afford freedom of movement to refugees needing to cross an international border to escape persecution. By emphasising the need to keep track of individuals and ensure refugees were tied to a state and territory, he made the idea sound compatible with the strategic concerns of statist governance. Accordingly, states shifted their policies and the 'passports' came into being.

The regime therefore helped convince states that the refugee problem was not only reaching far beyond the borders of the individual state, it was also a problem that extended beyond the capacity of any one state to deal with alone. State actors began to acknowledge that refugee movements had a considerable impact on both domestic and international politics, and therefore on peace and stability both within and between states. Refugee flows from one country affected others, just as increased immigration restrictions in one state could have severe repercussions on other states. Once it was perceived that the refugee 'problem' was no longer a concern of individual states, the issue became projected onto the international arena; in the words of Newman, 'constructivism in action'.[61] In the 1920s, for example, both Britain and France found themselves morally and financially responsible for Russian refugees, many of whom had been part of the White armies in the Russian Civil War that

---

[58] Skran, *Refugees in Inter-war Europe*, p. 195.
[59] Martha Finnemore cited in Checkel, 'The Constructivist Turn', 332.
[60] Skran, *Refugees in Inter-war Europe*, p. 290.
[61] Newman, 'Human Security', 247.

Britain and France had unsuccessfully supported. They tried to arrange repatriation agreements with the Soviet Union and eastern European states but failed. Since national policies would not solve the problem, international action was the only option. Similarly, many states hosting Russian refugees were supporting them alone: internationalising the issue would mean sharing the financial burden, thus it was in their interests to act in the context of an international regime. With these considerations in mind, the initial proposal of the Intergovernmental Committee on Refugees in 1921 for the appointment of a General Commissioner for the Russian Refugees met with little opposition.[62] States began to accept the necessity of intergovernmental action towards refugees and international organisations to coordinate such action. Norms of refugee protection that could prevent the instability that refugee movements cause gained an increasingly greater place in international relations and international politics, and in this way transnational norms of refugee protection extended the political discourse beyond the territorial limits of the sovereign state.

It is clear that the responses of sovereign states to the refugee problem were influenced by international norms and values propagated by international organisations and actors. Evidently states' interests and identities were affected by such norms and values, such that their perceptions of refugees, the refugee 'problem' and the way in which they were to be addressed were conditioned. Rather than acting entirely rationally according to self-interest and merely being constrained by international norms, state responses to the refugee question in the 1930s showed that such norms actually helped determine and mould state behaviour. The international refugee regime that was emerging and developing throughout the inter-war period acted to alter states' perceptions regarding how the refugee problem affected their national interests, and thus caused states to adjust their responses accordingly. In other words, states are social actors whose actions are shaped by social processes and constructions within the international system. State actors make a choice as to how they treat the refugee problem, a process known as 'issue constructivism'.[63] But in making this choice, they are influenced by international norms and values: 'Threats and security are

[62] Skran, *Refugees in Inter-war Europe*, pp. 89–92.
[63] Ole Wæver cited in Lars-Erik Cederman, 'Exclusion Versus Dilution: Real or Imagined Trade-off?', in Lars-Erik Cederman (ed.), *Constructing Europe's Identity: The External Dimension* (Boulder, Colo.: Lynne Rienner Publishers, 2001), 249.

not objective matters, security is a way to frame and handle an issue.'[64] As Skran concludes, within the League of Nations decision-making 'was not simply the sum total of government positions; it had its own dynamics', and refugee agencies under the auspices of the League 'clearly had the ability to play a leadership role independent of the wishes of any one member state'.[65]

And so the refugee 'problem' in the international system once again conjures up a paradox: the refugee as a concept and the 'problem' she entails were from the outset defined in state-oriented terms, such that the state became the referent object whose sovereignty and security had to be protected against the threat of the refugee. However, intergovernmental action on behalf of refugees in the inter-war period was promulgated by international organisations and norms that worked to influence state behaviour and change state interests and identities towards refugees. In this regard, the state may have remained the referent object, but its control over the refugee was not absolute. States were of course more willing to extend protection and assistance to refugees when it coincided with their foreign or domestic policy objectives, when the refugees had been forced out of enemy states, when the refugees had similar ethnic backgrounds to the majority population, or when there was a need for immigrant labour. Similarly, states were more ready to help other host countries if they were allies or of strategic importance. In this respect, states party to the norms may have seen the emerging refugee protection regime as nothing more than a set of 'collective aspirations' which they had only limited intention of actually upholding. Yet, by taking part in the international refugee regime, to whatever extent, state identity was altered. The norm of protection did more than simply regulate statist behaviour. Rather, states were given meaning through the international social context in which they were interpreted at the time. An international norm of refugee protection emerged and by adhering to the norm the state was redefined as an agent capable of protecting 'outsiders'. In this regard state sovereignty was compromised one bit further with an element of humanitarianism, and the pluralism–solidarism balance in international society shifted once again.

---

[64] Ole Wæver, 'European Security Identities', *Journal of Common Market Studies* 34 (1996), 108.
[65] Skran, *Refugees in Inter-war Europe*, pp. 274, 286.

Inter-war 'solutions'

Rather than acknowledging the rights of the refugee to claim membership in a state, the inter-war system of dealing with refugees was actually based on the coercive displacement of different groups of individuals. Peoples, rather than borders or territory, were to be moved to create homogeneous nations, which would eliminate the 'problem' of refugees. Whole populations could be shifted to a different political jurisdiction, where their individual rights would be protected by the new state and their sentimental communal attachments would be safeguarded via membership in a homogeneous nation. The right of states to expel or cleanse themselves of national minorities was not questioned as such, even where this resulted in mass refugee flows; rather, the international community sought ways to prevent states finding further cause to do so. The ideas of population transfer and exchange were therefore a corollary of the concept of the refugee. Indeed they are based on the same type of thinking that creates refugees, and such practices have the potential themselves to cause mass refugee flows. Whether such movements of persons were brought about by ethnic cleansing or more humane applications of forced population transfer, the goal was the same; the creation of a homogeneous nation-state. Population transfer and exchange aimed to bring about a better fit between political boundaries and ethnicity.[66] They were an attempt to reorganise the ethnic, religious and socio-political identities of peoples in accordance with the sovereign territorial state. The 'other' had to be removed from the designated national homeland of the 'citizen' for the process of nation-state building to succeed. Population transfers, it was held, would realign nations with their assigned states, a legitimate means of making territory and peoples coincide and of therefore preventing the creation of refugees.

Thus when national self-determination was pronounced as the organising principle of the 1919 peace settlements, forced population transfer became viewed as an internationally legitimate means of overcoming discrepancies between boundaries or geography and ethnicity or identity, so as to accomplish ethnically homogeneous nation-states. Yet ethnic cleansing and forced population transfer and exchange can be seen as another example of state action that may create mass displacements of people both within and across international borders. Indeed, they are

---

[66] Jennifer Jackson-Preece, 'Ethnic Cleansing as an Instrument of Nation-State Creation: Changing State Practices and Evolving Legal Norms', *Human Rights Quarterly* 20 (1998), 820.

intended to create refugee flows with the caveat that those moved will immediately or very quickly become (ethnic) citizens of their (new) host states, such as was supposed to be the case when moving Anatolian Greeks to Greece under the Greco–Bulgarian exchange of 1919. Homogeneous nation-states, however, are by and large a myth, and moving peoples around generally resulted in mass refugee flows that were difficult to resolve. Population transfer is evidence once again, therefore, of the inherently constructed nature of the refugee category and of the potential for exclusion once arbitrary selection criteria are employed with the aim of 'sorting out' peoples and territory.

In the inter-war period, population exchange that took place was frequently organised under the auspices of the League of Nations. The Congress of Berlin of 1912 and the Convention of Adrianople of 1913 initiated the practice of population exchange, but the transfers had been aborted with the outbreak of the First World War. Revisionist strategies were then renewed in the inter-war years. The 1919 Treaty of Neuilly saw around 100,000 Bulgarians exchanged, 'voluntarily' at least in principle, for 35,000 Greeks. The 1923 Treaty of Lausanne used religion as the indicator of national affiliation to compulsorily relocate 1.5 million Greeks and 400,000 Turks, with populations being forcibly removed and those who had fled the war prohibited to return.[67] But both sides then used the religion criterion as a means of expelling other undesirable minorities: the Turks removed groups of Armenians, Serbs, Russians, Romanians, Gypsies and even Arabs, whilst Greece forced out many Macedonians and attempted to eject Albanian Muslims. The logical implication of the ideal of population exchange and redistribution, therefore, was the creation on a vast scale of persons – refugees – 'to whom suddenly the rules of the world around them had ceased to apply'.[68] Attempts to settle displacement led to further displacement, and refugees were the inevitable by-product of such revisionism in a world that had come to be imagined in favour of nations and their representative agents, sovereign territorial states.[69] If the rules of the world had ceased to apply to the refugee, she showed that there was an 'outside the rules', a place in between states. The refugee acted to demonstrate, therefore, that belonging to a sovereign territorial state was not a natural given.

---

[67] Jackson-Preece, 'Ethnic Cleansing', 824. [68] Arendt, *The Origins*, p. 267.
[69] Soguk, *States and Strangers*, p. 274, note 7.

The initial practice of population transfer in the early League of Nations years was, of course, later continued by Nazi Germany, which aimed to both cleanse Europe of its Jews and bring ethnic German minorities back to the Reich to realise an ethnically homogeneous German nation-state.[70] But in the face of mass numbers of Jewish refugees in the 1930s there were problems with relying on population transfer since they had no 'national homeland' to be transferred to. Population transfer as a 'solution' therefore began to break down in the face of mass forced emigration of Jewish refugees.[71] Denationalisation of Jewish refugees who had fled the Reich began in 1933. Article 1 of the Law of 14 July 1933 Regarding the Withdrawal of Naturalization and Loss of German Nationality applied to all persons who had been naturalised in Germany between 9 November 1918 and 30 January 1933, if the nationality of such persons was now regarded as 'undesirable'. Article 2 applied the law to German nationals residing outside Germany if their nationality now 'prejudiced German interests by attitudes contrary to his duty of loyalty' towards the Reich. 'Undesirable' was determined according to national racial principles, such that it applied overwhelmingly to eastern European Jews. The Reich Citizenship Law of September 1935 left all 'non-Aryans' either stateless or without diplomatic protection. It reduced almost one million persons immediately to the status of guests or wards of the state and denied them all civil and political rights, thus having the effect of creating a mass of stateless refugees in the countries neighbouring Germany, and in depriving those refugees of state protection. By 1 January 1937 Germany had made 4,545 withdrawals of nationality.[72] As the League noted in its monthly summary of action in 1936, there was a real danger posed by the increase in the number of refugees, 'particularly owing to the growing practice of invalidating the passports of refugees abroad, thus rendering them stateless'.[73] The creation of hundreds of thousands of stateless persons and refugees led to a perceived threat to

---

[70] Jackson-Preece, 'Ethnic Cleansing', 825.

[71] Of course, the post-1945 'solution' found for the Jewish refugees who did not fit the logic of states and national homelands was the albeit artificial creation of the politico-territorial state of Israel in the (mythical) homeland of the Jewish minority. The problem of boundedness is immediately revealed in this scenario, whereby state creation initiated a zero-sum conflict between Israelis and Palestinians over a finite territory. It was, of course, a 'solution' to a 'problem' that is still searching for a peaceful resolution.

[72] Oscar I. Janowsky and Melvin M. Fagen, *International Aspects of German Racial Policies* (Oxford University Press, 1937), pp. 60–2.

[73] League of Nations, *Monthly Summary* Vol. XVI No. 1 (January 1936), 26.

host states not just in terms of a burden on resources; the masses of Jewish refugees had the potential to alter 'the ethnic, cultural, religious and linguistic composition of host populations',[74] particularly so given the historic role of Jews as the 'other' within (Christian) Europe.

Since these denationalisations were generally applied to those already outside Germany – namely refugees – their effect was immediately and directly felt in the territorial domains of the states of refuge. Once refugees became stateless the host state was in effect denied its right to expel or deport the refugees back to their country of origin if it so desired. Germany had a duty under international law to continue protection of its nationals 'until and unless it [could have been] withdrawn without violating the rights of other states'.[75] The forced emigration of thousands of individuals from the Reich's jurisdiction was therefore a clear violation of the territorial sovereignty of other states. Speaking about Russian policies towards its Jews in 1891, US President Harrison warned that such persecution was not a local question: 'A decree to leave one country is, in the nature of things, an order to enter another – some other.'[76] The US Secretary of State claimed that 'the mutual duties of nations require that each should use its power with a due regard for the results which its exercise produces on the rest of the world'.[77] Note, therefore, that Germany was not in breach of its duty to protect those individuals it sought to expel – protection of individual human rights was largely undiscovered until the post-1945 era. Rather, the violation of international law consisted in the burden placed on receiving states by expelling the refugees, forcing them into their territories and thus infringing their territorial sovereignty.

Since forced emigration and the refugees it produced were unattractive to potential host states, there were several formal attempts in the inter-war period at the expulsion of unwanted groups with the actual consent of the prospective host country. Such arrangements were known as 'collaborative relocation', 'one possible response to human rights abuses' whereby threatened individuals or groups from one territory are resettled in another.[78] As an alternative to population transfer, the practice attempted to formalise the idea of forced

---

[74] Loescher, *Refugee Movements and International Security*, p. 41.
[75] Janowsky and Fagen, *International Aspects*, pp. 67–8.
[76] Cited in Janowsky and Fagen, *International Aspects*, p. 52.
[77] Cited in Janowsky and Fagen, *International Aspects*, p. 57.
[78] Robert Darst, 'Guaranteed Human Beings for Sale: The Collaborative Relocation of Jews from Axis Europe, 1933–45', *Journal of Human Rights* 1, 2 (2002), 207.

emigration tried in the 1930s as a way to deal specifically with the increasing number of Jewish refugees. For a transfer agreement to work there had to be positive incentives for both sides. Collaborative relocation emerged as an option for the international community when the following four, or at least the first three, conditions were met: first, there had to be a third party with an interest in the relocation of the individuals in question; second, those willing to carry out the relocation – the 'rescuers' – had to have access to the political and economic resources necessary for it to be successful; third, the state currently 'housing' the individuals – the 'captor' – also had to have an interest in the relocation of these individuals, believing that their removal would promote their own goals of ethnic homogeneity, political stability or national security; and finally, the interests of the would-be emigrants and of the residents of the place of relocation had to be, or should have been, taken into account.[79] In other words, the 'solution' to the 'problem' had to be constructed in such a way that demonstrated the act of collaborative relocation as being in line with the interests of both the state of origin and the state of destination.

The Nazi–Zionist 'Transfer Agreement' of 1933–9 was the most successful of these attempts, with the conditions for a successful relocation of individuals largely being met. Whereas European Jewish refugees themselves had tried to survive threats simply by being left alone, Zionists were attempting to protect themselves from further threats by forming their own government. Accordingly, Palestine was seen as a good option for the relocation of Jewish refugees; it would be possible to literally reinstall the Jewish refugees in a territory where their identity fitted in, in accordance with the idea of making territory and identity coincide and granting every nation a state. The Zionists (the third party) had an active interest in encouraging Jewish immigration into Palestine, not only to stop persecution of fellow Jews, but also in accordance with their programme of 'ethnic bolstering' for the sake of helping to construct a Jewish National Home and hence protecting the Jewish identity.[80] Moreover, bringing in capital would build the economy and thus expand the immigration quota. The Nazis (the captors) for their part put in place an increasingly intense programme of persecution to encourage emigration of the Jews to Palestine. This started with forced emigration of a somewhat 'voluntary' nature, and led to the Directive of January 1939

[79] Darst, 'Guaranteed Human Beings', 210–11.
[80] Darst, 'Guaranteed Human Beings', 207.

that provided for the establishment of a Reich Central Office charged with promoting Jewish emigration 'by every possible means', a step that acted more or less as an official expulsion order and had the effect of causing 50 per cent of all Jewish refugee flows from Germany and Austria in that year alone.[81] The views of the would-be Jewish emigrants, however, were not totally convergent with the plan: whereas the Zionists saw German Jews primarily as Jews 'with a duty to immigrate to Palestine', German Jews identified themselves first and foremost as Germans, distinguished from other Germans by religion, not nationality. Indeed, prior to 1933 only 1 per cent of the Jewish population in Palestine had come from Germany. Thus those who did eventually take advantage of the Transfer Agreement 'did so not for ideological reasons, but because the Nazis and the Zionists collaborated to make that path relatively more attractive than it otherwise would have been'.[82] The transfer agreement was in line with security and identity ideas of both the Zionists and the Nazis; less so for the German Jewish refugees.

Despite facilitating the (forced) migration of 52,000 German Jewish refugees to Palestine, however, the Nazi–Zionist Transfer Agreement was ultimately a victim of its own success. As numbers of Jewish refugees fleeing to Palestine soared with the intensification of persecution in Germany and central and eastern Europe, the Arab population responded violently, and the British mandate reacted by sharply cutting quotas. Between 1933 and 1935 the Jewish population in Palestine rose from 192,000 to 355,000. When the British curbed immigration, numbers of Jewish arrivals fell from 29,700 in 1936 to 10,500 in 1937.[83] The refugees became more and more trapped in Europe, just when Nazi Germany set out on its policy of forcible expulsion. This, in turn, meant a huge increase in the number of Jewish refugees seeking asylum in western states, more often than not totally destitute and completely reliant on the host state or charity. Accordingly, the nature of future attempts at collaborative relocation changed, and it became harder to construct potential transfer agreements as beneficial to the interests of a host state; rather, refugees were increasingly viewed as a potential burden. Indeed, whereas the Zionists had been keen to encourage the immigration of Jewish refugees into Palestine, after 1938 governments of countries receiving, or potentially receiving, refugees were all motivated 'by

---

[81] Fox, 'German and European Jewish Refugees', 77.
[82] Darst, 'Guaranteed Human Beings', 212.
[83] Darst, 'Guaranteed Human Beings', 213–14.

a strong interest in directing German Jewish migration toward any destination but one: their own territory'.[84] Thus a Transfer Agreement between Germany and the Intergovernmental Committee on Refugees, which was to see the emigration of 400,000 Jews from the Reich, was flawed from the start. American Jewish organisations viewed the agreement as effectively sanctioning the expropriation of the remaining assets of German Jews, while the British government was strongly opposed to encouraging further refugees to Britain or Palestine. When it finally looked like the plan would go ahead, the Second World War broke out and put a stop to it.

Throughout 1940 and early 1941, Nazi Germany and the Romanian government collaborated with the Zionists to enable the illegal immigration of thousands of Jews to Palestine, but from mid-1941 the Reich blocked emigration entirely and turned instead to deportation and extermination.[85] Towards the end of that year the Romanian government offered to release and allow the relocation of its remaining 70,000 Jews to the western Allies for 200,000 lei per refugee – equivalent to about $1,300. These were the survivors of the 135,000 Jewish refugees interned in concentration camps in the Transnistria region of the Soviet Union. This action would have freed Romania of the rest of its unwanted Jewish outsiders, demonstrated independence from Nazi Germany and appeased the western Allies. Yet the proposal met with rejection, once again because no state was willing to accept such a large number of refugees. Extermination was undesirable, but so was another mass influx of Jewish refugees. Thus, as Darst points out, advocates of collaborative relocation were caught between Hitler's determination to exterminate the Jews and Allied governments' opposition to any more large numbers of refugees seeking sanctuary on their territory. Given these preferences, 'the mass termination of the European Jews proved to be the "equilibrium outcome" from which neither Nazi Germany nor the western Allies had any incentive to move'.[86]

Jewish refugees were found throughout Europe, running in all directions, escaping yet exiled beyond the state–citizen–territory hierarchy. Even when Germany put a ban on Jews leaving the country and trapped them within its borders, the refugee continued to be viewed as the outsider in the international system. The prohibition of emigration from Germany effectively 'relieved the major powers of a Jewish

[84] Darst, 'Guaranteed Human Beings', 214.   [85] Darst, 'Guaranteed Human Beings', 217.
[86] Darst, 'Guaranteed Human Beings', 220, 223.

refugee problem as such'.[87] Yet governmental protection had failed, and the refugees were physically unable to cross an international border which, now more than ever, meant life or death.

Conclusions

The refugee concept developed alongside the consolidation of a modern international states system, grounded in a positive view of sovereignty whereby the state was responsible for all citizens within its territory. A continual presence of international organisations dealing with refugees not only set the precedent for intergovernmental action to deal with the refugee 'problem', but, further, such a presence in the international system also acted to ensure that the refugee was problematised from a statist perspective. The refugee space was opened and maintained and intergovernmental action took place within this space, always in regard to the concept of the state. But the refugee showed that at times this responsibility would be avoided, at others there would be no actual state into which a particular group of individuals could be reinstated. While this constructed a specific refugee figure, state identities were also constructed and reconstructed by evolving international norms. As such, at certain times states were socialised as moral actors willing to take part in the evolving international refugee protection regime, at other times they guarded their sovereignty fiercely.

In its search for solutions the international community sought to shift peoples to fit sovereign territories, but this did not or could not always work. Moreover, human rights abuses that took place in the process did nothing to protect the very individuals fleeing the human rights abuses such solutions were supposed to avoid. It was perhaps only a question of time before the intergovernmental protection regime, as it took shape in its initial years, would break down. The solutions were not working, the numbers of refugees were increasing, and the experiment in the Wilsonian belief in nation-states and self-determination as a means of organising peoples then proved disastrous in failing to stop the persecution of thousands upon thousands of Jewish refugees during the Second World War. We now examine the shift in response to the refugee issue in the post-war years.

---

[87] Fox, 'German and European Jewish Refugees', 78.

6 Refugees and international protection in the Cold War era

> The attitude of the totalitarian states towards the would-be exiles is necessarily ambivalent. They would like to get rid of them – but they are also reluctant to let them go.   Paul Tabori[1]

The refugee issue cannot be divorced from the political context in which it operates at any one time, and international responses to the 'refugee problem' soon became entangled in the Cold War environment. But the changing refugee regime was also indicative of the international system as it developed in the post-war years, affected by a shift to fixed borders, negative sovereignty and individual human rights. The post-war years indicated a reorganisation of the map and a shift in state–citizen relations, but this did not remove the 'problem' of the refugee.

This chapter first asks how the Cold War period represented a continuation from the decades of international refugee regimentation preceding it, before examining the fundamental changes and differences. It then considers the Berlin Wall as representative of impermeable borders that were erected in this period as a barrier to refugee creation. Fourth, it discusses non-European displacements of persons as inherently contradictory to the Cold War (western) understanding of 'refugees'. Finally, it analyses what the Cold War normative responses towards refugees meant in terms both of refugee identities and the identity of international society itself.

Continuities in the refugee regime

If the creation of refugees leading up to the First World War and during the inter-war years saw the start of the 'modern' extent of the refugee

[1] Tabori, *The Anatomy of Exile*, p. 328.

problem, the mass of refugees created by the Second World War was on an even greater scale. In 1938 Thompson noted that 'a whole nation of people, although they come from many nations, wanders the world, homeless except for refuges which may any moment prove to be temporary'.[2] Millions of individuals spilled over their designated borders and boundaries. When Germany invaded Poland at the outbreak of the War, for example, 300,000 people were immediately forced out of the country as refugees. Likewise, when Alsace-Lorraine was occupied 100,000 French-speaking persons were expelled. In 1940 some five million refugees were sweeping across France, fleeing the Netherlands, Luxembourg and Belgium. As northern Transylvania was ceded to Hungary in August 1940, 200,000 Romanians moved back to Romania and 160,000 Hungarians were forced back to Hungary. And 12 million refugees were created as the German armies advanced across Russia.[3] In 1945 Europe was thus a continent awash with refugees. War had displaced over 30 million people throughout Europe, both within countries and across external frontiers, either forcibly transferred, deported or dispersed. The scene, as Wyman evocatively describes it, was one of 'a long, slow-moving mass of humanity'.[4] In the words of Marrus, 'Europe choked with refugees'.[5] From the end of 1944 each Allied advance had brought 'a crescendo of refugees', such that seven million individuals were roaming western Europe by the summer of 1945, 'fleeing, or heading home, or searching for family members, or simply trying to survive'.[6]

As the international community began to recover, it was thought that the 'refugee problem' would be resolved. Indeed the consensus of the international community was that refugees and displaced persons (DPs) were a creation of war, hence an end to the fighting would mean an end to the existence of such individuals. Refugees and displaced persons would now be able to return to their countries of origin since the factors causing them to leave had been eliminated. Successive organisations were established to expedite this return: the Intergovernmental Committee on Refugees (IGCR), the United Nations Relief and Rehabilitation Administration (UNRRA) and the International Refugee Organization

---

[2] Thompson, *Refugees: Anarchy or Organization?*, p. 5.
[3] All figures from Eugene M. Kulischer, *Europe on the Move: War and Population Changes, 1917–47* (New York: Columbia University Press, 1948), pp. 255–60.
[4] Mark Wyman, *Displaced Persons: Europe's Displaced Persons, 1945–1951* (Ithaca, New York: Cornell University Press, 1998), p. 15.
[5] Marrus, *The Unwanted*, p. 297.   [6] Wyman, *Displaced Persons*, p. 17.

(IRO).[7] Taking over from their inter-war predecessors, these bodies were established with the aim of 're-territorialising' the displaced. Thus intergovernmental responses to refugees in the post-war years were a continuation of what the LNHCR had started in the inter-war era.

The IGCR emerged from the Evian conference of 1938 and bridged the gap between intergovernmental action in the refugee field during the Second World War and early post-war activity. The underlying purpose of the conference is a matter of dispute – whether it was a response to the successive failures of the League of Nations and its High Commissioners for Refugees, a response almost completely to the Jewish refugee problem, or a more general, large-scale project to deal with what had become an international problem. What is clear is that it was no exception in containing elements of both politics and humanitarianism, such as had coloured the refugee issue from the start. Certainly the number of refugees in Europe seeking protection at this time, particularly Jewish refugees, was increasing rapidly. Yet the international community saw refugees as a potential strain on their already burdened economies, and a possible contributing factor to growing inter-state tension.[8] Whichever the favoured thesis, however, the IGCR can be viewed as the next on the list of consecutive attempts at intergovernmental action on behalf of refugees that took the state–citizen relationship as the norm, the refugee as the unstable exception. The organisation was instrumental in forming another site of intergovernmental action for the continued statist construction and control of refugees.[9]

UNRRA was established in 1943 to coordinate and administer measures for the relief of 'victims of war' in all areas under Allied control, which included displaced persons and refugees. It was tasked with the repatriation of displaced persons. Many such individuals were able to reach their former homes relatively quickly and easily. In May and June 1945, 80,000 individuals were repatriated each day, amounting to 5.25 million displaced persons.[10] At the end of September 1945 total figures included two million Soviet nationals repatriated from the

---

[7] For detailed accounts of each of these organisations, see respectively Tommie Sjöberg, *The Powers and the Persecuted: The Refugee Problem and the Intergovernmental Committee on Refugees (IGCR), 1938–1947* (Lund University Press, 1991); George Woodbridge, *UNRRA: The History of the United Nations Relief and Rehabilitation Administration* (New York: Columbia University Press, 1950); and Louise W. Holborn, *The International Refugee Organization. A Specialized Agency of the United Nations: Its History and Work, 1946–1952* (Oxford University Press, 1956).

[8] Loescher, *Beyond Charity*, pp. 44–5.   [9] Soguk, *States and Strangers*, p. 150.

[10] Marrus, *The Unwanted*, p. 310.

western zones of Germany, Austria and Czechoslovakia, 230,000 from western European countries including France and Norway, and 200,000 Yugoslavs. Between November 1945 and July 1947, UNRRA repatriated another 202,000 displaced persons from Austria, 742,000 from the western zones of Germany and 18,000 from Italy.[11] But at the end of September 1945 there were around two million displaced persons still in Europe, a figure that had only fallen to 1.7 million by the start of 1946. It included 850,000 individuals refusing repatriation, 250,000 pre-war refugees such as Armenians, Assyrians, Russians and Saarlanders, and 320,000 refugees from Germany, Austria, the Sudetenland and Republican Spain.[12] Due to changes in boundaries and acts of denationalisation that had occurred during the Second World War, it became evident that large numbers of DPs could not actually return to their pre-war country of origin. Thousands of displaced persons were now stateless, and 'going home' would not necessarily provide the governmental protection that should be accorded citizens.[13]

Hence, just when UNRRA was trying to build momentum for large-scale repatriation, this very 'solution' began to show signs of resistance and the post-war belief in repatriation started to fade. With the changing East–West international climate and increased political tension, western powers had to face the realisation that forced repatriation was no longer an option. It became apparent that many DPs would literally refuse to be returned to their state of origin: 'The great wave of repatriation came immediately after the end of fighting in Europe in 1945 and later declined until it became a mere trickle. The pool of the uprooted, however, still did not go dry. Initially some 100,000 people, mainly eastern European or Soviet nationals, declined offers of repatriation. Then their numbers began to swell.'[14] Accordingly, a 'hard core' of displaced persons looked set to remain: one million Poles, 170,000 Balts, more than 100,000 Yugoslavs and 54,000 Soviet citizens, 844,000 of whom were still receiving UNRRA aid in March 1946.[15] They were the 'non-repatriables', 'the politics around whose lives heralded and expedited the emergence of the cold war between the East and the West'.[16] Meanwhile political changes in eastern Europe were not only making past refugee flows irresolvable,

[11] Wyman, *Displaced Persons*, p. 64.
[12] Wyman, *Displaced Persons*, p. 37; Gordenker, *Refugees in International Politics*, pp. 23–4; and Tabori, *The Anatomy of Exile*, pp. 283–4.
[13] Wyman, *Displaced Persons*, p. 36.
[14] Gordenker, *Refugees in International Politics*, p. 23.
[15] Wyman, *Displaced Persons*, pp. 60, 69.   [16] Soguk, *States and Strangers*, p. 156.

they were also bringing new ones, and UNRRA became trapped within East–West politics.

Emerging from the ashes of UNRRA and constituting the penultimate link in the 1921–51 chain was the International Refugee Organization. As a non-permanent, specialised agency of the United Nations, the IRO was 'to bring about rapid and positive solution of the problem of *bona fide* refugees and displaced people'.[17] It was mandated with the repatriation, protection and resettlement of the so-called 'last million' whose cases UNRRA had failed to solve. Eastern European states successfully managed to include the provision that the main task of the IRO be 'to encourage and assist in every way possible their early return to their countries of origin'.[18] In other words, as Holborn notes, the IRO was to 'reestablish the refugees in a normal life'.[19] It was very successful: by the end of its four-year life-span the IRO had settled, resettled or repatriated over one million displaced persons and refugees.[20] Yet all the while it was solving existing cases, new ones were being created, with one group of refugees merely being replaced by another. Flows of refugees were continuing to arrive in the West from eastern European states. They included two main categories of '*infiltrées*' – Jewish refugees and 'political' refugees. Then a new group started to appear: the ethnic Germans. These refugees had lived in areas of Poland and central Europe or parts of Germany transferred to Polish sovereignty by the Potsdam Agreement. Indeed, refugee movements of ethnic Germans were in part at least the result of the great power agreement at Potsdam. And of course, the 'hard-core' refugee cases, the 'non-repatriables', remained just that, such that 'thousands of them were rotting mentally and physically in the bleak camps, without hope and without a future'.[21] As a consequence, under the IRO only 54,000 DPs returned to Communist-controlled areas in the three years between 1947 and 1950.[22] Approximately eighteen months after the end of the War, the IRO estimated that 1.25 million refugees and displaced persons still awaited repatriation or resettlement.[23] And as the phenomenon grew, the factors that set displaced persons apart from other refugees were coming into focus. Demobilised soldiers, evacuees,

---

[17] Zolberg *et al.*, *Escape from Violence*, p. 22.
[18] Article 1, Constitution of the International Refugee Organization cited in Holborn, *The International Refugee Organization*, p. 50.
[19] Holborn, *The International Refugee Organization*, p. 50.
[20] Tabori, *The Anatomy of Exile*, p. 286.   [21] Tabori, *The Anatomy of Exile*, p. 287.
[22] Wyman, *Displaced Persons*, pp. 74–7.
[23] United States Office of Public Affairs, Department of State, *The IRO: Background Summary* (March 1947), p. 1.

forced workers or political prisoners, for example, were all trying to return home. But 'displaced persons', today's refugees, had become a stateless people with nowhere to go.[24]

As with previous intergovernmental action towards refugees, these organisations acted to ensure the refugee figure continued to be imagined in statist terms, in opposition to the fixed, stable identity of the national citizen. Further, each organisation was created before its predecessor withered away, thus guaranteeing that the 'refugee space' as a place of statist regimentation was kept open. Thus we can identify a continuum in the growing international refugee protection regime, a chain with successive links being added from the first forms of intergovernmental action in the days of the League of Nations all the way to the 1951 boundary. Each organisation was designed to re-establish the refugee 'with a space of particularity, a territorial inside, a country of origin, represented and protected by a state',[25] so as to restore the 'normal' order of life. Rather than a genuine commitment to the humanitarian concerns of the refugees, it is once again possible to discern the influence of political concerns.

Further, all intergovernmental organisations working within the refugee field acted to define a certain image of the refugee. By limiting the types or groups of individuals to whom the status applied, a specific type of refugee could be the subject of intergovernmental protection, leaving other refugee identities, perhaps just as much in need of assistance, out of the equation. Indeed, the constructed character of the refugee is revealed when consideration is taken of the ever-changing definitions of the 'refugee' in the eligibility criteria of individual organisations. The purpose of intergovernmental action was to redefine the refugee's relationship with a bounded place of territory. But international opinion regarding who was in need of such reterritorialisation at any one time led to differing definitions of refugees and therefore constructed varying images of the refugee figure depending on changing spatio-temporal contexts. The IGCR, for example, constructed a 'refugee problem' in terms of Jewish and political refugees from the inter-war period, while UNRRA's image of whom the 'refugee problem' included used the generalised category of 'victims of war'. Viewed in human terms, the definitions and eligibility criteria found within the refugee regime quite often determined how an individual or group case would be resolved. For example, in June 1945 there were

[24] Wyman, *Displaced Persons*, p. 35.   [25] Soguk, *States and Strangers*, p. 159.

11,000 Baltic refugees in the western zones who found themselves in the category 'non-repatriables'. A few months later this number had become 131,000 due to changes in the eligibility requirements.[26]

Another example of the manipulation of categories can be found in the distinctions drawn between refugees and displaced persons. In the immediate post-war years, DPs were regarded as individuals who had been forcibly moved or deported during the war, but who would be able to return to their country of origin now that the war was over. The masses of individuals crowded into displaced person camps in the aftermath of the war were assumed to be awaiting repatriation, with the camp as a temporary means of stopping further displacement. The term 'refugee', on the other hand, was reserved strictly for individuals who could not be or would not be repatriated and, as we have seen, this category gradually grew in size as it became clear that many 'DPs' would never be able to return 'home' with the onset of the Cold War.[27] If the international community decided the Jews were displaced persons, for example, they would have to be returned to their countries of origin – largely eastern European states that had forced them out. If, however, they were to be labelled refugees, they would be entitled to resettlement in third countries. Yet the main third country in question at the time was Palestine, and there were growing political difficulties in allowing more Jews to resettle there. Instead of assisting Jewish refugees to reach Palestine, arguments were often used that these individuals were no longer leaving Germany for fear of persecution, and their movement was therefore restricted.[28] In the end, however, most of the remaining Jews in European DP camps were given refugee status and the majority sought resettlement in Palestine. Of course, as the Jewish refugees were transformed into Israeli citizens in 1948, the problem of Palestinian Arab refugees began, a problem that persists over fifty years later. It is perhaps one of the most enduring reminders of the attempt to make nations, states and territory coincide, a blatant example of the political exploitation of refugees and refugee warriors, and involving the only group of refugees to be excluded from the UNHCR system and given its own separate system of protection organised by UNRWA, the United Nations Relief and Works Agency for

---

[26] For a discussion of the different categories of displaced persons that could be counted at the end of the war, see Kim Salomon, *Refugees in the Cold War* (Lund University Press, 1991), p. 67.

[27] Salomon, *Refugees in the Cold War*, p. 39.   [28] Loescher, *Beyond Charity*, p. 69.

Palestine Refugees in the Near East. Gradually a shift took place in the normative understanding of the concept of a 'displaced person'. The IRO constitution made the distinction as early as 1947, when it specifically talked of 'refugees' as pre- and post-war victims of Nazi and Fascist regimes or of racial, religious or political persecution, and 'DPs' as those who had been displaced in the course of or soon after the Second World War for reasons solely related to the conflict. The new understanding of displacement no longer applied to those persons outside the borders of their home state who could be and ought to be sent home; rather, a displaced person became an individual forcibly uprooted from her home but remaining within the confines of her home state and thus outside the scope of the international refugee protection regime – today's 'internally displaced persons'.

The establishment of UNHCR in 1950 and the subsequent formulation of the 1951 Convention have to be viewed against this background: 'Thirty years of organizational growth and intergovernmental activities had firmly established the refugee field as a field of statist problematisations.'[29] Also operating under a temporary mandate, UNHCR has continued the trend in intergovernmental regimentation of the refugee problem developed over the three decades preceding its inception, and has acted to ensure that the refugee continues to be viewed in statist terms. The birth of UNHCR and the 1951 Convention were the next steps in a succession of statist regimentation and intergovernmental action in the field, demonstrating just one more readjustment of inherited practices. Indeed, Article 1 of the 1951 Convention refers to earlier Conventions as well as the Constitution of the IRO. When the post-war refugee protection regime was instigated in 1951, the way refugees were defined and dealt with by the international community did not constitute a major shift in direction from previous policy; rather, the statist image and statist ontology surrounding the refugee had already been established pre-1951. Accordingly, the 1951 'moment' should not be seen as the major watershed it is often made out to be. If different people were now refugees and different organisations now dealt with their plight, the meaning of being and becoming a refugee had not changed. Post-1945 refugee phenomena were caused by the same factors as those *circa* the First World War – in other words, the desire to attach all individuals to a state within a given territory and the failure of such states to guarantee the protection of those

---

[29] Soguk, *States and Strangers*, p. 162.

individuals within their domestic political community. By the time UNHCR was instituted, the refugee category had already been 'invented'.

Negative sovereignty and Cold War refugees

In the immediate post-war years, cracks in the inter-war regime began to appear. The flaw in the international system between a peace system in the form of the League of Nations and the ideal of national sovereignty had been taken to disastrous levels when Nazi Germany exploited self-determination as a principle of disintegration: 'The last shreds of the mask of international idealism were now dropped, and the grim visage of power politics again dominated the scene that in reality it had never left.'[30] The Holocaust showed the extremes to which excessive nationalism could be taken and the degree to which states could fail to represent and protect individuals. It had been seen that constitutional guarantees within states were no guarantee for the protection of citizens. Abuse of the power to make and unmake citizens was now understood to be a danger inherent in sovereignty. Above all, it was evident that sorting all individuals into nation-states, divided by clearly defined territorial borders, could not always work. And the fact that so many refugees had been denied refuge in European states during the Second World War highlighted the moral difficulties inherent in a system of dealing with refugees that had simply acted to condone the exclusive sovereign right of certain states to create refugees, and others to close their borders to individuals fleeing persecution and seeking asylum.

The post-war years therefore saw a change in the normative understanding of how the 'problem' of refugees could be resolved, according to what was now considered acceptable and not acceptable in the new era of human rights guarantees. A shift in the practice of rectifying the contradictions found in the international system took place and, with it, a development in the means used to try to 'solve' the refugee problem. From an inter-war focus on nationality whereby peoples and borders were moved with the aim of aligning nation and state, the post-war answer to the refugee issue was to focus on the state within fixed boundaries. This is evidenced in the incorporation of the reference to 'self-determination of peoples' in the UN Charter, as distinct from the discredited League of Nations idea of

---

[30] Cobban, *The Nation State*, p. 97.

'national self-determination'. Rather than seeking complete congruency between states and nations, now the stability of states and borders was to be paramount. A state would no longer be allowed to make claims on the territorial integrity of another state or to challenge another state's sovereign jurisdiction, as had occurred during the Second World War. The security of the international states system was now to be ensured by preserving the sanctity of state boundaries. State borders thus became much more rigid and impermeable as part of the normative rejection of the Wilsonian concept of national self-determination and a trend, instead, towards the rule on boundaries defined as *uti possidetis juris*, or 'as you may possess so you may possess'. And the onset of the Cold War, of course, also began to freeze the international system and its borders.

With the new emphasis on individual rights, as immortalised in the 1948 Universal Declaration of Human Rights, refugees were recognised as individuals with a right to protection in a state, in line with a negative, procedural view of sovereignty. If states failed to protect their citizens, the individuals forced to flee would be protected as if they were citizens by the international community responsible for the implementation of such universal norms – a sign of a potentially radical development in international society, even if it continued to reflect traditional thinking about the state–citizen relationship. To give the refugee access to this protection, the international community looked for a permanent solution to refugee movements via repatriation, integration in the first country of asylum or resettlement in a third country. In this way the emphasis shifted from the nation to the individual as embedded within the state. While the positive view of sovereignty endorsed by the League of Nations saw a state's internal sovereignty as the guarantee of the protection of individuals *qua* citizens, the negative view of sovereignty upheld by the United Nations saw a state's external sovereignty as the guarantee of the protection of individuals *qua* individuals. Since the model of international society required all individuals to belong to a state and act as individuals within that state, international corrective mechanisms would stop individuals existing between states. The birth of the 1951 Convention was one such corrective mechanism. Although the direction the post-war refugee regime took was conceived with recent history in mind in formulating this tool, the contemporary international climate quite clearly also had a substantial influence. Indeed, it is clear that it was formulated with the intention of serving specific political objectives. A look at the *travaux préparatoires* shows a great deal of emphasis being put on both Article 2 – that every refugee has duties in the host country to conform to its laws and regulations, a provision introduced to restrict the political activities of refugees – and Article 9 – that contracting states may take provisional measures which it considers essential to its national security, a response to concerns that enemy aliens may profess to be refugees.[31] This points to the intensely political and strategic nature of the construction of the 1951 Convention within the Cold War refugee debate.

During the onset of the Cold War the refugee question revolved around the ideological opposition between capitalism and socialism, and the recognition of refugees as victims fleeing Communism worked to stigmatise eastern European states as violators of the rights of their citizens. Welcoming and even encouraging flows of refugees from the East allowed western governments both to weaken the Soviet enemy ideologically and achieve greater political legitimacy in the Cold War environment.[32] Western states were keen to emphasise the plight of 'refugees fleeing Communism' to highlight the weaknesses of the regimes in eastern Europe in terms of protecting their citizens. The more individuals who could be shown to be fleeing persecution behind the Iron Curtain and quite literally 'voting with their feet', the greater the opportunities to denounce the human rights abuses and, by extension, the Communist regimes in government. As Westin notes, 'not only were they admitted and recognized, each single *émigré* was a propaganda triumph for the West'.[33] Using refugees to illustrate the individual's right to flee persecution acted to underscore a fundamental difference between East and West ideology, such that refugee policy touched on a central issue of the Cold War – the rights of the individual.[34]

Drafted between 1948 and 1951 at a time of a divided world, the 1951 Convention thus resulted in a definition of a refugee attributed with two main characteristics: a strategic conceptualisation of the refugee and a Eurocentric focus for its application.[35] Both aspects highlight the way a

---

[31] Paul Weis, *The Refugee Convention, 1951: The Travaux Préparatoires Analysed, with a Commentary by Dr Paul Weis* (Cambridge University Press, 1995), pp. 36–8, 60–1.

[32] Loescher, *Beyond Charity*, p. 59. Note also that this was particularly evident in the aims of the United States Escapee Program (USEP), an American organisation set up in 1952 specifically to encourage flight from the Communist bloc so as to gain information on and destabilise the Communist regimes – see p. 63.

[33] Charles Westin, 'Regional Analysis of Refugee Movements: Origins and Response', in Ager, *Refugees: Perspectives*, 33.

[34] Salomon, *Refugees in the Cold War*, pp. 249–50.

[35] Hathaway, *The Law of Refugee Status*, p. 6.

particular problem was constructed centring specifically on 'refugees fleeing Communism', which acted to form a restricted image of the refugee. The inclusion of the criterion of persecution as the defining factor in granting refugee status allowed for the privileging of Cold War refugees as those to whom refugee status applied. Reserving the refugee label solely for individuals who feared 'persecution' acted to promote western liberal values at the expense of Soviet values in two ways. First, it was 'a known quantity', having already been used to embrace dissidents from the Communist bloc in the immediate post-war years.[36] Western states saw that the concept of a 'fear of persecution' was sufficiently broad to allow for the continued granting of international protection to ideological opponents of eastern regimes. Second, the persecution standard was qualified by insisting on reasons of civil or political rights – the criteria of race, religion, nationality, membership of a particular social group or political opinion – rather than persecution for reasons of lack of respect for socio-economic rights. Such a qualification meant that it would apply largely to those from eastern European Communist states rather than the West, meaning that western states could use it as a tool against the East but not the other way round: 'By mandating protection for those whose (Western inspired) civil and political rights are jeopardized, without at the same time protecting persons whose (socialist inspired) socio-economic rights are at risk, the Convention adopted an incomplete and politically partisan human rights rationale.'[37] Hence the adoption of 'persecution' as the defining factor in refugee determination allowed the 'refugee problem' to be constructed during the early Cold War years almost entirely as a problem of 'refugees fleeing Communism', in accordance with western ideas of refugees. This acted to construct another specific spatio-temporal understanding of refugees in the long line of categories and definitions. Paradoxically, despite now officially having to prove individual persecution, the refugee became imagined under a group label as 'refugees fleeing Communism'.

Along with the persecution criterion, the 1951 Convention definition also rested on an individualistic concept of the refugee, as first developed in the IRO Constitution. According to Article 1, to be granted refugee status an individual had to prove a 'well-founded fear of being persecuted'. This was not an ontological innovation, argues Soguk, and

---

[36] Hathaway, *The Law of Refugee Status*, p. 7.
[37] Hathaway, *The Law of Refugee Status*, p. 8.

did not change the way the refugee was defined in relation to the state; rather, it meant a change in strategy, 'affording governments yet one more level of control and regimentation – the individual level'.[38] The criterion of individuality corresponded with the western image of Cold War refugees; only small numbers were managing to escape from behind the Iron Curtain, and western states were more than happy to assume that all those who did make it to the West were escaping political persecution. With the emphasis on individuals fleeing persecution, the image of Cold War refugees took a step back into the past to align itself more closely with that of famous political exiles of the nineteenth century than with the huge groups of refugees seen in Europe in earlier decades of the twentieth century. History, of course, has understood the exile as the romanticised figure welcomed abroad and offered sanctuary, while the refugee will be accompanied by several thousand others, potentially upsetting the delicate political, social and economic balance of host societies. Cold War refugees arrived individually, promulgating a certain heroic image in the eyes of western states that fitted the western discourse of freedom. Playing upon this image, notes Hathaway, and maximising the international visibility of the migration coming out of eastern Europe was an important tool in the ideological battle between East and West.[39]

Even in the face of mass influxes of persons, therefore, the individualistic exilic image of the refugee persisted. In February 1948 and in the following few months, huge refugee flows were generated by the Communist coup d'état in Czechoslovakia. By the time the exodus stopped, 50,000 individuals had crossed into western Europe.[40] Owing to reasons of geography the majority of these refugees found themselves in the American-controlled zone, where their applications for refugee status should have been rejected. The United States administration had imposed a 'freeze order' on any further '*infiltrées*' being granted asylum with a cut-off date of 21 April 1947, hence the Czechoslovakian refugees were not officially eligible for IRO assistance and protection. However, on 19 June 1948 the Prague government announced an amnesty for 'illegal emigrants'; if the refugees returned within three months their flight would go unpunished. Western states understood that refusing refugees protection or allowing them to languish alongside the thousands of others still living in bad conditions in DP camps would

---

[38] Soguk, *States and Strangers*, p. 160.   [39] Hathaway, *The Law of Refugee Status*, p. 7.
[40] Salomon, *Refugees in the Cold War*, p. 83.

have afforded the Communist regime its very own propaganda material. Accordingly, the United States authorities introduced a new label –
'hardship exceptions to the dateline order'. Individuals who had
entered the US zone within five months of the onset of the persecution
or fear of persecution in Czechoslovakia were to be considered eligible
for IRO care. The definitional category was extended en masse, without
ever questioning what had actually caused the individuals to leave; they
were automatically considered to have fled Communist persecution and
hence imagined as 'political' refugees. IRO estimates, however, put the
actual number of political refugees at 25 per cent of the total, the other
75 per cent having taken advantage of the open border and economic
prospects in the West.[41] As a result, between July 1947 and December
1951 a total of only 525 Czechoslovakian refugees returned home.[42]

Similarly, when revolution broke out in Hungary in October 1956,
250,000 refugees fled across the border into Austria and Yugoslavia
before Russian tanks moved in.[43] Without stopping to establish whether
all of these individuals really were fleeing persecution or a fear of
persecution, western states assumed them to be refugees eligible for
UNHCR support. The Hungarians were granted prima facie group eligibility as refugees, with the justification being that the events driving
them from their state of origin were a result of changes brought about
by the Second World War, and thus in line with the 1951 Convention
criteria. A small proportion of mostly child refugees were repatriated.
The majority were found permanent resettlement within two years, a
project into which more funds were poured than went into the United
Nations Refugee Fund to deal with refugees in the immediate post-war
years. Loescher points out that such generous and rapid intergovernmental action differentiated itself greatly from concern shown to other
refugees still wandering Europe over a decade after the end of the war.[44]
Thus definitions were once again twisted to fit a large group of individuals because extending refugee status would serve specific ideological,
political and foreign policy objectives.

The Soviet position towards refugees was that the only international
response should be repatriation. There was, in fact, no 'refugee problem';
rather, the problem consisted of the 'continued presence of large

---

[41] Salomon, *Refugees in the Cold War*, p. 86.   [42] Tabori, *The Anatomy of Exile*, p. 247.
[43] Tabori, *The Anatomy of Exile*, p. 254.   [44] Loescher, *Beyond Charity*, pp. 69–71.

numbers of ... "quislings, traitors and war criminals" in the DP camps, refusing to return home'.[45] Eastern European nationals in exile communities had the potential to rouse opposition towards the Communist governments, which threatened to destabilise their regimes. Moreover, the displaced persons who refused to return were 'an uncomfortable demonstration to the world that all [was] not well within the Soviet Union'.[46] This was an important shift in government policy towards refugees, 'a totally new and complicated situation in which governments desired to have returned to their countries of origin persons who disagreed with them politically',[47] rather than attempting to drive them out of their territory as had usually been the case until now. UNRRA had no choice but to stop any attempts at forced repatriation when refugee camps began to witness an increase in suicides from refugees too frightened to return to their countries of origin, while stories came back from the East of train-loads of *repatriés* being massacred on arrival in their former homelands.[48] Instead, some refugees were integrated into the first country of asylum, while resettlement in a third country was the solution most favoured by the international community. Yet in failing to encourage repatriation, UNRRA was viewed as an instrument of western foreign policy directed against the East; the Soviet Union actually prevented UNRRA from operating in the zones under its command. At the same time western states, largely the United States, which provided the organisation with its main source of funding, held that helping refugees in the East acted to allow the Soviet Union and other eastern European countries to continue their policies of persecution and hence consolidate control in the region.[49] UNRRA therefore became an accomplice in the emerging ideological battle between East and West. It acted in the midst of differing East–West conceptions of who should and should not be considered a 'refugee', bringing a politics of identity into play in the refugee debate.

Thus it was during the Cold War years that a particular refugee identity was constructed. Although their humanitarian needs were undeniable, 'refugee' movements such as those of the Czechs and the

---

[45] Cited in Marrus, *The Unwanted*, pp. 340–1.
[46] Wyman, *Displaced Persons*, p. 84.
[47] John G. Stoessinger, *The Refugee and the World Community* (Minneapolis: University of Minnesota Press, 1956), p. 89.
[48] See chapter 3 'Repatriation', in Wyman, *Displaced Persons*.
[49] Soguk, *States and Strangers*, p. 156.

Hungarians fitted 'fortuitously' into the West's image of refugees as victims of Communism.[50] Apart from these rare mass outpourings of refugees, numbers emerging from behind the Iron Curtain were minimal: refugees could not escape. Accordingly, any refugee who made it to the West was seen as an exile of the twentieth century, cousin of the nineteenth-century émigrés from Russia and all the individual exiled figures that the world had known previously. The West held a romantic image of the Cold War refugees, in stark contrast to the image afforded large groups of refugees at the end of the nineteenth century and throughout the inter-war period. They were individual figures who had been expelled due to dictatorial governments, individuals to whom the West owed thanks and support for attempting to bring democratic values to non-liberal societies. They contrasted with the masses of destitute refugees who threatened to 'swamp' 1930s economies, as they would be perceived to do again when the Wall came down.

The Berlin Wall as a border

As the Cold War set in there was less and less risk for the West of being overwhelmed by applications for asylum, since the Iron Curtain ensured that numbers of refugees arriving would be minimal. Many if not most putative refugees from eastern Europe were literally locked in, physically unable to leave and cross an international border to seek international protection. Unlike today, entering a host state was easier than leaving the state of origin. During the Cold War years the refugee's right to enter a state was more or less guaranteed, while her right to exit was threatened.[51] Eastern European government policy often made it illegal to leave, and numerous physical barriers were erected in an attempt to prevent nationals from exiting their countries. Ironically, then, an international refugee protection regime was consolidated and firmly established in the UNHCR Statute and 1951 Convention, just at a time when the refugee 'problem' as such in Europe was drying up. Western states could therefore appear to be more liberal in their refugee policy since there was little danger of being 'flooded' with thousands of refugees, as had been the case during the Second World War. As with

[50] Gordenker, *Refugees in International Politics*, p. 34.
[51] This is not to say that the right to leave one's country is upheld by all states today; however, it is important to note the relative ease of entering a host state as opposed to leaving the state of origin in the Cold War years, a balance that has by and large been turned around in the post-Cold War era.

contemporary debates, the refugee was only viewed as an individual in need of protection and assistance once she had crossed an international border, but this meant managing to get through the Iron Curtain. Those individuals who remained on the eastern side were out of reach of international protection.

The construction of the Berlin Wall in 1961 is, in this respect, both highly symbolic as an external border and exemplary of all borders that were closing eastern Europe in and thus denying the right to seek asylum. Exit from East Berlin into the West was quite literally walled up. In 1962 it was noted that, whereas the great walls of the past had been erected to repel invaders, the Berlin Wall was unique in its aim to prevent individuals behind it from reaching freedom.[52] The Wall was to keep individuals in, the implication being that potential insecurity could emanate from the state's own citizens rather than outsiders. The wall currently being built between Israel and the Palestinian territories, where one of the largest refugee populations in the world has been living for over half a century, bears a striking resemblance to the Berlin Wall of the Cold War era. The key difference, however, is that it is designed to keep people out of Israel rather than inside the Palestinian territories, hence it is more representative of the use throughout history of fortifications and enemy defence.

In 1950 almost 200,000 refugees left the German Democratic Republic (GDR) for West Germany, a figure that peaked at 330,000 in 1953 and then remained around 200–250,000 every year until 1961.[53] Estimates put the total number of refugees who managed to leave Soviet-occupied areas of Germany for the West as high as four million.[54] In the early years the GDR government saw it as only a good thing that individuals critical of the regime should leave the state. Gradually, however, East Germany was being threatened with a complete drain of skilled labour. Indeed between 1954 and 1961, the refugee flows were made up of considerable numbers of skilled workers: 3,371 doctors, 1,329 dentists, 291 vets, 960 pharmacists, 132 judges and state attorneys, 679 lawyers and notaries, 752 university lecturers, 16,724 teachers, and 17,082 engineers and technicians.[55] Refugees who 'voted with their feet'

[52] International Committee of Jurists, *The Berlin Wall: A Defiance of Human Rights* (Geneva: 1962), p. 5.
[53] Albert Hirschman, 'Exit, Voice, and the Fate of the German Democratic Republic: An Essay in Conceptual History', *World Politics* 45, 2 (1993), 180.
[54] International Committee of Jurists, *The Berlin Wall*, p. 13.
[55] International Committee of Jurists, *The Berlin Wall*, pp. 13–14.

were an embarrassment to the Communist government, as well as a potential cause of 'brain drain'. Accordingly, in the lead-up to the construction of the Wall a succession of measures was taken to make travel out of the GDR more and more difficult, with the overall aim of thwarting the flow of refugees escaping the GDR. Initially East Berliners could make temporary visits to the western side of the city without restrictions, while longer stays or transfers of residence entailed certain emigration regulations. Meanwhile the 52,000 'trans-frontier workers' who lived in the East were allowed to continue work-ing in the West.[56] The Passport Act of 15 September 1954 then made a passport and visa obligatory for every border crossing into or out of the GDR. Failure to provide the necessary documentation could be met with three years' imprisonment. When passing sentences for such breaches of the Act, the wording of the courts was very clear: putative refugees from the GDR were seen as a 'considerable danger to society' in trying to cross the state border and leave illegally.[57] In 1957 the East German government introduced the offence of *Republikflucht* or 'fleeing the Republic', also punishable by imprisonment. Finally, the Act of 11 December 1957 invented the crime of 'false proselytism' – literally 'recruiting away' or 'suborning into leaving the German Democratic Republic' – punishable by up to fifteen years' imprisonment and con-fiscation of property.

Legislation to prevent the movement of refugees to the West was complemented by physical restrictions even before the Wall was erected. First, a 122-kilometre long closed area was established along the border between East and West Berlin, as well as one running for a stretch of 1,550 kilometres along the entire border between East and West Germany. In 1952 the border area was forcibly evacuated; the GDR government called it 'voluntary removal' from the 'danger area of the state border',[58] yet the evacuation was carried out under the control of armed police and the operation resulted in yet another increase in refugee flows to the West. Construction of the actual Wall began in August 1961. It represented a clear embodiment of the East German government's final, drastic attempt to prevent refugees escaping en masse across the border. Initially consisting only of barbed wire, it

---

[56] International Committee of Jurists, *The Berlin Wall*, p. 30.
[57] Finding of the Municipal District Courts in East Berlin in August 1961 cited in International Committee of Jurists, *The Berlin Wall*, p. 15.
[58] International Committee of Jurists, *The Berlin Wall*, p. 18.

was gradually replaced by a wall up to one metre thick made from hollow bricks covered in slabs of concrete, at which point the sealed border became a wall and a physical obstacle to leaving. By August 1964 it stretched for 15 kilometres, with wire fences and barriers covering a total of 130 kilometres. There were 165 observation towers and 232 bunkers and gun emplacements, along with vehicle barriers, fencing fitted with sensors, guard dog runs and armed border police, all in an attempt to make the border impermeable.[59] In 1968 sections were replaced with industrially manufactured concrete slabs with horizontal joints and piping along the top; in 1971 a 2.9 metre-high barbed wire barrier was added to the top; and in 1974 concrete segments were sunk 2 metres into the ground to stop potential refugees trying to tunnel under. And so as to keep potential 'border violators'[60] as far from the border as possible and thus reduce the risk of refugees somehow seeping through, there was a back-up wall 50 to 70 metres in front of the actual wall. Accordingly, what the West knew as the Berlin Wall most East Berliners never actually saw until 1989; as Flemming notes, 'when East and West Berliners talked about the Wall they had a picture of completely different things in their minds'.[61] And a further irony was that the Wall never actually marked the real border between East and West but was, instead, entirely on East Berlin territory approximately 1 metre from the actual border.

The denial of freedom to leave the GDR was an infringement of the basic rights guaranteed by the Constitution of the Republic of 3 August 1950. Article 8 upheld freedom of movement within the GDR while Article 10 guaranteed freedom to emigrate. The introduction of the obligatory possession of passports and visas is only compatible with freedom of exit and emigration if the citizen is given legal entitlement to the issue of such passports and exit visas. This was not upheld in the 1954 Passport Act. The penalties for fleeing the Republic and for the crime of false proselytism were also irreconcilable with the right to leave a state and the guarantee of fundamental human rights. And of course, the Universal Declaration of Human Rights had declared, in Article 13, that 'everyone has the right to leave any country, including his own' – a right clearly denied by the Berlin Wall. Since the individual had to cross an international border to become a refugee, the Wall can

---

[59] Thomas Flemming, *The Berlin Wall: Division of a City* (Berlin: be.bra-verlag, 2000), p. 35.
[60] Cited in Flemming, *The Berlin Wall*, p. 17.
[61] Flemming, *The Berlin Wall*, p. 36.

be seen as the epitome of a more general, albeit less extreme, trend towards the hardening of international frontiers so as to preserve international and indeed domestic stability. We talk of trickles, streams and floods of refugees, such that the Berlin Wall can be seen as a kind of dam. Its purpose was to try to plug the flows of refugees and stem the tide of individuals trying to leave the GDR. Eastern Europe was leaking, and allowing this 'human leakage' to continue would have had political and economic consequences. Yet this dam had cracks in it that allowed small but steady rivulets to keep flowing through. A trickle of refugees succeeded in penetrating the wall throughout its twenty-eight years in existence: 16,700 refugees managed to leave in 1962, with numbers gradually settling at around 5,000 individuals per year by the mid-1960s.

The Wall was also a site of danger, further emphasising its role as an international border. Between 1961, when the Wall went up, and 1989, when it came down, 27 border soldiers and 800 refugees were killed at the Wall and at the inner-German border.[62] In border troop jargon attempts at escape were known as 'border breakthroughs'. Shooting to kill was supposed to be a last resort as too many deaths would damage East Germany's international reputation, yet the wording in the 1965 Handbook for Border Soldiers regarding the use of weapons was unambiguous: 'shout out, give a warning shot, then take an aimed shot which prevents the border violator from moving any further'.[63] The visual imagery of the refugees attempting to penetrate the Wall made television and newspaper headlines across the world. One such attempt, which was particularly exploited as western propaganda, was the death of the eighteen-year-old Peter Fechter, shot as he was climbing the Wall. As he bled to death on the East Berlin side of the Wall, neither East German border police, West German police nor American soldiers on the western side moved to save him. All just watched, unwilling or unable to take action.

Despite the general prohibition on exit, the boundary represented by the Berlin Wall was manipulated via a policy of authorised emigration of certain individuals or outright expulsion of those who constituted a threat to the cohesion of the regime. Individuals were variously allowed, encouraged or obliged to leave for the West. In this way the Communist regime systematically caused the deliberate creation of refugees across the border. Coupled with the small numbers of refugees

---

[62] Flemming, *The Berlin Wall*, p. 50.   [63] Flemming, *The Berlin Wall*, pp. 17, 32.

that continued to make it across the border following the construction of the Wall, therefore, was another flow of forced migrants – those 'authorised' to leave by the East German authorities, the *Übersiedler*. This group consisted in part of older individuals allowed to go and join their families who had already left, but also those who the GDR wished to expel for political reasons. These 'authorised migrants', or more correctly 'authorised refugees', constituted greater numbers than those who managed to escape the East on their own. Figures stood at around 10,000 per year, and peaked in 1964, when just over 30,000 individuals left with authorisation.[64] In addition, some political opponents were literally sold to the Federal Republic of Germany (FRG). Over 1,000 refugees were created each year in this way almost constantly from 1974 to 1988, with a peak of nearly 2,700 individuals being sold in 1985 alone. This was a clear attempt at controlling 'voice' within: dissension could cause instability, thus forced exit was used to reduce the potential for instability. Where the conversion of voice into exit involved a sale, refugees became a valuable source of hard currency for the East German government.[65] Thus the GDR authorities engaged in the deliberate creation of refugees. This bears striking resemblance to the transfer deals struck between the Nazi regime and Zionists regarding the sale of European Jews, discussed in the previous chapter; both involved the deliberate forced removal of unwanted individuals as refugees at a price acceptable to both parties. Hence certain strategies undertaken in this period hark back to the League of Nations methods of moving peoples to fit territory, practices discredited and prohibited by the international community in the post-1945 era of human rights.

Non-European 'refugees'

The refugee regime that became immortalised in the 1951 Convention was formulated as a specific response to the post-war situation in Europe, and, accordingly, the refugee continued to develop as a concept invented in and for Europe. Indeed, it first applied only to European refugees and it was not until 1967 that the refugee concept was 'universalised' with the removal of the geographical limits of the 1951 Convention via the Protocol. In spite of this formal opening-up of the concept to beyond Europe, however, non-European refugees

---

[64] Hirschman, 'Exit, Voice', 179, 181.　　[65] Hirschman, 'Exit, Voice', 184–5.

continued to be kept outside the refugee regime during the Cold War years. This is evidenced, for example, by the statistics regarding the main groups of refugees admitted to the United Kingdom between 1939 and 1980: 250,000 Polish nationals, 50,000 other eastern Europeans, 17,000 Hungarian nationals, 5,000 Czech nationals and 19,000 south-east Asians.[66] No large groups of refugees from Africa, where mass displacements were then occurring, found their way to Britain for resettlement. Indeed, refugee identities that did not fit with the 'Cold War victim' image did not feature on the international agenda. Huge refugee movements were starting to occur in the 1960s and 70s in developing countries, brought about by the struggle involved in the decolonisation process and the unrest often left behind once colonial rule was over. The violence inherent in decolonisation inevitably created refugee movements, mirroring those generated by the collapse of European empires earlier in the century. Following independence a variety of factors continued to provide the necessary ammunition for mass refugee flows: political repression, vulnerable economies and ethnic conflict, especially where the arbitrary drawing of international borders had separated ethnic groups, all acted to make many newly independent states potential powder kegs.[67] And once the violence erupted, refugees were once again the unavoidable side-effect.

The displacement of millions of individuals outside Europe was beginning to pose a serious challenge to international stability. In Africa alone a few examples serve to illustrate the scale of the emerging phenomenon: in the early 1960s, 150,000 Tutsi refugees fled Rwanda for Uganda, Burundi, Tanzania and Zaire; more than 80,000 refugees from Zaire could be found in Burundi, the Central African Republic, Sudan, Uganda and Tanzania by 1966; the first Sudanese war that ended in 1972 created 170,000 refugees and displaced another 500,000 persons internally; and there were 250,000 refugees from Rhodesia in Mozambique, Zambia and Botswana by the end of the 1970s. Estimates put the total refugee population of Africa at 400,000 in 1964, a figure that had reached one million by the end of the decade and several million by the end of the 1970s.[68] But these large-scale movements of refugees were constructed by western states as 'national problems', outside the scope of the

---

[66] Institute for Public Policy Research, *Asylum in the UK: An IPPR Fact File* (London: IPPR, 2003), p. 7.
[67] Loescher, *Beyond Charity*, p. 78.
[68] Loescher, *Beyond Charity*, pp. 78–9; and Zolberg *et al.*, *Escape from Violence*, p. 38.

'international', yet in practice heavily European, refugee protection regime. As Westin notes, despite the vast movements of refugees that began to be generated in developing states, the discourse on refugees – theoretical, political and legal – has been mainly fashioned by the European experience, and not refugee occurrences in Africa or Asia.[69] Loescher points out that most incidences of non-European refugees of this era did not grab the attention of western states: 'With the exception of anti-Castro Cubans and (later) anticommunist Vietnamese, the new refugees were generally not seen as serving the political or ideological interests of the United States or the other major Western powers.'[70] As such they did not directly impinge on the West and its interests. The few non-European refugee flows reaching the West were largely those accepted under resettlement schemes. Taking in certain refugees under such agreements, as was the case with the Vietnamese boat people, scored ideological points against Cold War political rivals. Thus certain refugee episodes that did not automatically fit the 1951 Convention discourse of a refugee nonetheless affected the West, but only when the West saw reason to let them do so.

Another non-European refugee group welcomed in the West was one that brought obvious advantages to the host society. On 4 August 1972, Idi Amin ordered all Asians to leave Uganda within ninety days. This affected a community of 71,000 individuals of whom even the 26,000 who possessed Ugandan citizenship were not exempt. Between 12,000 and 16,000 had their citizenship documents confiscated, leaving them stateless. Airlifts began in mid-September with the help of UNHCR, and almost 42,000 individuals were flown out of Uganda within six weeks. Britain accepted some 24,000 of these, and a total of nearly 40,000 Asian refugees from across East Africa by the end of 1972.[71] Other countries of resettlement included India, Canada, Pakistan and the United States. By the end of the refugee movement 70,000 individuals had fled Uganda. Of course, Uganda, like much of East Africa, had been a British colony, such that many Asians were still British subjects or 'protected persons'. Britain therefore felt a moral obligation to accept refugees, particularly those who possessed British passports, so as not to attract a negative image of a colonial power that caused refugee flows. But the fact that the Ugandan Asians represented a highly educated and skilled group also went in their favour, and

---

[69] Westin, 'Regional Analysis', 31.   [70] Loescher, *Beyond Charity*, p. 76.
[71] Zolberg *et al.*, *Escape from Violence*, pp. 65–6.

Britain, like other host countries, could see the benefits that could be reaped from allowing these refugees in.[72]

Refugees from developing countries constituted a problem for the West quite different from that posed by European refugees. First, as they were fleeing widespread violence and civil war, the 1951 Convention criterion of individual persecution rarely applied, yet these were individuals quite clearly fleeing for their lives, unable to remain in their country of origin. Second, most refugee flows were regionalised and by extension therefore outside the West, both for reasons of geography and due to ethnic, linguistic and cultural ties. Groups of refugees attempted to remain close to similar groups of people in the hope of being able to return home once conditions allowed. Thus the emphasis on resettlement that underpinned the entire Cold War European approach to solving the refugee problem was inappropriate for the new refugees of the 1970s and 80s. Of course, in the initial post-war phase of refugee protection, the boom in refugee flows in and from developing countries had not yet begun. While numbers remained small, western states could apply the same resettlement policies that they had developed as a response to European Cold War refugees. But once the new categories of refugees encompassed ever higher numbers and western economies went into recession, other responses had to be sought. Finally, granting refugee status immediately made a statement about the state of origin, and where the refugees were arriving from former colonies of western powers, such powers were reluctant to admit that their policies were the cause of refugee flows.

In terms of 'solutions' to the non-European displacements, UNHCR got round some of the political problems involved by focusing initially on emergency assistance in the 1960s, then repatriation and some attempts at integration in neighbouring countries in the 1970s. An estimated 15 million refugees were repatriated during the 1970s, a figure that included 10 million Bangladeshis, 200,000 Burmese, 300,000 Cambodians and 250,000 Nicaraguans.[73] In this way the non-European face to the refugee problem was kept away from Europe, whilst western states could in fact appear to be doing something and thus meeting their obligations as moral international actors. Refugee flows from the military

---

[72] This is not to say, of course, that accepting such a group of refugees met with no controversy among the British public. On the contrary, the influx of the Ugandan Asians was the context for Enoch Powell's infamous 'Rivers of blood' speech, the reactions against which led to the introduction of the Race Relations Act in 1976.

[73] Loescher, *Beyond Charity*, p. 82.

coups in South America and the 'boat people' from the Vietnam War which displaced 10 million individuals were the two main exceptions, both of which were resolved with resettlement. Like the refugees from eastern Europe, these episodes also attracted much publicity and sympathy, which pushed western states to accept resettlement as a solution. Of course, helping these particular refugees also served to make specific political statements and thus was in line with foreign policy objectives. Meanwhile, the 'good offices' concept generally helped avoid the political sensitivities of labelling former colonial subjects 'refugees', which had the potential to offend member states. This allowed UNHCR to extend assistance to certain groups of refugees without making a statement about either the former colonial power or the newly independent state, as well as obviating the need to make individual determinations of eligibility according to the 1951 Convention criteria.[74]

Of course, while the majority of the world's refugees were originating in developing states and staying there, the West had little problem with accepting the extension of UNHCR's mandate to cover areas outside Europe. If non-European refugees were far enough away not to affect western politics, stability or identity, the refugee discourse could be extended to these non-Europeans without any risk to the states involved in the regime. European refugees were Cold War refugees and thus automatically fulfilled the 1951 Convention criteria; non-European refugees were offered assistance and limited protection by UNHCR outside Europe even if they did not. Any refugees from developing states who did reach Europe's borders could, in any case, usually find entry as immigrants if their application for asylum failed, at least until the oil crisis of 1973. Despite being indicative of severe limitations of a system that prioritised one type of refugee over another, it was 'a pragmatic and principally nonlegalistic approach that served the interests of most states and most of the world's refugees for the next two decades'.[75] But by the 1980s this situation was starting to change. Refugees from developing countries were arriving in their thousands to seek asylum in western states as the refugee-producing conditions persisted and intensified. At this point western states started to be involved in internal and regional conflicts outside Europe, both directly or indirectly, which further complicated the refugee problem for political and moral reasons. Western powers made regional allies either with the regimes themselves or with the 'refugee warriors' or 'freedom

---

[74] Loescher, *Beyond Charity*, pp. 80, 86.   [75] Loescher, *Beyond Charity*, p. 81.

fighters', as and when it fitted with foreign policy objectives. For example, when three million Afghan refugees fled to Pakistan in 1979 and formed a base for resistance to Soviet-backed control of Afghanistan, the United States, China and several Arab states all provided military assistance. The US poured in large amounts of money for humanitarian aid in the refugee camps to indirectly help the rebels and anti-Communist forces hiding there in line with American political aims.[76] And the provision of arms to developing states, of course, also began to play a role in exacerbating regional conflicts and thus increasing refugee movements.

The West's refusal to either take notice of or offer assistance to certain non-European refugee episodes in this period further illustrates the way the refugee developed as a specifically European concept. With Indian independence and partition in 1947, more than two million refugees were created within two months. In the four years that followed, 8.5 million Hindus fled to India and 6.5 million Muslims to Pakistan.[77] It was one of the last experiments in population exchange, left over from the inter-war methods of dealing with clashes between nations, states and territory. Yet these mass movements of persons were hardly noticed by the international community, since there was little political or ideological value in recognising these non-Europeans as refugees. The Hindu and Muslim refugees were outside the 1951 Convention understanding of the refugee, and so India and Pakistan were left to deal with the huge task of resettlement pretty much alone. Of course, there were some exceptions to this trend of simply acting when it suited strategic aims, but in spite of some subtle variations, by and large the international community was stimulated to act as and when it served political purpose.

The formulation of the 1969 Organisation of African Unity (OAU) Convention Governing the Specific Aspects of Refugee Problems in Africa is further evidence of a system of protection apparently universal in nature yet Euro-centric in application. First, it broadened the definitional scope of the refugee category, adding to the 1951 Convention criterion of persecution a wider list of factors that may cause flight:

> The term 'refugee' shall also apply to every person who, owing to external aggression, occupation, foreign domination or events seriously disturbing public order in either part or the whole of his country

[76] Loescher, *Beyond Charity*, pp. 88–9.   [77] Tabori, *The Anatomy of Exile*, p. 232.

of origin or nationality, is compelled to leave his place of habitual residence in order to seek refuge in another place outside his country of origin or nationality.[78]

This definition reflected historical experience in Africa in the same way as the 1951 Convention reflected European experience. It was a response to the instability and violence then producing mass movements of refugees, which African states felt were causal factors of refugee movements inadequately covered by the 1951 Convention. It was also an expression of political solidarity with fights against white rule both in southern Africa and, retrospectively, Algeria.[79] The definition highlighted that the persecution criterion was by no means the only determining factor for refugee status, and that such status should be accorded on a group basis as well as individually. Indeed, in the context of widespread generalised violence, a system of individual determination was both irrelevant and impractical. The OAU definition acknowledges that if an individual or a group of individuals fears the accidental but nonetheless dangerous consequences of armed conflict, this is sufficient grounds for the granting of refugee status. Such a basis in effect allows the individual to decide for herself when she believes flight and international protection to be the only option to guarantee her safety.[80] The OAU Convention highlights once again, therefore, the western understanding of the refugee figure that was consolidated in the 1951 Convention, which put the emphasis on the criteria of persecution and individuality to serve political purpose at a certain time. The timing of the adoption of the 1967 Protocol also needs to be seen in the context of the African refugee movements. The Protocol deleted the temporal and geographical restrictions of the refugee definition which had limited refugee status to those fleeing persecution or a fear of persecution 'as a result of events occurring before 1 January 1951'.[81] The OAU planned to establish an African Refugee Convention independent of the 1951 Convention, which western states and UNHCR feared could politicise refugee problems on the African continent and act as a possible conflict of authority and source of competition to the

---

[78] Article 1(2), OAU Convention Governing the Specific Aspects of Refugee Problems in Africa.

[79] Zolberg *et al.*, *Escape from Violence*, p. 29.

[80] Eduardo Arboleda, 'The Cartagena Declaration of 1984 and Its Similarities to the 1969 OAU Convention – A Comparative Perspective', *International Journal of Refugee Law*, special issue (1995), 94–5.

[81] Article 1(2), 1951 Convention.

(supposedly) universal regime.[82] Thus the Protocol was added to the 1951 Convention and the OAU was appeased to adopt, instead, a complementary instrument in the form of the 1969 Convention.[83]

In short, there was a strong distinction placed on the Cold War definition of a refugee as it emerged from a western perspective. Individuals in need of protection within Europe were almost automatically considered eligible for refugee status according to the terms of the 1951 Convention. As regards individuals outside Europe, however, the definition was constructed to have limited application. While such 'refugees' remained territorially insignificant to Europe – in other words, far from Europe – they could be mostly ignored, and during the Cold War years this was generally the case. There was little political or strategic reason to attempt to extend a protection regime beyond Europe that was in large part relevant only to a very specific Cold War refugee figure.

A new politics of identity

During the Cold War the refugee's identity was reconstructed with the issue being narrowed down into a 'refugees fleeing Communism' problem. This consequently acted to alter the identity of the refugee in the international states system in such a way as to reverse the 'other' status of the refugee that had developed and been established over the previous thirty years. The refugee's identity was rewritten so that she became the innocent victim of the enemy, rather than the potential security risk or burden. The image of the refugee was altered so as to fit into the East–West political environment. As a result, this was a period of respite for the refugee; she was transformed from a burden into a victim. The refugee helped widen the gap between East and West, becoming implicated, albeit involuntarily, in the perpetuation of opposing ideological and political identities. International organisation towards refugees tended, as Stoessinger noted at the height of the Cold War, not to bring East and West together but to actually push them further apart.[84] And in this way, the refugee became an insider in the statist regimentation of refugees, rather than the outsider she had been until now. The refugee, innocent victim of the (Soviet) enemy, was

---

[82] Loescher, *The UNHCR and World Politics*, p. 125.
[83] See Paul Weis, 'The Convention of the Organisation of African Unity Governing the Specific Aspects of Refugee Problems in Africa', *Human Rights Journal* 3, 3 (1970), 3–70.
[84] Stoessinger, *The Refugee*, p. 206.

evidence of the threats located on the 'outside'. She was to be literally encouraged out of the dangerous (eastern) 'outside' and welcomed into the secure (western) 'inside'.

The refugee acted within the discourse of danger that was being played out in an international society concerned not with potential breaches of a state's territorial borders, but feared transgressions of a nation's boundaries of identity defined in ideological terms.[85] If the Cold War was 'an ensemble of practices in which an interpretation of danger crystallized around objectifications of communism and the Soviet Union',[86] the refugee was the visceral proof of this 'danger', transformed from her role as the 'other-outsider' to the 'other-insider'. 'The cold war,' says Campbell, 'was a powerful and pervasive historical configuration of the discursive economy of identity/difference'.[87] Within this discursive economy the refugee was strategically and purposefully positioned between 'identity' and 'difference' to draw attention to the distance between the two concepts. She acted, once again, to blur the boundaries between inside and outside. The refugee was now employed as an indicator of identity and difference in an inclusionary, not exclusionary, fashion.

This inversion of the refugee's position from outside to inside illustrates both a continuation of and a break with previous state responses to the refugee problem. Western states felt a sense of guilt and responsibility over the fate of so many millions of, predominantly Jewish, refugees during the Second World War. They proclaimed a responsibility to help 1950s refugees to prevent the tragedy that befell 1930s refugees ever happening again. In this sense, state responses to Cold War refugees were formulated in identification with, as well as in opposition to, their own earlier responses to previous refugee movements. This highlights once again how state responses to Cold War refugees were a continuation of earlier responses, not a separate reaction standing alone; and, by extension, that the formulation of the 1951 Convention was not a one-off, novel step forward in the refugee protection regime but was instead the result of thirty years of such practice. States were therefore forced to establish a relationship of both identity and difference with their previous attitudes to refugees. Difference from their indifference to earlier refugees was as fundamental as the

---

[85] David Campbell, *Writing Security: United States Foreign Policy and the Politics of Identity* (Minneapolis: University of Minnesota Press, 1992), p. 164.
[86] Campbell, *Writing Security*, p. 195.   [87] Campbell, *Writing Security*, p. 249.

identification with their indifference to earlier refugees.[88] Yet helping 1950s refugees would be both necessary and problematic. On the one hand, it was necessary to offer refugee protection to live up to historical responsibility, namely the earlier neglect of refugees. On the other hand, it was problematic to the extent that helping refugees inevitably meant striking a balance between, and therefore compromising, sovereign rights and human rights. Refugees were in need of legal protection and humanitarian assistance, yet offering this could lead to further refugee flows and therefore a much larger infringement on sovereignty and state resources than envisaged. The issue of helping 1950s refugees launched western states into the heart of a contradiction in the way they understood who they were: the question was explosive considering the clash with sovereign rights that refugee protection entails, yet to overcome their historical failures in helping Second World War refugees, protecting 1950s refugees seemed inevitable.

The dilemma was resolved by the reconstruction of the 'refugee problem' as a problem of 'refugees fleeing Communism'. Humanitarian concerns and preoccupations over the protection of sovereignty remained in conflict, but such a clash could be overcome by the façade of helping 'refugees' in general, whilst limiting the boundaries to whom such a status would apply. And choosing the 'refugees fleeing Communism' category as opposed to any other group of refugees wandering Europe at the time fitted in nicely with the strategies of the East–West ideological battle. Thus the vision of 'never letting it happen again' was strictly limited so as to speak to one specific refugee identity. Indeed, the 'Jewish refugee problem' was largely downplayed; not only did it fail to fit into or serve the ends of any ideological strategy, moreover it risked upsetting international relations, particularly between Britain and Palestine. Ironically, therefore, any surviving Jewish refugees who had suffered disproportionately during the War were given little attention on the international agenda. In effect, the action of western states towards Cold War refugees then worked to obscure the earlier neglect of refugees, highlighting the contingent and inherently contradictory character of expressions of state identity towards refugees. Western states were able to make an appearance at this point as observers of humanitarian principles and concerned actors in the refugee

---

[88] Maja Zehfuss, *Constructivism in International Relations: The Politics of Reality* (Cambridge University Press, 2002), p. 86.

regime, which in effect hid their past, multiple histories in which refugee protection had not always been top of their list of priorities.

The change of emphasis in the early Cold War era to focus on 'refugees fleeing Communism' demonstrates the socially constructed nature of the refugee regime. Western states developed an interest in offering protection to this restricted category of displaced individuals due to the changing normative context in which they were operating. The normative international environment shaped states' conceptions of identity and interest. This points to the social nature of international politics; normative understandings are created between international actors, understandings which then shape values, expectations and behaviour in the international system.[89] A shift in the conceptions of identity between East and West caused a repositioning of western states' interests relative to refugees and hence a redefinition of the refugee category. It was this redefinition that became inscribed in international legislation via the 1951 Convention and the Statute of UNHCR. A modification in states' interests and identities, influenced by the evolving international normative context, acted to transform the refugee from a security issue into a seemingly stable regime by way of its codification in an international Convention.[90] In this way the 'refugee problem' ceased to be a security issue for international society, and the earlier attention given to the reterritorialisation of the refugee into the state–citizen–territory trinity took a back seat in favour of a reconstruction of the refugee's identity as the innocent victim of a new enemy. In other words, state responses to the 'refugee problem' were only a response to part of the 'refugee problem', namely 'refugees fleeing Communism'. Thus it is evident that it was not just the necessity to stabilise the movement of refugees and their potential security risk that pushed states to formalise intergovernmental action in another Convention and another intergovernmental organisation in the early Cold War era; the wider, territorial discourse of the refugee as the exceptional figure outside the 'normal', stable state–citizen–territory hierarchy was not the only nor the most important discourse being constructed. The refugee – rather, the 'refugee fleeing Communism' – was now called upon to play a more important part in an international

---

[89] Martha Finnemore, 'Constructing Norms of Humanitarian Intervention', in Peter J. Katzenstein (ed.), *The Culture of National Security: Norms and Identity in World Politics* (New York: Columbia University Press, 1996), 157–8.

[90] See Ronald L. Jepperson, Alexander Wendt and Peter J. Katzenstein, 'Norms, Identity, and Culture in National Security', in Katzenstein, *The Culture of National Security*, 73.

discourse of identity, of inside and outside, self and enemy, into which she was, ambiguously, brought.

Accordingly, the Cold War period can be seen as another stage in the ongoing process of (re)writing refugees' identities. However, the making and breaking of states and shifting of boundaries and borders common to the international system could not occur in the frozen political climate of this period, and those characteristics of international society that under 'normal' circumstances create the stimuli for the generation of refugee flows were thus not at work. Instead, the boundaries of identity and belonging began to shift, such that the refugee found herself situated more prominently in a discourse of identity than a discourse of spatiality or territoriality. Further, she found herself included in the identity discourse, rather than excluded from the territorial discourse as she had been. It follows that the Cold War period can be seen as a period of exception for the refugee; international society was more interested in a particular type of refugee for identity reasons than in maintaining the territorial status quo of the international states system that the refugee had until now threatened to upset. The refugee was no longer a threat to the international system; rather, she was a pawn in an ideological political game, a game in which 'normal' political and international transformations could not take place. The Cold War period can therefore be seen as a period of exception in the 'refugee history'.

The territorialisation and statist regimentation of the 'refugee' had already been consolidated by the time of the Cold War, but it was precisely in the Cold War period that the refugee was brought inside so as to serve a specific identity politics. Her threat of destabilising the international system and the correlative need to reinstall her in the state–citizen–territory hierarchy was relegated to secondary importance. The period constituted a period of exception in the refugee's identity, and it was in this period of exception that the entire refugee regime was established. Accordingly, the reification of the establishment of UNHCR and the formulation of the 1951 Convention is somewhat distorted and should not be seen as the major watershed it is so often made out to be: the 'refugee' had already been constructed before this date. The Cold War continued to construct and reconstruct the refugee's identity, but reconstructed it in the opposite way from that which had occurred until now and that which would continue after the Cold War. During the Cold War period the international system stood still, and identity politics took the upper hand, such that the image of the refugee was reversed. She moved inside. The international refugee regime was therefore an expression of a particular geopolitics that put less emphasis on territoriality, but one that acted, nonetheless, as a continuation of statist intervention and construction of a 'refugee problem'.

Conclusions

The Cold War years clearly highlight the extent to which the refugee is caught up in the very workings of international society. With the end of the League of Nations set-up and the onset of the Cold War, politics froze within fixed borders. The refugee never broke free of the statist definitions that surrounded her, such that she continued to be imagined as the outsider to be reinstalled in the state–citizen–territory hierarchy. But such reterritorialisation was now sought via resettlement arrangements, rather than transfer or exchange agreements. Small numbers of European refugees still managed to leak through the East–West border and they fitted nicely with the strategic, ideological conceptions of persecution and political exiles. The exilic approach to refugees was in line with a negative, external view of sovereignty whereby individuals were the bearers of human rights. The large numbers of refugees beginning to rock the international system outside Europe were on the whole too far away to cause the West too much concern, and western states could thus pick and choose specific groups that they considered eligible for protection.

During the Cold War period the 'refugee problem' was therefore constrained, strictly defined to be applicable only to certain individuals by way of a particular identity discourse of 'refugees fleeing Communism' consolidated in the 1951 Convention. But Conventions are only as stable as the normative context in which they operate. Once that normative context changed following the end of the Cold War, the potential for instability increased due to the growing disjuncture between institutionalised norms and practices and emerging political realities. In 1989, of course, the putative refugees spilled over what had been almost impenetrable for three decades, and in so doing signalled the beginning of the end of the GDR. The movement of refugees across the Wall and other eastern borders acted to undo the system. Thus it was the refugee who provoked the construction of the Wall and, almost three decades later, the refugee who pushed the Communist regime into opening it. The East German government believed that taking the Wall down would actually stop the desire for escape, yet as soon as the plug was let out refugees poured through.

They began to leave East Germany in their masses in the spring of 1989, and by the end of the year almost 340,000 individuals had crossed the German–German border.[91] Refugees caused the construction of the border, and refugees caused its destruction.

The inherent instability of a Convention drawn up under very specific circumstances has allowed the 'refugee problem' to re-emerge as a politicised issue on a scale larger than before. The refugee 'problem' has now become blurred with other movements of persons, and the refugee has found herself trapped in a changing world unsure of its values and unsure of what it means to belong. States and regional entities have had to seek new ways of responding to the refugee issue, and it is this contemporary 'refugee discourse' to which we now lastly turn.

[91] Hirschman, 'Exit, Voice', 188.

PART III

The refugee: a contemporary analysis

7 The external dimension of EU refugee policy

> Providing security and long-term solutions for such refugees is a humanitarian imperative. And to the extent that it can contribute to this objective, then the notion of 'protection in regions of origin' must be welcomed. At the same time, we should not expect this approach to provide any easy answers to the asylum and migration dilemmas of the world's more prosperous states. Jeff Crisp[1]

This book has thus far set out a normative rethinking of the refugee concept from an international society perspective and considered how this created a statist understanding of the modern refugee as she evolved over the inter-war and Cold War periods. This chapter now turns to the contemporary period to ask how the statist construction of the refugee affects the way in which the international community formulates contemporary refugee policy. By using the English School to view the EU as a particular example of a regional international society, it highlights how EU refugee policy has become more protection oriented, which can be explained by the diffusion of norms and socialisation of states to move to a more comprehensive agenda.

It first looks at the context in which refugee policy is now made, in particular the increasing difficulty of distinguishing refugees from other migrants. It then analyses the recent phenomenon to externalise EU refugee policy and looks at the specific example of proposals for Regional Protection Programmes as one form of this externalisation. Finally, it asks what this trend in regional protection has meant as a normative response to the need to balance pluralist and solidarist elements in EU international society.

---

[1] Jeff Crisp, 'Refugee Protection in Regions of Origin: Potential and Challenges', http://www.migrationinformation.org/Feature/displau.cfm?id = 182 (December 2003).

The refugee and contemporary international society

In the contemporary period the 1951 Convention and surrounding protection regime have found themselves in uncharted waters. Having been formulated at the start of the Cold War under such specific circumstances, the 1951 Convention is now unsure of its status. It was drawn up at a time when politics and borders were frozen such that movements of persons were too. But when the Iron Curtain came down in 1989 and the Soviet Union began to collapse in 1991, the potential for large-scale refugee flows into or within Europe became a reality. As international relations thawed, politics and peoples started moving again and the international system began to evolve, develop and meta-morphose as it always had done before. As a response western states – the very states that had welcomed escapees who managed to infiltrate the East–West border – have since acted to take steps to avoid potential mass movements that now have the opportunity to transform them-selves from theoretical flows into actual flows.

At the end of 2005 the total global refugee population stood at 8.4 million, the lowest level since 1980.[2] Ideological persecution, as asso-ciated with refugees of the Cold War era, is no longer an issue and therefore no longer a useful indicator telling potential host states who they are and are not supposed to assist. Rather, forced migration is induced today by exactly the same factors as those that prevailed during the inter-war period: we have returned to a time of refugee flows being generated by the breakdown of states, the formation of new states and persecution based on ethnic, national and religious grounds. All these events produce violent, often internal, conflict. Indeed, by far the main causes of refugee flows today are intra-state violence and civil war. Forced migration has become not just a con-sequence of war but a tool and an objective, such that mass population displacement may act as a political strategy in claiming control over a particular territory.[3] The experience in the Balkans region is indicative of this. Population transfer as a means of making peoples and territory coincide, such as was tried in the inter-war period, made a reappear-ance in the 1990s with the devastating effects of genocidal warfare and

---

[2] Provisional data: UNHCR, '2005 Global Refugee Trends', 3. The total population of concern to UNHCR at the end of 2005 was 20.8 million persons.

[3] Gil Loescher cited in Julie Mertus, 'The State and the Post-Cold War Refugee Regime: New Models, New Questions', *International Journal of Refugee Law* 10, 3 (1998), 332.

the redistribution of population. During the war in the Balkans huge numbers of people were uprooted and compelled to seek refuge in foreign states. The Serbian policy of ethnic cleansing in Kosovo led to what the newspapers described as the biggest refugee movement since the Second World War. Millions were literally forced out of their homes and European states were left facing the same 'refugee problem' as in the 1930s and 40s, despite the legal refugee regime that had grown up over the years specifically designed to manage such events. Of course, population transfer in the inter-war years was, in principle at least, intended to be orderly and humane, carried out under international supervision and regulated by treaty stipulations, which contrasts sharply with the much more ad hoc and correspondingly more violent practice of ethnic cleansing associated with population transfer of the end of the century. Yet the same results were produced – refugees.

With the end of the Cold War the spotlight turned to refugees from the South: the boat people of the 1980s began to reach western states as the jet people of the 1990s, and these individuals have since provided the focus for the 'new threat' posed to international society by the refugee. But of course, such refugee flows are not a new phenomenon. As was discussed in the previous chapter, refugee movements were being created on an increasingly large scale in developing countries as early as the 1960s, yet at that time they were largely constructed as extraneous to western states and the refugee regime. Refugees from developing countries stayed in developing countries or regions and so were physically irrelevant to Europe. But when the Cold War reasons for accepting refugees disappeared, and the scale of European refugee flows began to pale into insignificance compared to those being created across the globe, non-European refugees found themselves situated outside the regime and thus with restricted eligibility for entry into the West. Indeed, when refugees started to arrive on Europe's doorstep, the 'myth of difference' was constructed to make the refugee from the South seem incompatible with the international refugee regime. As Chimni observes, it was in the 1980s and 90s that:

> The foundations for a paradigm shift in international refugee policy and law began to be laid *inter alia* through the creation of the myth of difference: the nature and character of refugee flows in the Third World were represented as being radically different from refugee flows in Europe since the end of the First World War. Thereby, an image of a 'normal' refugee was constructed – white,

male and anti-communist – which clashed sharply with individuals fleeing the Third World.[4]

When non-European refugees began to be a physical reality in Europe, not just something happening across the other side of the world, the 'threat' of the non-European refugee became both visual and credible. Contradictions to the western image of the refugee were a contradiction to the refugee regime consolidated in the specifics of the Cold War political environment. If the contradictions became too powerful, the entire regime could be destabilised and collapse. And so a series of myths and exceptions to the regime have been constructed to create the image of a regime still relevant to western perceptions of the refugee problem.

International society has imagined a reinterpretation of the past: refugees from outside Europe have been constructed as a new experience, caused by apparently new factors and on a scale never seen previously. This conceals three truths: that non-European refugees have been colouring the international landscape for decades, even since before the 1951 watershed mark; that refugees from the South are not fleeing conditions wholly different from their predecessors, indeed today's causal factors have many similarities with pre-1951 flows; and that the numbers of refugees across the globe are not bigger than ever before, since pre-1951 flows were vast and, in comparison with total world population figures, proportionately bigger even than today.[5] It is this reinterpretation that has led to the construction of an 'asylum crisis' in Europe today.

A major influencing factor bolstering the construction of this 'crisis' has been the increased blurring of economic and forced migration. While numbers of refugees in developing countries were on the increase in the 1970s, the demand for labour began to decrease in western Europe, and states started to introduce reductions in refugee resettlement programmes alongside restrictions in accessing the asylum system. With the decline in opportunities for asylum and resettlement, the distinction between economic migrants and political refugees collapsed, and they were forced into one single migration route – asylum seeking.[6] The result was to effectively transform the image of the 'refugee' into that of the 'asylum-seeker'. Meanwhile, the end of the

[4] Chimni, 'The Geopolitics of Refugee Studies', 351.
[5] Skran, *Refugees in Inter-war Europe*.
[6] Khalid Koser, 'New Approaches to Asylum?', *International Migration* 39, 6 (2001), 88.

Cold War removed the ideological motivations that had been hidden behind refugee assistance programmes with the aim of rescuing 'victims of Communism'. This marked the beginning of the end of the 'interest convergence' that had characterised relations between western states and refugees throughout the Cold War period.[7] Western foreign policy began to diverge from refugee protection, while political refugees and economic migrants in fact began to converge.

For these reasons, the distinctions between voluntary and involuntary or forced migration are not as clear-cut as we once might have assumed: 'Today, more than ever, refugees are part of a complex migratory phenomenon, in which political, ethnic, economic, environmental and human rights factors combine and lead to population movements.'[8] The result is a blurring between the simple distinction refugee versus migrant. UNHCR has grappled with this blurring for some time now. Many officials were fixed on the 'refugees are not migrants' line. But with the reality of dealing with mixed flows and governments more and more interested in 'managing migration', it has proved impossible to maintain a strict separation of categories. The latest official position, therefore, holds that refugees are a distinct group of people, and that it is feasible to make a valid distinction between refugees and other moving people. At the same time, UNHCR recognises that there are specific points at which the issues of refugee protection and international migration intersect, and UNHCR has a legitimate interest in these moments. According to a recent UNHCR position paper:

> Refugee and migratory movements now intersect in a number of different ways ... Movements of people from one country and continent to another may include some who are in need of international protection and others who are not. This is likely to be the case when, as often happens, a country of origin is simultaneously affected by human rights violations, economic decline and an absence of livelihood opportunities. Such flows of people, involving both refugees and migrants, are commonly referred to as 'mixed movements'.[9]

---

[7] James C. Hathaway (ed.), *Reconceiving International Refugee Law* (Cambridge, Mass.: Kluwer Law International, 1997), p. xix.

[8] UNHCR cited in Jeff Crisp, *Policy Challenges of the New Diasporas: Migrant Networks and Their Impact on Asylum Flows and Regimes*, New Issues in Refugee Research, Working Paper No. 7 (Geneva: UNHCR, 1999), 3.

[9] UNHCR, 'Refugee Protection and International Migration', June 2006, 1–2. See also UNHCR, 'Addressing Mixed Migratory Movements: A 10-Point Plan of Action', June 2006.

There are many factors that contribute to the blurring of the distinction between refugees and migrants: unauthorised or undocumented movements that use similar routes or using the services of the same smugglers; a refugee movement in time becoming a 'mixed movement'; a mixture of motivations that often lie behind an individual's decision to leave her country; or the undertaking of a secondary movement by the refugee, for example for economic or family reunification reasons. The current high-visibility crossings of the Mediterranean are one example of the mixed nature of movements and the problems this poses for the international community. Boatfuls of migrants continually arrive on the shores of southern EU Member States, and some of these claim asylum. Turning a boat back in international waters or in the territorial waters of a third country could be equal to *refoulement* if the opportunity to claim asylum on board the ship is not guaranteed. Not only is there the difficulty of distinguishing between reasons for migrating – and with that the complexity of categorising motives as forced or voluntary – but also an individual who starts out in one category may not necessarily stay in that category. As Koser and Van Hear have noted, 'it has been increasingly recognized in recent years that asylum migrants enter other kinds of migration streams, joining those who move in search of employment, education, professional advancement, marriage or for other purposes'.[10] The convergence of economic and forced migration has caused big problems in attempts to define, categorise and distinguish those 'real' refugees fleeing persecution and others moving to seek a better quality of life. The result is that the refugee is imagined now more than ever as the non-refugee, linked to the illegal immigrant and economic migrants. While definitional difficulties have been at the heart of the refugee debate since its establishment in modern international relations, these difficulties are today perhaps more pronounced than ever. It is this latest blurring of concepts and categories that is at the heart of the so-called 'asylum crisis' sweeping Europe. In other words, the refugee 'problem' once again comes down to a question of semantics.

Interestingly, therefore, the debate has gone right back to where it started – a debate about who exactly falls into the refugee category, and how to differentiate between seemingly equally deserving individuals.

[10] Khalid Koser and Nicholas Van Hear, 'Asylum Migration and Implications for Countries of Origin', United Nations University, World Institute for Development Economics Research Discussion Paper No. 2003/20, 4.

Karatani has argued that this blurring of categories can be traced back to the immediate post-war years, when refugee and migrant regimes were being consolidated separately, albeit inadvertently, and that the 'basic weakness of the current regimes derives from the artificial distinction between "refugees" and "migrants" created after the Second World War'.[11] According to Lavenex, the blurring of the normative core of the asylum concept is due to increases in migration flows across the globe coupled with the end of the Cold War, and that as a consequence, 'today, the emergent European refugee policy faces a fundamental confusion, namely the difficulty to determine who deserves which kind of protection – and who does not'.[12] This is the context in which current policy is made. What has this contemporary blurring of categories and concepts and the emergence of the asylum-seeker meant for the policy world? The next section analyses one response which has been sought by EU refugee policy.

EU refugee policy

This book has examined the refugee concept through an English School lens, in which the refugee is seen as an inevitable if unintended consequence of the system of separate sovereign states. In this system states interact with each other according to agreed rules of the game. The international society approach can be usefully applied to the regional context of the European Union. As Diez and Whitman have noted, 'from an English School perspective, the EU presents itself as an international society that has been formed within a particular regional context and is embedded in a wider, global international society'.[13] Wight's description of a 'society of states' is particularly applicable to the EU:

> A community of states ... sharing certain common purposes and values, responsive to each others' views and interests (or at least some of them), accepting the formal rule of law in some matters as well as the authority of common institutions, and behaving in relation

---

[11] Rieko Karatani, 'How History Separated Refugee and Migrant Regimes: In Search of Their Institutional Origins', *International Journal of Refugee Law* 17, 3 (2005), 517.

[12] Sandra Lavenex, *The Europeanisation of Refugee Policies: Between Human Rights and Internal Security* (Aldershot: Ashgate, 2001), p. 7.

[13] Thomas Diez and Richard Whitman, 'Analysing European Integration: Reflecting on the English School – Scenarios for an Encounter', *Journal of Common Market Studies* 40, 1 (2002), 45.

to many other matters as if they were bound by formal legal rules, even if they are not.[14]

Indeed EU Member States interact with one another according to a complex set of agreed rules and norms as set out in several treaties, conventions and other instruments, while keeping control of elements of their sovereignty in the Council. Scholars have long debated the peculiar make-up of the EU as a hybrid mixture of intergovernmentalism and supranationalism, and of various combinations and degrees in between, in which states remain the key actors but renounce aspects of their sovereignty to be decided at the EU level. Although the EU institutions keep an eye on the Member States to a certain degree – a degree that of course varies across policy domains – and have specific powers to hold them to account in several areas, there is no overarching government as such. EU international society therefore operates much in the same way as global international society, a system without a government. It consists of a constant balancing act between integration and the maintenance of national sovereignty. In English School speak, this mixture can be examined from the point of view of the balance and interplay between pluralist and solidarist elements. Individual sovereign Member States' (pluralist) behaviour is constrained by (solidarist) human rights instruments, the concept of European citizenship and the Fundamental Charter of Human Rights, for example.

Buzan has rethought the concepts of pluralism and solidarism, arguing that they should not be understood as mutually exclusive positions that identify two distinct types of international society, 'but as positions on a spectrum representing, respectively, thin and thick sets of shared norms, rules and institutions'.[15] In this way, the EU can be seen as a solidarist inter-state society: Member States have entered into the realm of solidarism by acknowledging common values 'which they agree to pursue by coordinating their policies, undertaking collective action, creating appropriate norms, rules and organisations, and revisiting the institutions of interstate society'.[16] Member States interact with one another within a regional international society in which norms, judgements, values, institutions and interests all converge

---

[14] Cited in Roger Morgan, 'A European "Society of States" – But Only States of Mind?', *International Affairs* 76, 3 (2000), 563.

[15] Barry Buzan, *From International to World Society?: English School Theory and the Social Structure of Globalisation* (Cambridge University Press, 2004), p. 139.

[16] Buzan, *From International to World Society?*, pp. 146–7.

and play an important role. The EU has entailed, in other words, a redefinition of how sovereignty and boundaries operate.[17] The idea of 'world society' links the English School to debates about the EU. World society can be identified at the EU level, according to Diez and Whitman, by references in the discourse to a common European history, common values and common transnational activities. There is an ambiguous relationship between international and world society, and it is this relationship that gives the EU its legitimacy. Such a relationship, they argue, constantly needs balancing through political practice: 'Elements of a "European world society" provide the necessary basis for the shared values of the European "community of states", which in turn has allowed integration to proceed.'[18] Yet too much progress in the world society direction would undermine the sovereignty of Member States and thus threaten the make-up of international society in which sovereignty is a fundamental norm. International society exists, of course, amongst other things, to perpetuate the existence of independent sovereign states, hence the continual debate over European integration versus sovereignty.

We have already seen how refugee policy is a complex mixture of the political and the ethical or the humanitarian at the national level of the state. In domestic refugee policy there is a constant tension between humanitarian principles and political concerns over state sovereignty and control of who may or may not enter the state's territory. EU Member States have had to grapple with the 'asylum crisis' in their politics and policies, balancing the political need to both lower numbers and appear in control with the need to meet, and be seen to be meeting, humanitarian obligations. At the EU level the debate on refugee policy is perhaps even more fraught. Indeed, Lavenex has noted that there are fundamental paradoxes intrinsic to the Europeanisation of refugee policies, and these paradoxes have emerged along two dimensions: state sovereignty versus supranational governance, and internal security versus human rights and human security.[19] Integration means renouncing a certain element of state sovereignty, and when this element is linked to border control the decision to move some power to the EU level becomes even more sensitive. The tension between politics and humanitarianism, or pluralism and solidarism, has meant progress

[17] Buzan, *From International to World Society?*, p. 152.
[18] Diez and Whitman, 'Analysing European Integration', 45, 51–3.
[19] Lavenex, 'The Europeanization of Refugee Policies', 852.

in the development of EU refugee policy grew from a desire on the part of Member States to retain control of their borders and to preserve their sovereignty. For this reason refugee policy at the EU level developed in its initial years with a minimum influence of humanitarian norms, limited transfer of political authority to supranational institutions, and limited cooperation among Member States.[20] This has changed, however, since 1998, when the focus started to shift to the external aspects of migration – that is, the extension of policy-making in asylum and immigration to beyond the borders of the EU.

There have been two aspects to the externalisation process of refugee policy that have become known as 'control' and 'prevention'. The first aspect refers to attempts to use domestic or EU tools of migration control in countries of transit on the borders of the EU. This has included border control measures to try to combat illegal migration and smuggling and trafficking in human beings, capacity-building of immigration and asylum systems in transit countries, and readmission agreements to facilitate the return of asylum-seekers whose claims have failed and illegal migrants back to third countries. It has been a restrictive, control-oriented approach, in part a response to the abolition of internal borders in the Schengen area and the (perceived) need to compensate by strengthening the external borders, in part a result of enlargement to eastern Europe and the (perceived) need to control the new external border of the EU. This aspect has been, in short, an extension of the logic of asylum and migration management that prevailed in EU Member States in the late 1990s to countries outside the EU.[21] No new way of imagining the refugee debate has had to be conjured up, rather the externalisation of control mechanisms has been a continuation of the securitisation of asylum and migration of the post-Cold War period, complicated by the blurring between refugees and economic migrants.

The second aspect, and that which is now much more in favour on the international agenda, has been a more holistic approach which seeks to address the root causes of forced migration and provide protection in regions of refugee origin. This agenda has appealed to the ethical side of state actors, who see it as a way to cooperate internationally and be seen to be advocating human rights and refugee protection, while

---

[20] Lavenex, *The Europeanisation of Refugee Policies*, p. 138.
[21] Christina Boswell, 'The "External Dimension" of EU Immigration and Asylum Policy', *International Affairs* 79, 3 (2003), 622–3.

acknowledging that such an approach can reduce the pressure of numbers arriving in Europe at the same time. It has coincided with an international environment more disposed to humanitarian intervention, human rights monitoring, peace-building and post-conflict reconstruction, which in turn has allowed international organisations dealing with refugees to become more and more active and involved in countries of origin, not just in running refugee camps but also in offering protection to internally displaced persons, assisting returnees and helping with institutional capacity-building.[22] The export of control mechanisms has undoubtedly had consequences for individuals seeking asylum and protection as refugees, not just for 'economic' migrants seeking to come to Europe legally or illegally, and international and non-governmental organisations have repeatedly pointed out that these measures may deny 'genuine' refugees access to asylum processes. The preventive approach, on the other hand, can be seen to have given rise to a more protection-oriented EU agenda. This agenda is highlighted by the language employed in successive Communications of the European Commission and Council Conclusions from 1998, as well as the creation of the High Level Working Group on Asylum and Migration that specialises in the external dimension of migration.

The Conclusions of the European Council held in Tampere in 1999 demonstrated the first major reference to linking EU refugee policy with external relations. This was a special Summit on Justice and Home Affairs, convened in the light of mass movements of refugees being created in Kosovo at the time. Tampere committed the EU both to creating a common European asylum system as well as to working in partnership with countries of origin. The Conclusions stated:

> The European Union needs a comprehensive approach to migration addressing political, human rights and development issues in countries and regions of origin and transit. This requires combating poverty, improving living conditions and job opportunities, preventing conflicts and consolidating democratic states and ensuring respect for human rights ... To that end, the Union as well as Member States are invited to contribute ... to a greater coherence of internal and external policies of the Union.[23]

Thus European heads of state and government linked the domestic and the external in this field, explicitly, for the first time. The importance of

[22] Boswell, 'The "External Dimension"', 625–6.
[23] Presidency Conclusions, European Council, Tampere, 15–16 October 1999, paragraph 11.

addressing the root causes of migration in countries of origin was therefore underlined, while the Conclusions also called for full commitment to the obligations of the 1951 Convention and other relevant human rights instruments. Conclusions of the Laeken and Seville European Councils followed a similar theme. Laeken in December 2001 called for 'the integration of the policy on migratory flows into the European Union's foreign policy', and also referred to protection of refugees and the 1951 Convention.[24] Similarly, Seville in June 2002 reinforced the external dimension of asylum and migration by stating that 'an integrated, comprehensive and balanced approach to tackling the root causes of illegal immigration must remain the European Union's constant long-term objective'.[25]

In 2002 the Commission issued a Communication, 'Integrating Migration Issues in the European Union's Relations with Third Countries'.[26] This document represented the Commission's first real attempt to push forward a strategy that used external relations tools to address the root causes of migration and forced migration, with prevention and protection measures clearly marked out as priorities and the Commission arguing for a complementary approach with existing development programmes. Indeed, this Communication was the first main step towards bringing EU migration policy and development policy together. The Hague Programme adopted in November 2004 built on these previous objectives and stated that 'a comprehensive approach, involving all stages of migration, with respect to the root causes of migration, entry and admission policies and integration and return policies is needed'.[27] Most recently, the link between external relations and asylum and migration policy was made explicit once again under the UK Presidency in the second half of 2005. In December 2005 the European Council adopted the 'Global Approach to Migration: Priority Actions Focusing on Africa and the Mediterranean'.[28] Several references to strengthening protection for refugees appeared in the text, alongside a strong theme of working in partnership with countries of origin and an emphasis on the need to

[24] Presidency Conclusions, European Council, Laeken, 14–15 December 2001, 11.
[25] Presidency Conclusions, European Council, Seville, 21–22 June 2002, 10.
[26] European Commission, 'Communication on Integrating Migration Issues in the European Union's Relations with Third Countries', COM(2002) 703 final.
[27] Presidency Conclusions: 'The Hague Programme', European Council, Brussels, 4–5 November 2004, 16.
[28] Presidency Conclusions: 'The Global Approach to Migration: Priority Actions Focusing on Africa and the Mediterranean', European Council, Brussels, 15–16 December 2005.

formulate a comprehensive, balanced approach, representing a clear shift away from the control agenda. These European Council Conclusions were followed up a year later by a Commission Communication that looked at how to develop and strengthen the 'global approach', in which refugee protection featured as a section in its own right. The Commission underlined in particular 'the need to ensure access to asylum processes for those in mixed migratory flows who might need international protection', noted the importance of keeping asylum and protection issues as a key element of dialogue with third countries and suggested building on UNHCR's '10-Point Plan of Action' to foster operational cooperation in this domain.[29]

The second aspect to the preventive approach to asylum and migration policy has been the establishment of a Council working group dedicated to bringing together migration and asylum with development and external relations. The High Level Working Group on Asylum and Migration (HLWG) was formed on a Dutch initiative in 1998. Its mandate is to develop a cross-pillar, integrated approach to the internal and external dimensions of EU asylum and migration policy. Unlike the other working groups dealing with asylum and migration issues, which report directly to the Justice and Home Affairs Council, the HLWG reports to the General Affairs and External Relations Council, which means asylum and migration issues frequently find themselves on the agendas of foreign affairs and development ministers. Although the original task of the HLWG was to prepare action plans for six countries – an initiative that according to most accounts saw limited success – its recent mandate has evolved into focusing much more on the prevention and protection agendas. Indeed, the HLWG was the lead group to examine the Commission proposals on enhancing the links between migration and development, developing ways to increase dialogue and cooperation on migration and asylum issues with African states and regional organisations, and applying the 'Global Approach to Migration', all of which demonstrated increasing attention to the protection agenda of external refugee policy. Even those agenda items that focused more on migration than asylum, such as developing an action plan for cooperation on illegal migration with Libya, highlighted a strong focus on protection: Member States repeatedly made respect for international human rights

---

[29] European Commission, 'Communication on the Global Approach to Migration One Year On: Towards a Comprehensive European Migration Policy', COM(2006) 735 final, 9.

instruments, including the 1951 Convention, a prerequisite for assistance to Libya from the EU. The HLWG also took the lead on one specific recent development – the proposals to create Regional Protection Programmes – which demonstrates the shift to the protection agenda particularly well, as the next section will show.

Regional Protection Programmes

The response of the EU to the mass movements of persons that took place in Kosovo in 1999 was the first real experiment in external refugee policy in practice. Such large-scale movements had of course already occurred on the EU's doorstep in the former Yugoslavia in the early 1990s, and the international community responded with the creation of 'safe areas'. Much has been written on the intervention that took place, but what is of interest here is the very concept of attempting to offer protection to the displaced populations on the territory of the former Yugoslavia, and what this experiment meant in normative terms. In fact, intervention can be seen as interference in the state–citizen–territory trinity for the sake of preserving the trinity. Without intervention, mass flows of refugees may have arrived in EU Member States. Seen from this perspective it had a very pluralist flavour. However, intervention also aimed to protect the displaced, thus bringing the solidarist element into the picture at the same time. The same happened when mass movements of Kosovar Albanians began to occur in 1999, and the international community pushed once again for protection in the region, with little use being made of the durable solution of resettlement. The use of 'safe areas' was therefore an early experiment in the externalisation of refugee protection policy.

Both these experiences took place before the commitments were taken by EU international society to develop the external dimension of refugee policy with its protection ethos that, as discussed above, evolved from 1998. A more recent development, and the culmination of the externalisation of EU refugee policy to date, has been the move towards the idea of protection of refugees in regions of origin. The Commission Communication of December 2002, 'Integrating Migration Issues in the European Union's Relations with Third Countries', devoted attention to outlining the different Community actions in favour of refugees, including humanitarian assistance being provided to refugee populations. A further Communication issued by the Commission in June 2003, 'Towards More Accessible, Equitable and Managed Asylum Systems', stressed that possible new approaches should be focused on action outside the EU, within a framework of genuine burden and responsibility sharing.[30] Preparatory actions were to be taken to test the ground for what could be done in regions of origin within this scope, and a budget line, B7–667, was set up for this purpose. Those projects selected were conducted through UNHCR and focused on issues such as gaps analyses of protection, how to strengthen international protection and institution-building of asylum systems in regions of origin, for example the Comprehensive Plan of Action for Somali Refugees.

Following a mandate from the Thessaloniki European Council in June 2003, the Commission then issued a Communication, 'On the Managed Entry in the EU of Persons in Need of International Protection and the Enhancement of the Protection Capacity of the Regions of Origin: "Improving Access to Durable Solutions"'. It noted that:

> A reduction in the numbers of asylum seekers in the EU does not necessarily mean an overall reduction of the numbers of refugees and persons seeking international protection at a global level and it is clear that there remain many regions and countries in the world where human rights violations and consequent displacement cause protracted refugee situations, with still some 85% of these persons being hosted by the under-resourced neighbouring countries in regions of origin.[31]

Here the Commission clearly placed the focus on protection and attempted to push Member States to acknowledge that the control agenda risked denying protection to refugees. The Communication noted that according to UNHCR 'there is a collective duty of the broader community of States ... to equip States receiving or likely to receive asylum-seekers with the means to live up to international standards in their treatment of refugees'.[32] This suggested that a system of international burden or responsibility sharing is implicit in international relations between states and, as such, showed once again that the international refugee regime creates obligations on sovereign states. The Communication committed the Commission to bringing forward a proposal for the creation of 'Regional Protection Programmes' (RPPs).

---

[30] European Commission, 'Communication on Towards More Accessible, Equitable and Managed Asylum Systems', COM(2003) 315 final.
[31] European Commission, 'Communication on the Managed Entry in the EU of Persons in Need of International Protection and Enhancement of the Protection Capacity of the Regions of Origin: Improving Access to Durable Solutions', COM(2004) 410 final, 3.
[32] European Commission, 'Communication on the Managed Entry', 13.

Such proposals would respond specifically to the world's protracted refugee situations – some thirty-three situations affecting 5.7 million refugees – in which the great majority of refugees continue to live in a state of limbo, unable to return home, unable to integrate in the country of asylum, and unable to find resettlement in a third country.[33] Programmes would be 'part and parcel of the overall strategy towards the country or region concerned and synergies with the various components of the strategy (in particular good governance, judiciary reform, institution building, democratisation and human rights etc) [would] be fully exploited'.[34] The Hague Programme called for the Commission to present an action plan for one or more pilot RPPs, which should be situation specific and protection-oriented, showing the shift towards protection had now taken hold in the Council.

The Communication on 'Regional Protection Programmes' was presented by the Commission in September 2005. It held that RPPs would be flexible and tailor-made with the objective of enhancing the protection capacity of third countries and creating the conditions for one of the three durable solutions to take place. Each RPP would consist of practical actions 'that deliver real benefits both in terms of protection offered to refugees and in their support of existing arrangements with the relevant third country'.[35] Thus RPPs would be a key policy toolbox to address protracted refugee situations, comprising projects that could improve protection capacity in host countries, establish an effective Refugee Status Determination procedure, improve reception conditions, benefit the wider local community, and provide training in protection issues for those dealing with refugees. The toolbox approach would be important for assessing what kind of protection should be available in regions of origin, not just the standards of that which is currently available. Indeed, according to Phuong, 'protection should take on a broader meaning to refer also to access to durable solutions . . . [serving] to determine what practical actions are required from donor countries to improve both the enforcement of refugees' rights and

---

[33] United Nations, Office of the United Nations High Commissioner for Refugees, *The State of the World's Refugees: Human Displacement in the New Millennium* (Oxford University Press, 2006), p. 10. This figure does not include the 4.3 million displaced Palestinians who fall under the mandate of UNRWA–UNHCR, '2005 Global Refugee Trends', 3.

[34] European Commission, 'Communication on the Managed Entry', 17–18.

[35] European Commission, 'Communication on Regional Protection Programmes', COM(2005) 388 final, 3–4.

access to durable solutions in regions of origin'.[36] The proposals further suggested a voluntary resettlement commitment, in the aim of providing durable solutions. This element especially was intended to be an important factor in demonstrating the partnership approach of RPPs between the EU and third countries, but would also remove the need for refugees to move on from their country of asylum, for example by way of irregular secondary movements.

The proposals emphasised the scope of RPPs as protection oriented, building on and complementing existing initiatives in the region by working closely with international organisations, UNHCR in particular, so as to provide more effective protection closer to home and as early on as possible. Some concern was voiced by UNHCR and various NGOs that protection could be outweighed by the desire to better manage migration. Indeed, the two were somewhat unhelpfully linked in the proposal by the suggestion that projects could include those aiming to establish effective refugee status determination procedures to 'help host countries better manage the migration implications of refugee situations'.[37] In response, UNHCR underlined its expectation that the main focus of the programmes would remain on improving protection and access to durable solutions.[38] The concern was perpetuated by the choice in location of the two pilot programmes: one in the Great Lakes region, but the other in eastern Europe, and this latter, a transit migration region on the eastern border of the EU, most likely had the desire to reduce numbers of asylum-seekers entering Europe in mind. However, the Communication emphasised that RPPs should be established to fill existing 'protection gaps', and the underlying concept of regional protection generally received wide support.[39] Discussions on the proposals in the High Level Working Group were overwhelmingly focused on the protection element, and the Council Conclusions adopted by the General Affairs and External Relations Council two months later once again underlined the insistence of Member States that protection should remain at the heart of the whole exercise.

---

[36] Catherine Phuong, 'The concept of "effective protection" in the context of irregular secondary movements and protection in regions of origin', *Global Migration Perspectives* 26 (April 2005), 12.

[37] European Commission, 'Communication on Regional Protection Programmes', 4.

[38] UNHCR, 'Observations on the Communication from the European Commission to the Council and the European Parliament on Regional Protection Programmes', 3.

[39] European Commission, 'Communication on Regional Protection Programmes', 3.

AENEAS, the funding programme for providing assistance to third countries in the field of migration and asylum, is being used to fund the first Regional Protection Programmes. Projects will be implemented by UNHCR for both RPPs that build on UNHCR's ongoing work in these regions. For eastern Europe, projects will include improving access to asylum procedures and training of border guards. For Tanzania, a larger-scale RPP will consist of projects designed to strengthen the capacity of national authorities to protect refugees, improve security in refugee camps, promote voluntary return of Burundian refugees, enhance access to resettlement and improve the registration of refugees. The designation of €6 million for the initial exercise is only a beginning and will need to be increased if regional protection is to make a noticeable and positive difference to the quality and scope of refugee protection. However, it is an important start in the right direction, and no doubt further funding will be set aside if the pilot programmes prove to be a success. Moreover, the designation of UNHCR as the main implementing actor should help increase international legitimacy of the initiative.

Normative considerations of regional protection

It is interesting to note that there is a key difference between the Regional Protection Programmes currently being tried and the previous experiment with external protection tested during the Kosovo War. In 1999 EU Member States were faced with the prospect of mass numbers of refugees arriving on their territory. Now, however, external protection is being offered outside a time of imminent mass influxes. The Great Lakes region, for example, has long hosted a protracted refugee situation and the large majority of the refugees will continue to remain there. This is therefore an attempt to increase protection via capacity-building even when there is no impending arrival in the EU of particularly large numbers of individuals seeking asylum, pointing towards the solidarist beginning to supersede the pluralist. Mass flows of refugees in and from the developing world and growing distrust of and blurring with so-called 'economic refugees' and 'illegal migrants', coupled with the reality that many refugees can now actually return to their country of origin, means that resettlement in a host state has lost its status as option number one, as it was used during the Cold War. Regional protection has stepped in to fill this gap. This has altered the former exilic bias of international refugee protection, whereby the refugee had to flee her country of origin and cross an international border, and then became a ward of the international community.

If regional protection gets off the ground it could have several positive effects. As Crisp notes, regional protection has the potential to deprive human smugglers of their customers, as well as to reduce pressure on asylum systems in western states, thus countering hostile attitudes towards refugees and asylum-seekers and leading to a more rational debate on refugee policy. Reducing asylum costs and the costs of repatriation and reintegration could then make further funds available for development assistance in regions of refugee origin. And offering protection in the region should also allow refugees to go home more easily once conditions allow.[40] However, the aim of regional protection is to provide 'effective' protection, and the refugee should not be confined to areas where this cannot be guaranteed. Indeed, as UNHCR has emphasised, durable solutions will not always be available in regions of origin or transit for all individuals in need of protection.[41] A key part of the thinking behind the development of RPPs was that they should enhance the protection capacity of third countries so that they become 'robust providers of effective protection'.[42] But this is to all extents and purposes a debate about protection per se since, as Phuong has pointed out, 'protection that is not effective is simply not protection'.[43] Resettlement should therefore remain a key tool for the most vulnerable in situations of high security risk.

Several authors have noted the constant and increasing focus that has been given to the external dimension of EU refugee policy in recent years, but the need for such a shift is generally explained as a consequence of the inadequacy of border controls and other domestic migration management measures in coping with increased flows of refugees and other migrants to Europe such that Member States have sought to find a response outside the EU. According to Lavenex, for example, the externalisation of refugee policy has actually been a way for Member States to impose the control agenda to their own advantage even more. She maintains that it has been easier for Member States to cooperate on the sensitive issue of asylum away from their territory than within it and, if successful, engagement of third countries 'reduces the burden of

---

[40] Crisp, 'Refugee Protection in Regions of Origin'.
[41] UNHCR, 'Observations on the Communication', 1.
[42] European Commission, 'Communication on the Managed Entry', 14.
[43] Phuong, 'The Concept of "Effective Protection"', 3.

control at their immediate borders and increases the chances of curtailing unwanted inflows before they reach the common territory'.[44] Rather than an increase in the protection agenda, therefore, externalisation in this field has perhaps exported control. In the words of Zolberg, externalisation can be seen as 'remote control', with control maintained but the centre of that control simply shifted further from the territory of Member States.[45] This, claims Lavenex, is the reason for such a rapid development of cooperation in the external dimension of European asylum policy, as opposed to the internal dimension. Everything somehow seems less sensitive when it takes place in another country.

In a similar vein, Geddes has also argued that the externalisation of refugee policy has been driven by domestic interests. Geddes looks at the relationship and balance that must be maintained between territorial, organisational and conceptual borders. While territorial borders are usually understood as the site where sovereign power controls who may or may not enter a state's territory, organisational borders are the sites where the conditions of membership for the putative refugee in the host society are laid out, such as access to the labour market, the welfare state and national citizenship. Different types of migrants will experience a different relationship between territorial borders and organisational borders – for example, the asylum-seeker is allowed entry to make a claim, but may not be allowed to work while that claim is being processed. Finally, conceptual borders comprise notions of belonging and identity, and these too may not coincide with the other types of borders. According to Geddes, the desire to maintain key organisational borders – those of work, welfare and citizenship – impel EU Member States to 'project borders of territory and to use the EU as an institutional venue to pursue external aspects of EU migration and asylum policy'.[46]

The international society approach allows us to view the debate differently. The workings of international society necessitate a delicate balance between pluralist and solidarist elements. We have seen that the refugee is created precisely because of this mixture of norms. EU international society works in the same way. The society of EU Member States can only continue to exist while they show to each other, as well

---

[44] Sandra Lavenex, 'Shifting Up and Out: The Foreign Policy of European Immigration Control', *West European Politics* 29, 2 (2006), 337.

[45] Aristide Zolberg cited in Lavenex, 'Shifting Up and Out', 334.

[46] Andrew Geddes, 'Europe's Border Relationships and International Migration Relations', *Journal of Common Market Studies* 43, 4 (2005), 790.

as to global international society as a whole, that they are willing to play by the rules of the game. Among these rules are respect for human rights and human security, hence states want to be seen to be offering refugee protection even when it may not be a strategic national priority. Failure to play by the rules would jeopardise the entire EU structure and its recognition by global international society. EU states realise that their obligations under the 1951 Convention cannot be ignored. Offering refugees protection closer to home and as early as possible shows a commitment to those obligations. Further, within international society states' identities and interests are affected, influenced and changed by evolving norms. The norm of regional protection has been constructed as being in the interests of all states concerned, in terms of international protection, security, development and migration management, and thus states' priorities have shifted. Similarly, the EU institutions want to show to members of other regional international societies that the EU acts properly, and will thus socialise Member States to accept such norms. Protection-oriented ideas promulgated by the Commission, with the contributions and influence of UNHCR, have influenced Member States to adopt the language of protection and develop a protection agenda. Hence part of the reason for seeking to offer regional alternatives to refugee protection must by definition be of a solidarist nature.

The external dimension has been described by Lavenex and Uçarer as having become 'the most dynamic aspect of cooperation in asylum and immigration matters' since Tampere.[47] Developments from 1998 onwards have really consolidated the protection agenda, which has become more than just sporadic references to the 1951 Convention but something also carried out in practice. By shifting the focus from control mechanisms to keep potential asylum-seekers away from EU territory, to working with countries of origin to strengthen protection closer to home and to address the root causes of forced migration, external refugee policy has brought about a new emphasis on the protection agenda. In other words, the protection agenda only becomes pronounced in the EU debate on refugee policy when it is linked to the external relations agenda. The externalisation process has demonstrated explicit and frequently resurfacing references to norms of protection, illustrating that protection is something that the EU can more

---

[47] Sandra Lavenex and Emek M. Uçarer, 'The External Dimension of Europeanization: The Case of Immigration Policies', *Cooperation and Conflict* 39, 4 (2004), 427.

easily help make available outside the Union. Via regional protection Member States therefore contribute to the guaranteeing of refugee rights beyond the borders of EU international society. The debate over refugee protection has now become less about what the 1951 Convention upholds in the legal sense, and more about what exactly should be provided to which refugees, where and by which state. As Phuong has noted, 'protection is obviously not a new concept, but what is novel is the context in which it is discussed'.[48] The space of the analysis has moved from the national to the regional domain.

By offering protection outside the territorial confines of EU international society, protection has in effect been decoupled from sovereignty. Current practices of controlling refugees in Europe are strategies that attempt to place refugees in areas of 'protection' that are no longer dependent on state borders. The borders of EU Member States now extend further than ever, far from the state's territorial jurisdiction and its physical borders, and the state attempts to exercise its sovereignty away from its territory. Protection has effectively been deterritorialised. This points once again to the arbitrary nature of international borders as physical symbols of sustaining political communities, suggesting instead that the contents of substantive sovereignty could, in theory, be divided from territory. With this decoupling of sovereignty and borders, the concept of international protection has been transformed. Refugee protection was traditionally something to be found far away from the source of persecution. It was the territory of the host country, the sovereign space within its territorial borders, that was the necessary element for offering asylum. Now protection has become something states believe they can guarantee close to a refugee's home. With this change, the idea of protection in EU international society becomes something external to the EU. At the same time, and in clear contrast, security remains internal. A securitarian ethic is promulgated within the EU, while a protection ethic is spread outside the EU in countries or regions of origin. Or, to take this further, to maintain security inside protection is exported. This points to a tight link between the control agenda and the prevention agenda and, instead of one having given way to the other, rather the two go hand in hand but occupy different spaces. In other words, the externalisation of protection clearly underlines the links between the desire to increase control and security inside and the fostering of a more liberal, humanitarian

[48] Phuong, 'The Concept of "Effective Protection"', 14.

approach outside. Once again, international society demonstrates itself to be a complex and overlapping space of both pluralism and solidarism. Note the dichotomy: flows of refugees into the EU are posited under a security ethos, while intra-EU movement of persons is found under a liberalisation ethos with internal borders having been abolished.[49] Accordingly, 'security' becomes a given: the state, or in this case the EU, is the given norm, the refugee the given other, and security the given threat that exists in the relationship between them. If refugee flows are kept in their regions of origins, not only will the EU remain safe and stable, but the safety of the refugees can be guaranteed via the promulgation of extra-territorial protection norms by EU Member States.

From a normative perspective, the trend can be seen as a direct effect of the statist desire to keep people where they are, rooted in the state–citizen–territory hierarchy. Since refugees undertake transnational and transregional movements, the desire to examine ways of providing protection in regions of refugee origin, whatever the underlying motivation, is a distinct example of an attempt to maintain the pluralist architecture of international society. From the English School perspective, however, the paradox here is intriguing. Dialogue on protection in regions of origin on the one hand acts to maintain the pluralist make-up of international society, by keeping all individuals as close as possible to their state–citizen–territory hierarchy. On the other hand, protection in the regions also has a solidarist, human rights thinking: states believe that by addressing the root causes of forced migration fewer individuals will be pushed out of their homes as refugees, and those who are forced to flee can be offered protection as close to home and as early as possible during flight, rather than having to make precarious often covert journeys across continents in search of that protection. In other words, the externalisation of EU refugee policy is another example of the balance being maintained between pluralism and solidarism within EU international society. Paradoxically, concern for security within EU Member States can therefore be seen to have been framed within a liberal thinking rather than a realist thinking. Sovereignty becomes more than simply a pluralist conception, focused on non-intervention and territorial integrity, but encompasses the wider understanding of a

---

[49] Dora Kostakopoulou, 'The "Protective Union": Change and Continuity in Migration Law and Policy in Post-Amsterdam Europe', *Journal of Common Market Studies* 38, 3 (2000), 506.

responsibility to protect. The EU acting as a regional international society collectively promulgates a solidarist element to sovereignty, which transforms our understanding of both sovereignty and international protection. Although keeping refugees in their country or region of origin acts to maintain the pluralist architecture of international society, at the same time it promotes a solidarist, human rights thinking by evoking ideas of protection and consideration of the root causes of forced migration.

This demonstrates a shift from the emphasis that was placed on the 'right to remain' in the country of origin in the 1990s, to the granting of asylum by third countries in the region of origin. Arguments put forward by western governments in favour of 'within country' protection justify it on the grounds that people prefer to stay close to similar national, religious or ethnic groups; that it is no longer always the state that is the source of persecution, and the state may be able to provide sanctuary from a persecuting non-state group in another part of the country; and that it is easier for refugees to go home once the factors that caused the flight in the first place have been removed if they remain nearby. This shift also fits the liberal, human rights argument that sees resettlement as undermining and even violating the refugee's right to return home safely when conditions allow: membership in a society is not just a legal status that can be easily shed and acquired.[50] Human rights advocates maintain that the 'solution' is to prevent the conditions that compel flight in the first place, or remedy those conditions as soon as possible after flight.

There are of course risks associated with this approach. It shows, as Chimni stresses, a trend in internalist interpretations of the root causes of refugee creation.[51] By blaming conditions in the country of origin for the creation of refugees, the international community can lay the 'burden' of stopping refugee flows on that country of origin: if the state fails to comply with the norms of good governance that would ensure the protection of its citizens, it is its own responsibility to improve the internal situation. Hence there is a need to ensure that western states do not attempt to keep refugees in their country or region of origin by calling for an improvement in the human rights situation there whilst ignoring two important factors: first, that external factors play a large part in the creation of conditions that lead to refugee flows, not least

---

[50] Aleinikoff, 'State-centred Refugee Law', 261.
[51] Chimni, 'The Geopolitics of Refugee Studies'.

because refugees are intricately wrapped up in the workings of the entire international system; and second, that the international community has a role to play in the international human rights regime, which implies a conception of negative sovereignty that implicates international society as a whole, and not just conditions of positive sovereignty within states. As Gibney's Basic Rights Principle demonstrates, duties extend beyond borders such that states are obligated 'to play some part in meeting the basic rights of individuals in other societies even if they were not the cause of this need'.[52]

The shift to regional protection must be closely monitored. Even with the rhetoric of a protection agenda, working with countries of origin is inevitably due at least in part to a desire to control refugee flows that create both practical and theoretical problems for the international states system. Whether or not preventive protection and repatriation are conceptualised in human rights terms, these 'solutions' continue to be grounded in the aim of restoring all individuals to a state. The move to a preference in the international community for voluntary repatriation and concern with the root causes of refugee movements does not necessarily indicate a real change in the underlying premise of refugee law. If we were witnessing a true shift in response to the refugee problem from a communitarian bias to a cosmopolitan paradigm, the distinction made in the 1951 Convention between 'refugees' and 'internally displaced persons' (IDPs) would be called into question. At this point, notes Aleinikoff, 'refugee law would collapse into human rights law'.[53] But limited intervention on behalf of internally displaced persons shows that this has not yet taken place. The continued importance placed on distinguishing between the two shows the persistence of the different normative understandings of refugees and IDPs and the continued power and significance of political borders and state sovereignty. Protection in regions of refugee origin, therefore, regardless of whether or not the state is fully compliant with the human rights regime or norms of good governance, has the potential to return the refugee to a situation in which her basic rights fail to be protected.

Above all the right to seek asylum must be fiercely upheld. This right assumes an entitlement to be granted safety from persecution, as contained within the principle of *non-refoulement*, even if the right to be

---

[52] Mark Gibney, *Strangers or Friends: Principles for a New Alien Admission Policy* (Westport, Conn.: Greenwood Press, 1986), p. 103.
[53] Aleinikoff, 'State-centred Refugee Law', 264.

granted asylum per se is not written down. Regional protection could limit the opportunities for exit, thus undermining the fundamental individual right to seek asylum. And of course, in-country protection or the establishment of refugee camps in border areas cannot substitute entirely for international protection away from the source of flight and thus the source of danger: 'Those people who attempt to take refuge in a neighbouring or nearby state increasingly find that they simply swapped one situation of insecurity with another.'[54] History has shown that internal conflicts have a tendency to mushroom into regional conflict, meaning that conditions in neighbouring states no longer represent safety, while camps may be havens for armed rebels or targets for cross-border attacks by forces of the home government, thus severely undermining the guarantee of the refugee's safety.[55] As Mertus notes, the greater the involvement of host states in any episode of displacement, the more rights that become available for the individual, and 'although an international body can provide an uprooted person with "temporary protection" in a refugee camp in the middle of nowhere (or in an area in conflict), only a State can grant asylum and the rights necessary to start life anew'.[56] Protection is only fully guaranteed away from the source of danger.

Conclusions

With today's mixed movements of persons, the international community will need to continue looking for ways to respond to the specific needs of the refugee. The proposals for regional protection promulgated by the European Union are one recent example of this search. They clearly have not only the capacity to bring together pluralist and solidarist interests but also the potential to increase the protection ethic and move states towards a more cosmopolitan agenda, and in so doing EU international society could socialise other regional international societies to respond in the same way. The English School shows that the external dimension of EU migration policy goes beyond a functionalist desire to control borders, beyond realism. Protection

---

[54] UNHCR, *The State of the World's Refugees, 1997–8*, p. 5.
[55] Bill Frelick, 'Down the Rabbit Hole: The Strange Logic of Internal Flight Alternatives', *World Refugee Survey 1999: An Assessment of Conditions Affecting Refugees, Asylum Seekers, and Internally Displaced Persons* (Washington D.C.: United States Committee for Refugees, 1999), 22.
[56] Mertus, 'The State', 335–6.

norms have been diffused and accepted among Member States as one of the new ways of interacting with third countries on asylum issues at the EU level. Of course, national interest continues to play a role in the direction the external dimension of EU refugee policy takes, and the English School account of developments must take this into consideration. However, if the aim of theory is to provide a conceptual lens for examining real-world issues, the English School provides a useful means of analysing the direction that the externalisation of refugee policy has taken so far, and a tool to debate the direction it may take in the years to come.

8   The way ahead

> The ten years that I spent with refugees marked a period of continuous humanitarian crises ... Try as we might to protect the refugees and alleviate their suffering, humanitarian action alone could not lead to solving their problems. What was required was a convergence of interests covering humanitarian, political, and security action by major international and regional powers.   Sadako Ogata[1]

The post-Cold War era has left the refugee in a state of uncertainty. Refugee policy is now being reinterpreted in the light of countervailing forces in contemporary world politics. On the one hand is the growing security agenda, an agenda that at times gives states a cover for contracting out of their obligations towards refugees; on the other is the sovereignty as responsibility discourse, evidenced in the intervention of states on behalf of refugees and others in need of assistance. How can the pluralism–solidarism tension be balanced so that these two competing interests are taken into consideration when seeking responses to the refugee and refugee policy? This chapter first assesses the current position of the refugee in between the security agenda and the responsibility to protect agenda. It then suggests some ways to move forward with refugee policy. Last, it draws together the themes and findings of this book to analyse the value of the conceptual and historical approach for contemporary refugee policy.

The effects of the security agenda

Whereas during the Cold War threats to states were largely of a military nature, now they have become radically different. New threats emanate

---

[1] Sadako Ogata, *The Turbulent Decade: Confronting the Refugee Crises of the 1990s* (New York: W. W. Norton & Company, 2005), p. 317.

from the environmental, economic, political and societal sectors. The break-up of multi-ethnic states in the immediate post-Cold War years released or revived nationalism and xenophobia at a time when the traditional concept of state sovereignty was being challenged by the idea of European integration. In western Europe perceived threats to identity now came in part from mass increases in the numbers of immigrants arriving in western societies. Eastern European states, on the other hand, were still struggling to find a way to construct a state–society relationship along nation-state lines while building demo-cratic, market economies. Thus the end of the Cold War gave birth to a time of immense socio-political change across Europe, with boundaries between state and citizen being reconstructed. On both sides of Europe states began to undergo changes that included migration of peoples and the formation of new societal identities.[2] 'Societal security' resur-rected issues such as national identity and ethnic rivalries that were evident in European politics in the inter-war period. Changes in the international structure discredited accepted boundaries and erected new ones, while totalitarian regimes came and went and economies grew and declined. Within such a context the refugee easily became the 'other' against whom dissatisfactions with one's own identity could be directed.

The securitisation of an issue is intensely political. Constructing the refugee as an existential threat is a political technique able to foster integration.[3] In constructing an issue as a threat to security, the social boundaries in which the threat is to be perceived are at the same time constructed. Shore notes that identities are created by 'the manipula-tion of boundaries and the mobilization of difference for strategies of inclusion and exclusion ... [and it is] at the *boundaries* of states, nations and ethnic groups that problems of identity tend to be most acute'.[4] For example, Europe has no 'official' or defined identity as such, but 'evi-dence of a more "applied" definition can be seen emerging at the borders and boundaries of the new Europe, particularly in the spheres of immigration control and external customs barriers [where] the terms "non-EC nationals", "third countries" and "non-Europeans" are being

---

[2] Barry Buzan, Ole Wæver and Jaap de Wilde, *Security: A New Framework for Analysis* (Boulder, Colo., and London: Lynne Rienner Publishers, 1998), pp. 1–5.

[3] Jef Huysmans, 'The Question of the Limit: Desecuritisation and the Aesthetics of Horror in Political Realism', *Millennium: Journal of International Studies* 27, 3 (1998), 577.

[4] Cris Shore, 'Inventing the "People's Europe": Critical Approaches to European Community "Cultural Policy"', *Man* 28, 4 (1993), 783 (Shore's emphasis).

defined with increasing precision and thus, as if by default, an "official" definition of European is being constructed'.[5] The refugee in her position between sovereigns, confined to the gaps between borders and boundaries, is the 'other' who constitutes a threat to societal security and constructed identities. In the context of the international states system, security is about the ability of states and societies to survive as independent, sovereign entities. If state security is therefore imagined in terms of sovereignty and territory, then it is the security of people as a community or a society who will imagine the refugee in terms of a threat to their identity. Indeed, as Huysmans observes, in the construction of security 'the image seems to be not only one of insecure individuals threatened by "foreigners", but also one of an insecure collective identity which unites the insecure individuals'.[6] Thus societal security involves a threat, real or perceived, to the identity of the society. State or 'national' security are distinct from societal security but act in parallel: 'Sovereignty is the name of the game of survival for a state – if it loses its sovereignty, it has not survived as a state [while] survival for a society is a question of identity, because this is the way a society talks about existential threats: if this happens, we will no longer be able to live as "us".'[7]

The issue of asylum and refugees has effectively been 'securitised' in western societies. Immigration of any kind is linked to insecurity, and where this movement is seemingly illegal or out of control the insecurity increases. Thus refugees are constructed as a high-level threat even though being an 'illegal asylum-seeker' or 'illegal refugee' is, of course, a misnomer. According to Ceyhan and Tsoukala, this threat is articulated around four axes: the socio-economic, the securitarian, the identitarian and the political.[8] Within this discourse of 'danger' several myths are perpetuated: that the refugee causes unemployment; that the presence of the refugee indicates a loss of control over sovereign borders; that the refugee weakens the national identity of the host society; and that the refugee brings disease. Right-wing propaganda inflated with distorted facts and scare tactics reinforce this security discourse. Western

[5] Shore, 'Inventing the "People's Europe"', 786.
[6] Jef Huysmans, 'Migrants as a Security Problem: Dangers of "Securitizing" Societal Issues', in Robert Miles and Dietrich Thränhardt (eds.), *Migration and European Integration: The Dynamics of Inclusion and Exclusion* (London: Pinter Publishers, 1995), 53.
[7] Huysmans, 'Migrants as a Security Problem', 25–6.
[8] Ayse Ceyhan and Anastassia Tsoukala, 'The Securitization of Migration in Western Societies: Ambivalent Discourses and Politics', *Alternatives* 27 supplement (2002), 24.

societies are made to believe that there are precarious gaps in their borders which, if not closed, could allow danger to seep through. Yet this discourse suggests that states have always had complete control over their borders and that, before the onset of this 'asylum crisis', borders were totally impermeable. Of course, just as sovereignty has never been absolute, so state control over borders has long been compromised by the flow of individuals in and out of the state's territory, both legal and illegal. But states like to endow their borders with a sense of the magical. Borders are highly symbolic, demarcating the limits of political control and the boundaries between inside and outside, them and us: 'Each discourse associating the control of migration flows to the reinforcement of border-control measures relies ... on the myth of the existence of the sovereign state fully able to control its territory.'[9] Borders represent sovereignty, designate national identities and protect citizens against external threats. They are accordingly charged with power, and it is this inherent power that keeps the securitarian discourse of a 'European asylum crisis' alive. The logic of security that has come to characterise the normative understanding of the refugee problem in contemporary politics, therefore, rests on two interconnected assumptions: that a security problem exists in western Europe, and that refugees and asylum-seekers represent a security threat. Securitising the refugee 'implicitly constructs the political identity that is being rendered secure as unproblematic and as the desired political order'.[10] The object under threat becomes the norm, the refugee becomes the problem. Just as the refugee is silenced in this statist understanding of her, the political process of critically articulating and defining what constitutes a security threat is also rendered speechless.

The security agenda is perhaps more prominent now than it has ever been. Attacks such as those on the United States, Madrid and London in the past few years have heightened concern over international terrorism, and both state and societal security have taken on a new dimension. Any individual who is seen as 'other' is a potential threat. Borders must be controlled and movement must be legal and visible, otherwise it could bring danger. The result is that protection rules are increasingly under strain both from above and below: world powers feel the need to be seen to be taking appropriate measures to guarantee the security of

---

[9] Ceyhan and Tsoukala, 'The Securitization of Migration', 34.
[10] S. Dalby cited in Aninia Nadig, 'Human Smuggling, National Security, and Refugee Protection', *Journal of Refugee Studies* 15, 1 (2002), 16.

their states and nations, and their responses are at times putting human rights norms at risk – the global 'war on terror', for example, has led to large-scale movements of refugees and internally displaced persons due to the military offensives it has entailed; at the same time, citizens are increasingly unsure of what it means to belong and with whom they share values. Rather than forming a new threat focused on international terrorism, the increased uncertainty in world politics has acted to blur all potential threats into one, something not helped by the fact that international terrorism is a faceless, unknown quantity. Hence the refugee figure, the moving individual fleeing all that is dangerous and unstable, is a security risk to be controlled just like any other threat, in spite of the human rights implications involved.

Constructing sovereignty as responsibility

The competing value that pulls refugee policy in the other direction is that of 'sovereignty as responsibility', an agenda that also grew out of the 1990s. An increasing number of 'humanitarian' interventions have taken place over the last two decades. Between the Gulf War of 1991 and the violence in Kosovo that erupted in 1999, the UN intervened in a large number of conflicts to provide humanitarian relief and peace-keeping operations. Fourteen interventions took place in Africa alone, the majority in intra- rather than inter-state conflict.[11] Many of these episodes caused, or had the potential to cause, mass refugee flows. Yet this intervention has been controversial both when it has happened and when it has failed to happen.[12] As Mayall has pointed out, while in the post-Cold War environment western states have taken the lead in promoting the discourse of human rights, 'their willingness to inter-vene in the domestic affairs of states whose governments transgressed these norms [has] remained highly selective, particularly where their own interests were not directly involved'.[13] Rwanda will, of course, spring to mind.

The formulation of contemporary refugee policy comes at a time when more and more conflicts are causing and are likely to cause internal displacement. The number of internally displaced persons

---

[11] James Mayall, *World Politics: Progress and Its Limits* (Cambridge: Polity Press, 2000), p. 125.
[12] International Commission on Intervention and State Sovereignty, *The Responsibility to Protect* (Ottawa: International Development Research Centre, 2001), p. 1.
[13] Mayall, *World Politics*, p. 139.

has increased dramatically in recent years. By the end of 2005 UNHCR was reporting the presence of 6.6 million IDPs in sixteen countries, constituting the second-largest group under its mandate.[14] Quite simply, the crossing of an international border to become a refugee is not an option for the vast number of individuals now requiring protection from violence such as armed intra-state conflict.[15] Yet often the decision to move or not to move across an international border is not always a personal one taken by the individual. Fearing mass influxes of refugees from neighbouring countries, states may actively close their borders. Turkey did so in 1991, when 400,000 Iraqi Kurds arrived at its border with Iraq, and the former Yugoslav Republic of Macedonia attempted to do so when faced with mass flows of Kosovar refugees in 1999. Both acts sparked a response from the international community: in the former case, Northern Iraq was designated a United Nations 'safety area', so that Turkey was not in fact breaching the 1951 Convention with an act of *refoulement* by refusing entry; in the latter case, international pressure forced the former Yugoslav Republic of Macedonia to allow the refugees into its territory, but not before guarantees of responsibility-sharing had been received. Qualitative similarities between the refugee and the internally displaced person and the arbitrary nature of the borders separating them are hidden behind the labels in ignorance of the fact that the internally displaced may frequently be more at risk than the 'externally displaced'. Situated out of the reach of international aid agencies, risks of abuse of the human rights of IDPs are often more widespread than in the case of the refugee, yet means of international protection are not (formally) available.[16] Internal displacement is frequently the result of a failure of good governance on the part of the state in which the displaced person finds herself. As a refugee, the individual is entitled to international protection; as an IDP she may lack both national and international protection, being trapped 'in the vacuum of sovereignty'.[17]

The concept of sovereignty is as central to the IDP question as to the refugee question. But whereas the notion of the refugee works in

---

[14] UNHCR, '2005 Global Refugee Trends', 8.
[15] According to Bennett, for example, there were 94 conflicts in 64 locations across the world between 1989 and 1994, only four of which were inter-state conflicts – Bennett, 'Internal Displacement in Context', 16.
[16] Phuong, 'Internally Displaced Persons', 218–19.
[17] Francis M. Deng, 'In the Vacuum of Sovereignty: The International Challenge of Internal Displacement', *Forced Migration Review* 17 (2003), 56.

opposition to sovereignty, undermining the state's sovereign control of its population and challenging the territorial boundaries of the state, the term 'internally displaced person' actually reinforces sovereignty. Inherent in the distinction, and in the desire to continue distinguishing, between the 'refugee' and the 'IDP' are different normative understandings of how the displaced person interacts with the concept of sovereignty. The refugee encompasses a negative idea of sovereignty in that she has exited her state of origin by crossing an international border and hence has become an issue of concern on the international agenda and a ward of international society. On the other hand, the protection of the internally displaced person who remains within the confines of her state is theoretically the continued responsibility of her own government. Wrapped up in the definition of the IDP is the idea that sovereignty implies norms of good governance and that governments are responsible for the well-being of their citizens – sovereignty as responsibility. The IDP concept therefore rests on a positive idea of sovereignty. Indeed, the core principle that has guided the work of the UN Representative of the Secretary-General on Internally Displaced Persons has been 'to recognise the inherent nature of the problem of displacement as internal and therefore falling under state sovereignty and to postulate sovereignty positively, as entailing the responsibility to protect and assist citizens in need'.[18] In the case of IDPs, therefore, human rights become *part* of the definition of sovereignty rather than acting in opposition to it. Accordingly, the idea of protection for internally displaced persons involves an inherent contradiction: international assistance is necessary to ensure that the human rights of individuals are upheld by states fulfilling their responsibilities, while such protection involves strengthening the ability of the same state to carry out these responsibilities. There is a clash between the demand for international intervention and the demand for the offending state to sort out the problem of IDPs itself.[19] This points once again to the blurring of natural law and positive law where the national and the international meet.

Sovereignty means internal authority and responsibility for citizens. The emerging norm of international intervention is particularly contentious because any action the international community takes on behalf of

---

[18] Deng, 'In the Vacuum of Sovereignty'.

[19] Phuong, 'Internally Displaced Persons', 220; and Francis M. Deng, 'Flocks Without Shepherds: The International Dilemma of Internal Displacement', in Davies, *Rights Have No Borders*, 23.

IDPs by definition takes place within the sovereign jurisdiction of a state and because states should remain responsible for the individuals under their jurisdiction. Yet, although the IDP may remain within the territorial jurisdiction of her state, the substantive element of sovereignty that would ensure her protection and the guarantee of her basic rights is no longer functioning. Statist international refugee law may rely on the border-crossing criterion for the granting of refugee status, but the internally displaced person is created in exactly the same way as the refugee and has crossed this border, albeit fictitiously, following a breakdown in the state–citizen relationship. It is not just the physical, geographical act of moving that is important; borders are the symbolic representation of a state's sovereignty and a failure to be protected by sovereignty means falling outside these borders.

But perhaps it is more that the international community fails to see the *need* to take action when the displacement occurs within the confines of a state. While the IDP remains within her country of origin and does not represent a threat to international stability there is seemingly less need for other states to intervene. Indeed, the realist position views intervention in such circumstances as itself potentially destructive of international order. But internal displacement may not remain localised, and IDPs have the potential to quickly become refugees: 'massive internal displacement becomes the spark that ignites refugee flows'.[20] When the country of origin can no longer cope with the instability generated by the movement of persons, IDPs may be forced over borders to become refugees. Incidences of IDPs are further evidence of international society in motion, 'at their most benign burdening neighboring states with refugee flows and at their worst spreading violence and instability through entire regions'.[21] It is only when displacement spills over boundaries and threatens to disrupt and destabilise other states and the international states system as a whole that some sort of a response is required. If the humanitarian needs of the individual were the sole reason for intervention, the categories 'refugee' and 'IDP' would lose their distinction and the two would become one, subsumed within the broader category 'displaced'. Almost all Security Council resolutions allowing for international action in the

---

[20] David A. Korn, *Exodus Within Borders: An Introduction to the Crisis of Internal Displacement* (Washington D.C.: Brookings Institution Press, 1998), p. 3.

[21] Roberta Cohen and Francis M. Deng (eds.), *The Forsaken People: Case Studies of the Internally Displaced* (Washington D.C.: Brookings Institution Press, 1998), p. 14.

face of human rights violations in the 1990s were premised on threats to regional and international peace and security, rather than human suffering per se.[22] All recent examples of the designation of 'safe areas' show that the international community was only prompted to take action, and decided to take this specific course of action, precisely when mass refugee flows threatened to pour out of the country of origin. For this reason the 'safe haven' in Bosnia and Herzegovina, the 'safety area' in northern Iraq and the 'safe humanitarian zone' in Rwanda all showed a great blurring of politics and humanitarianism promoted by forced displacement on a huge scale.

In 2000 the Canadian government established the International Commission on Intervention and State Sovereignty. The Commission was mandated to try to build a better understanding of the problems involved in reconciling state sovereignty with intervention for human protection purposes. It set out with the understanding that today's international context expects different standards of conduct of states and individuals and has different expectations for action than the context within which the United Nations was born, not least because of evolving human rights norms.[23] It further noted:

> In an interdependent world, in which security depends on a framework of stable sovereign entities, the existence of fragile states, failing states, states who through weakness or ill-will harbour those dangerous to others, or states that can only maintain internal order by means of gross human rights violations, can constitute a risk to people everywhere.[24]

From the start the Commission also underlined that sovereignty does still matter – that the international environment may have evolved since 1945, and will undoubtedly continue to evolve, but that it seems unlikely that the sovereign state will wither and die. Further, it noted that, for the maintenance of international security, 'a cohesive and peaceful international system is far more likely to be achieved through the cooperation of effective states, confident of their place in the world, than in an environment of fragile, collapsed, fragmenting or generally chaotic state entities'.[25]

[22] Bennett, 'Internal Displacement in Context', 20.
[23] International Commission, *The Responsibility to Protect*, p. 3.
[24] International Commission, *The Responsibility to Protect*, p. 5.
[25] International Commission, *The Responsibility to Protect*, p. 8.

The Commission chose to talk not of the 'right to intervene' but of the 'responsibility to protect'. Thinking about the debate in this way, it maintained, focuses attention on human security, on precisely those individuals seeking protection or assistance, and thus takes the emphasis away from national or territorial security and the rights and prerogatives of states.[26] The Commission concluded that the emerging principle is such that the responsibility to protect lies above all with the state within which people are directly affected, but intervention for humanitarian protection purposes 'is supportable when major harm to civilians is occurring or imminently apprehended, and the state in question is unable or unwilling to end the harm, or is itself the perpetrator'.[27] At this point the international community has a residual responsibility to protect.

Sovereignty as responsibility, the Commission agreed, implies that states are responsible for protecting their citizens, that they are accountable to their citizens internally and to the international community externally through the United Nations, and that they are responsible for their actions and in-actions. With the emerging human rights culture, a shift can be witnessed from an international society framed by sovereign impunity to an international society based on national and international accountability. This is particularly so if we think about the establishment of the International Criminal Court and the international criminal tribunals set up to deal with crimes against humanity committed in the Balkans, Rwanda and Sierra Leone.[28] Tipping the balance towards the country of origin means insisting on a positive, substantive view of sovereignty couched in the idea that sovereign states have a responsibility and duty to protect their citizens. This is of course the ideal, but recalls the pre-1945 climate, which looked to solve refugee problems within the state. The state, it was held, was sovereign over its internal affairs and by assigning all individuals to a nation they would be protected within this sovereign jurisdiction. The post-1945 move to a negative view of sovereignty shifted the responsibility of protection to the international community, which was acceptable during the Cold War years, when movements of refugees in Europe were frozen and movement elsewhere stayed elsewhere. This emphasis on negative sovereignty could not stand up to the post-Cold War environment,

---

[26] International Commission, *The Responsibility to Protect*, pp. 15–17.
[27] International Commission, *The Responsibility to Protect*, p. 16.
[28] International Commission, *The Responsibility to Protect*, pp. 13–14.

however, when mass refugee flows once again became a reality in Europe. Accordingly, international society now insists on positive sovereignty as far as is possible, but expects negative sovereignty to step in when the duties of a state to protect its citizens fail. The refocusing of the discourse onto the issue of human security has put the debate surrounding intervention or the responsibility to protect onto the international arena – constructivism in action once again. States now recognise more and more that intra-state conflict can impact on the international system as a whole, thus a threat to national and international security is constructed. The new norm of the responsibility to protect is becoming accepted and shared since it is seen as necessary for the peaceful continuation of international society.[29]

Rethinking responses towards the refugee

The refugee highlights the imagined power of geographical space via the territorial boundaries of sovereign states and of moral space constituted by the ethical borders of identity. The refugee relies on borders for her being – is forced between such borders by statist, territorialised politics – and thus 'solutions' are founded on the 'need' to maintain the status quo of international society, rather than on a purely humanitarian, altruistic basis to international protection. Within a states system composed of uneasy dichotomies, blurred outlines and paradoxical situations, the refugee brings into stark view the clash between communitarianism and cosmopolitanism, forcing us to question the extent to which we can insist on the ethical within the political.

If we look for a 'solution' to the refugee 'problem' outside the state, we would opt for the cosmopolitan idea of international human rights norms, striving for a global entity beyond the current system of separate sovereign entities. We would assume that 'natural rights' are prior and superior to citizens' rights, and that belonging to a political community is not a necessary condition for upholding our fundamental human rights. Yet aspiring to a global community without borders means simultaneously assuming a world without refugees, since it is the existence of separate sovereign states, states that then fail to ensure a system of substantive sovereignty that would guarantee the protection of all their citizens, that brings the refugee into being. The refugee 'problem' must therefore be seen within the current international

[29] Newman, 'Human Security', 247–8.

system in line with the communitarian idea of granting the refugee a subset of citizen rights in an attempt to reinstate her into the jurisdiction of a political community. Even while admitting that states are the root cause of the creation of refugees, we must seek responses within the boundaries of individual states. They are both the source of the 'problem' and the location of the 'solution'. Finding an external response would be inconceivable, since outside the world of nation-states there would be no refugees. We have no choice, therefore, but to accept the international arrangement and take action within it.

If the refugee's situation is exceptional, the response would seem to be to restore the individual to a state where her rights can be protected by normal state responsibilities. Refugee status constitutes the dissolution of 'social bonds', so 'unmaking refugees demands the creation or reestablishment of such bonds', the recreation of the state–citizen relationship under 'normal' conditions of good governance so as to 'repair the tear in the state system fabric by ensuring that no individual goes without membership in some state'.[30] Protection is not a new obligation being imposed on states; rather, it is offered when states fulfil the responsibilities that come with membership in international society. As Warner explains, 'the protection function is normal: it is the situation on which the function must operate that is extraordinary'.[31] In theory it should not be important whether a person exists as a member of a political community or finds herself, instead, outside the jurisdiction of a sovereign unit. But the problem is perhaps just that: *in theory* it should not be important whether an individual is inside or outside a state's jurisdiction, but the reality is different. We can readily accept that the conception of individual rights has been expanded, but should not forget that this has only taken place within the framework of the state.[32] A realistic approach to refugee rights should, therefore, acknowledge the existence of the present states system and attempt to formulate 'a workable ethics' of refugee policy within it – a 'global covenant' that seeks to accommodate human diversity and human imperfection while trying to uphold common humanity.[33] Just as security is perhaps 'not a good in and of itself but only in relation to that which it secures',[34] so refugee policy must be seen not as a good in and of itself, but in relation to the society of states in which it must be

---

[30] Aleinikoff, 'State-centred Refugee Law', 260.   [31] Warner, 'The Refugee State', 264.
[32] Weiner, 'Ethics', 172.   [33] Jackson, *The Global Covenant*, p. 400.
[34] Jackson-Preece, 'Ethnocultural Diversity', 3.

formulated. Advocating global justice and open borders in a world of states is idealistic – and of course in an ideal and just world the refugee would not exist, hence such an approach is also irrelevant to the real world problems we face. Further, global ethics are inherently solidarist while refugees may only exist in the pluralist world. Since the two are logically in opposition, a globally ethical refugee policy would appear to be unattainable.

We need, perhaps, to distinguish between personal morality and the application of such moral principles to public policy.[35] An individual might advocate granting refugee status and protection to all those apparently fleeing persecution, but state policy-makers cannot make the same moral choices because of the costs this would involve. There is, perhaps, a limit to which state actors can be expected to go against their interest and those of their political masters.[36] If the state is a human activity it will never be completely altruistic; international politics, and particularly that area of politics involving clashes between 'equally compelling yet potentially incommensurate values' such as national interests versus human rights, is all about 'hard choices'.[37] As Berlin noted, 'a world in which what we see as incompatible values are not in conflict is a world altogether beyond our ken'.[38] There cannot be an apolitical humanitarian solution to 'the politically charged events of mass human displacement [and] refugee protection is a process of balancing the needs of refugees and other displaced persons against the interests of states'.[39] We need, therefore, to reimagine the refugee and our responses to her, and where a state's interests clash with those of the refugee we must continue to seek a compromise between the is and the ought.

So if we are opting for the equivalent of arms control rather than disarmament, what does arms control look like in the refugee debate? Is it possible to find a way forward within the current system, admitting that the refugee protection regime will remain an imperfect mixture of the political and the humanitarian? Moving forward has to mean acknowledging that finding a balance between a wholly pluralist and a wholly solidarist response is both desirable and feasible. The pluralist suspicions of international society that action on behalf of refugees or

---

[35] Weiner, 'Ethics', 192.
[36] Joseph H. Carens, 'Realistic and Idealistic Approaches to the Ethics of Migration', *International Migration Review* 30, 1 (1996), 163.
[37] Jackson-Preece, 'Ethnocultural Diversity', 24.
[38] Berlin, *The Crooked Timber of Humanity*, p. 13.
[39] Hyndman, *Managing Displacement*, p. 3.

those destined soon to become refugees will be subversive of inter-state order can be reconciled with the solidarist project that holds state leaders to account if they decide not to take action to 'save strangers'.[40] At such times as the international community is impelled to intervene in the internal affairs of a sovereign state, it should be possible to reconcile national interests with humanitarian action to protect another state's citizens. Preventive action costs less than responding to a conflict once it is underway or clearing up once it is over via military action, humanitarian relief or reconstruction projects. Further, it is in a state's national interests to prevent a mass refugee movement that might otherwise end up on its territory, with all the associated risks of inse-curity and escalating regional violence. And intervention to provide protection shows a state to be a good, moral international actor who plays by the rules of international society; hence action can help foster good international relations. The slowly diminishing importance of state boundaries with respect to the concept of humanitarian interven-tion shows that the concept is gaining legitimacy in customary law, a concept that was largely undreamt-of in the pre-Second World War days of sacred sovereignty.

According to Boswell, the granting of protection to refugees need not be considered contrary to a state's national interests, and there are several ways in which citizens of western states could be encouraged to adopt a more liberal approach to refugee rights. Political leaders could help develop a sense of national identity of which a fundamental constituent and defining element is a liberal attitude towards refugees. This, she notes, is exactly what appears to be developing at EU level, with the shift from a control agenda to a more solidarist, protection-oriented discourse and the EU promoting itself as upholder of human and fundamental rights. Such proclamations can create a self-reinforcing dynamic and thus generate a virtuous circle of government action. It is neither helpful nor realistic to restrict states to a stark choice between a moral course of action and a self-interested one, as if the two are forever in conflict with one another. Instead, suggests Boswell, such conflict must be reconceived as a normal feature of international society in which diverse values coexist, and ways of realising both sets of claims can be explored.[41]

---

[40] Nicholas J. Wheeler, *Saving Strangers: Humanitarian Intervention in International Society* (Oxford University Press, 2000), pp. 309–10.
[41] Christina Boswell, *The Ethics of Refugee Policy* (Aldershot: Ashgate, 2005), pp. 150–7.

Gibney has also tried to move the debate forward by seeking a policy response that is at once ethically informed and politically relevant, recognising that 'governments operate within the structure of the modern state, find their capabilities politically constrained by democratic politics, and have only a limited ability to determine the costs of entrance policy in advance'.[42] His proposal is the development of the principle of humanitarianism, which implies that states have an obligation to assist refugees when the costs of doing so are low. This is significantly narrower in scope than an impartial theory that calls for states to help all those in need or to open their borders. As such, it recognises that states have national interests and priorities and does not ask them to override these by being totally altruistic, and so is likely to be more politically digestible.[43] According to Gibney, a key element of humanitarianism means pushing western states to increase resettlement quotas. This would provide more protection to refugees at low cost to governments, since it would reduce asylum-processing costs within country; avoid confusion between asylum-seekers and economic migrants by determining who is a 'genuine' refugee before they arrive; allow governments some degree of control over numbers; and indirectly ensure *non-refoulement* by extending protection to those most in need and not only to those who arrive at the borders of a state requesting asylum. Some of these measures would also promote more positive public attitudes towards refugees and the institution of asylum, such that the amount of protection provided at low cost could be maximised.[44]

A further option is the concept of temporary protection, which has emerged to partly fill the gap between the decline in the willingness of western states to grant asylum and the trend towards protection in the country of origin. The idea here is that refugees are given protection in host countries on the specific understanding that it is for a limited amount of time, and that once conditions in the country of origin return to normal they will be required to return home. Moving away from a universal refugee protection regime, temporary protection has a tendency to provide assistance on an ad hoc basis to specific groups of refugees. It was provided to Kosovar refugees in 1999, for example, a

---

[42] Matthew J. Gibney, *The Ethics and Politics of Asylum: Liberal Democracy and the Response to Refugees* (Cambridge University Press, 2004), p. 230.
[43] Gibney, *The Ethics and Politics of Asylum*, pp. 231, 234.
[44] Gibney, *The Ethics and Politics of Asylum*, pp. 231, 239, 244.

defined refugee group identity bounded by nationality. This bears remarkable resemblance to the responses tried by the international community in the inter-war period with Russian refugees, Armenian refugees and refugees from Germany, to cite some examples. In Hathaway's well-known reformulation of refugee protection, he noted how international refugee law currently falls short in two key ways: first, it puts the onus on the states in which an individual applies for asylum to provide full legal responsibility and *non-refoulement*, irrespective of the potential impact refugee flows may have on the receiving state and their national interests; and second, refugee protection is often a route to permanent immigration, which is difficult to reconcile with today's 'managed migration' policies. However, the 1951 Convention ensures *non-refoulement* but only while there is an ongoing risk of persecution, meaning that refugee law is in fact based on the idea of temporary protection rather than permanent immigration.[45] Indeed, supporters of temporary protection point out that the whole spirit of the 1951 Convention itself is temporary, since it is clearly spelt out in the cessation clauses that refugee status should end when the conditions that forced an individual to flee have come to an end.[46] Refugee law reformulated would therefore look like a generalised temporary protection system, and would regain its relevance by acting 'to reconcile the need for a secure and dignified refugee protection system to the legitimate interests of the countries in which refugees are sheltered'.[47] Promoters of temporary protection argue that it serves many purposes: that it is a way to address the emergency needs of mass groups of individuals who would fail to meet the criterion of individual persecution for refugee status under the 1951 Convention, thus filling a gap in the humanitarian protection regime; that states are more likely to act in the face of human suffering on a vast scale if they can do so on their own terms and not feel under a legal obligation to do so; and that in contemporary Europe's securitised environment in which asylum has become a source of political tension and levels of asylum applications are high, temporary protection quells the fears of the public by

---

[45] Hathaway, *Reconceiving International Refugee Law*, p. xviii.
[46] Article 1.C(5) holds that the terms of the 1951 Convention shall cease to apply to any person falling under the definition of refugee status set out in section A if 'he can no longer, because the circumstances in connexion with which he has been recognized as a refugee have ceased to exist, continue to refuse to avail himself of the protection of the country of his nationality'.
[47] Hathaway, *Reconceiving International Refugee Law*, p. xxvi.

convincing citizens that the arrangement is not permanent and that the refugees will not be allowed to become a 'burden'. States can therefore be comfortable in the knowledge that the displaced individuals will only remain on their territory for a defined period of time. It would be useful to explore the use of temporary protection further in the years to come. Since temporary protection status means the individual will return home, it can provide a useful link between *non-refoulement* and a durable solution.[48] As always, however, care would need to be taken to ensure that states do not use such a concept to avoid future responsibilities under international law, whereby temporary protection could merely 'offer political cover for states disenchanted with refugee law and seeking to escape the individual-rights paradigm'.[49]

Finally, as discussed in the previous chapter, regional protection should offer another means to bring together solidarist action with pluralist goals. Protection in regions of refugee origin could certainly turn out to be the most frequently applied tool in refugee protection policy in the coming years. Indeed, in terms of balancing state interests with humanitarian obligations, the idea of offering protection away from a state's territory is certainly attractive. It cannot be the case any longer that refugee status depends on the successful completion of a long and illicit journey. If the obligations of the 1951 Convention can be met outside the state–citizen–territory trinity and protection can be extended without relying on sovereign boundaries, this is a step to be welcomed. It could open the way for a new understanding of states' refugee protection duties and overcome many of the obstacles that today's policy environment faces, such as negative public reactions, expensive asylum processes and the difficulties of identifying refugees in mixed migratory flows.

Of course, if state attitudes towards refugees are constructed, then so too are states' declared absorption capacities and social costs of admitting refugees into their societies. The conceptual analysis of the refugee reminds us that refugees are creations of a system in which identities and labels matter and that it is possible to construct protection as being in line with states' identities and interests when certain conditions are in place. There are no simple, magic 'solutions' to a field in which

---

[48] Morten Kjaerum, 'Temporary Protection in Europe in the 1990s', *International Journal of Refugee Law* 6, 3 (1994), 444.

[49] Joan Fitzpatrick, 'Temporary Protection of Refugees: Elements of a Formalized Regime', *American Journal of International Law* 94, 2 (2002), 281.

pluralist interests and solidarist concerns blur and interweave so intricately, but recognition of this fact, coupled with the recognition – set out in this book – that the refugee is as old as the states system and that she will remain as long as the states system remains, should allow us to begin to view the refugee question differently.

The importance of the conceptual and historical analysis

The conceptual analysis of the refugee figure set out in this book has argued that the refugee is not the consequence of a breakdown in the system of separate nation-states, rather she is an inevitable if unintended part of international society. The refugee only exists in as much as modern political borders exist and try to organise peoples and territories among nation-states, entities that then fail to ensure respect for substantive sovereignty. It is a characteristic of sovereignty that the attempt to place all individuals within (homogeneous) territorial spaces will inevitably force some between the borders, into the gaps and spaces between states and thus outside the normal state–citizen–territory hierarchy. Sovereignty sorts and classifies, and refugees are created in the process. Refugees are the sign of a failure of individual governments to protect their citizens, as well as a failure of the international system as a whole – the failure to assign every individual to a state and protect them as citizens of that state. Of course, if all states were akin to western liberal democracies in the context of a wholly peaceful international climate, the number of refugee flows would be reduced. But the reality is that refugees occur in the gap between theory and practice: international society assumes states will protect their citizens but responds ineffectually when they fail to do so. Thus refugees highlight an inherent failure in the international states system, a way in which the system is always bound to fail. The refugee in part defies simple definition since she only makes sense in relation to her alter image – the citizen. She is both excluded and included, outside the system but necessary for the continuation of the system and therefore inside it. As such she is paradigmatically *in between*, somewhere in the middle of outside and inside.

Alongside this conceptual approach, this book's historical analyses of state practices in the refugee regime over the inter-war, Cold War and contemporary periods have highlighted various common themes. In terms of 'root causes', it is particularly apparent that there are specific similarities between the inter-war and contemporary periods. Whereas all three periods saw refugee movements created by violations of human rights, persecution by states and conflict between states, the inter-war and contemporary periods caused mass movements of refugees specifically by the breakdown of states and the break-up of empires, while the Cold War era saw the biggest numbers of refugees caused by liberation movements. The inter-war period sought to solve the refugee problem in accordance with a positive view of sovereignty, such that the answer was sought in constitutional guarantees of protection within the state. The Cold War period shifted to a negative view of sovereignty, whereby refugees were to be protected by external guarantees between states. The contemporary period has returned to a positive idea of sovereignty, with the state increasingly linked to causation of refugee flows by its failure, not its actions, and the international community putting more and more pressure on states that fail to protect their citizens by insisting on sovereignty as responsibility.

The criteria for granting asylum, intervening to protect refugees or providing aid in the contemporary period also resemble those of the inter-war period. In the 1920s and 30s international action was extended when refugees were of certain nationalities or ethnic groups. Racial, ethnic and national prejudices continue to dominate grounds for international protection today, such that states' interests once again play a key role in deciding when to extend protection. The big difference, of course, is the shift that has taken place from judging such racial, ethnic and national criteria on a group basis, as was the case in the inter-war period, to an individual basis as consolidated in the 1951 Convention. The Cold War period, on the other hand, concentrated on extending rescue to specific refugees in line with political objectives. Ideology and geopolitics were more important than issues of race, ethnicity, religion and nationality, which acted to portray an important image of rescuer to western opponents. Now there are fewer strategic points to earn, and instead public perceptions have become highly influential in the political domain.

Similarities between the periods in terms of the elements of the refugee protection regime itself are also evident. Since the refugee field became one of international cooperation there have been certain principles, norms and rules, both formal and informal, as regards the granting of assistance and asylum and finding other 'solutions' to reterritorialise the refugee. The regime has always constituted a space where sovereignty and humanitarianism overlap, such that the right to seek asylum has been evident from the outset, but not the right to be granted it. The principle of *non-refoulement* has been a defining factor of the regime since the 1951 Convention was adopted at the start of the Cold War, a principle which still acts to bridge the gap where the right to be granted asylum is missing. Further, UNHCR, like LNHCR, operates around one central High Commissioner with staff in Geneva and in the field working under a 'non-political' mandate. Perhaps most significantly, the regime under the League of Nations and the current one under the United Nations have both worked to formalise a distinct category for the refugee figure. Although the refugee question forms part of wider migration and immigration debates, intergovernmental regimes have helped afford the refugee specific legal protection, specific material assistance and a specific status within the society of states.

Finally, the refugee continues to be constructed in certain ways according to specific spatial and temporal factors. Just as the League of Nations and its associated refugee agencies had to construct the issue in a way that brought about a change in the interests and identities of states party to the refugee regime, so UNHCR continues to do. As Loescher has demonstrated, 'successful High Commissioners have convinced states to define their national interests in ways compatible with refugee needs' so that UNHCR not only acts as 'transmitter and monitor of refugee norms but [has] also socialized new states to accept the promotion of refugee norms domestically', playing upon the importance of their international image and the need to gain legitimacy from the international community.[50] UNHCR, like its inter-war predecessors, has not been merely a 'passive mechanism with no independent agenda of its own', but has become a 'purposeful actor in its own right with independent interests and capabilities'.[51] High Commissioners have seen that sovereignty and humanitarianism may be compatible 'in circumstances where sovereignty represents the best hope for the attainment of humanitarian objectives'.[52] Successive High Commissioners have understood that to make a positive impact in the field of refugee protection in a world of sovereign states, they have to convince states of the need to define and redefine national interests in line with the humanitarian requirements of international refugee protection. Exercising moral leverage on states has been one strategy; linking protection issues

[50] Loescher, *The UNHCR and World Politics*, pp. 5–6.
[51] Loescher, *The UNHCR and World Politics*, p. 6.
[52] Skran, *Refugees in Inter-war Europe*, p. 68.

to a state's material interests another. In the latter case, certain states have been willing to act in accordance with norms of protection where doing so meant receiving large quantities of humanitarian assistance to help failing economies. International organisations such as UNHCR or the EU construct and promulgate norms and ideas that act to influence and change state interests and identities and hence alter the refugee debate as a whole. While different people are now made refugees, the underlying reasons for and construction of responses to the 'problem' have not changed. Refugees were already tied up with security concerns and constructed as a threat to both state and societal security in the inter-war period. The refugee underscores the way identity and constructions of 'inside' and 'outside' within the modern European states system have not altered since the system was established.

Thus what comes to light is a real parallel between the construction, perpetuation and understanding of the refugee across the three key periods of refugee regimentation. Contemporary refugee debates are normatively the same as inter-war and Cold War debates; the concept of the refugee has not changed. Parallels between the periods serve to highlight the arbitrary nature of both borders and definitions of who is and who is not a refugee. If we acknowledge the relevance of earlier examples of refugee movements and responses of the international community to them, we can perhaps avoid reinventing the wheel. Certain aspects of our international imagining of the refugee will persist and thus some types of action that have been tried and tested in the past need not be tried again. Rather, it would be expedient to admit that the refugee is an inherent side-effect of the society of sovereign states, and to rethink both our statist definitions of her and our sovereign attempts to control her.

While there are commonalities that link the three periods, differences and divergences of course exist. One important distinction is that the Cold War era can also be seen as an exception to the understanding of the refugee in international society, and it was in this era of exception that the 1951 Convention was drawn up and the whole refugee protection regime consolidated. Just when the international community thought it was establishing a formal regime in 'normal' times to deal with 'abnormal' situations, it was actually attempting to stabilise a 'normal' and inevitable side-effect of the international system – refugees – during a time of exception – the Cold War era. The 1951 Convention was an endeavour, albeit unknown by regime actors, to end a phenomenon that cannot realistically be ended in the present international system of separate states. But this truth was masked by the fact that borders were locked, rather than being the changing, moving constructs that they naturally are, and politics was a bi-polar battle between East and West. Refugees served the specific political strategy of scoring points against Communist enemies and so were constructed and perceived in a different way from how they were perceived before and from how they would be perceived forty years later. The illusion of a solvable problem was shattered when the Cold War ended and mass flows of refugees began once again to annotate the international landscape. But the refugee issue had been born before the onset of the Cold War, and the mass refugee flows that ensued when Communism fell at the end of the 1980s were no different to those that Europe had witnessed in the 1920s and 30s. Refugees were an inevitable part of the turbulent war years, just as the contemporary period could not be rewritten without them. They were and still are the consequence of erecting political boundaries and failing to protect all individuals as citizens, hence pushing insiders outside.

The conceptual and historical analysis demonstrates that one individual in one political context in one particular political space will be recognised as a refugee, while a similar individual in a different political context who finds herself in a different political space will fail to be recognised as a refugee. In other words, there is, and always has been, a response and a non-response. Russian refugees of the 1920s attracted refugee status, some Cold War refugees such as the Hungarians in 1956 attracted refugee status, and some recent displaced individuals such as the Bosnians of 1999 attracted refugee status. But individuals will only be imagined specifically as 'refugees' if the political conditions are right. Many Jewish individuals of the 1930s failed to enter the legal domain of refugee protection. The hundreds of thousands of individuals who fled from Laos and Cambodia in the 1970s were largely excluded from the international protection regime. And today's 'asylum-seekers' who arrive in the EU from Iraq or Afghanistan will sometimes be excluded from the safe world of the refugee label. While the individual may cross the physical or imagined borders necessary for her to become a refugee, she can only do so if international society allows it. And this should provide us with lessons for the future. A non-response is not the answer to solving the refugee problem, because this is abandoning people whose fundamental human rights are being undermined. An examination of the refugee 'problem' from the beginnings of a mass phenomenon shows that there has been a continuation of help and non-help, response and non-response, taking notice and not taking notice, always depending on the international political climate and the individuals in question. And frequently the atrocities that meet refugees who cannot leave would have been prevented not only by a way out, but also by a response from the outside world showing the persecuting agent that such action is not acceptable, and that the international community will not stand by and watch if such action continues or threatened action starts. As Timothy Garton-Ash has observed, it was perhaps only after overpowering the Hungarian revolution of 1956 that Soviet leaders could be quite sure the West would not intervene militarily: 'Everyone knows that Russian tanks crushed that revolution, setting the pattern of Soviet responses (and Western non-responses) to East European revolutions for the next thirty years.'[53]

It is thus vitally important to understand the refugee in both her conceptual and historical contexts, linking the twenty-first-century 'asylum-seeker' to the inter-war displaced person and refusing to accept the refugee as a simple, pre-given figure. As Campbell writes, 'in considering the issue of where we go from here there is a tendency to uncritically accept a particular story of how we got to here'.[54] We must not forget the history tied up in today's refugee. The conceptual and historical analysis highlights that sovereignty has never been absolute, nor has humanitarianism ever been completely apolitical. International society continues to take an interest, albeit in a somewhat non-uniform manner, in the internal affairs of sovereign members of international society when the management of the state's internal affairs impinges upon the peaceful co-existence of states in the international system. As such, the refugee uncovers the proximity of the national and the international, the communitarian and the cosmopolitan, the pluralist and the solidarist. We must use this appreciation to push for new ways of studying international relations, new ways of looking at political identity and community, and new ways of analysing the individual in the international. By refusing to accept the refugee as a pre-given figure, we are forced to question ideas of inside and outside, belonging and not belonging, and otherness, movement and identity. In this way we are faced with the opportunity of changing our understanding of the

---

[53] Timothy Garton-Ash, *We the People: The Revolution of '89 Witnessed in Warsaw, Budapest, Berlin and Prague*, 2nd edn (London: Penguin, 1999), p. 47.

[54] Campbell, *Writing Security*, p. 17.

concept of the refugee and redesigning our responses to her. If we can admit that a different construction of the refugee is both possible and desirable, the way could be opened for a rethinking of the refugee and new policy options.

Like any subject of contemporary politics, the refugee field remains a field in continuous construction. Refugees will continue to spill over their designated borders and boundaries and the individual will continue to move within a cycle of displacement, wherein different ways of being forced to move from home interact with, influence and feed off one another in an unending succession of movement within, between and across borders. But the sooner we can understand the refugee domain as a space of possibility and a space to reimagine that which we have for too long taken as different, dangerous and unstable, the sooner we can begin to truly understand the refugee figure and respond accordingly. And this could mean a change of direction in the dangerous and unjust paths that millions of individuals have been forced to travel, and millions more will travel, across the globe in the foreseeable future.

Select Bibliography

Primary sources
Treaties and legal instruments

- Convention Relating to the International Status of Refugees (1933)
- Convention Concerning the Status of Refugees Coming from Germany (1938)
- Constitution of the International Refugee Organization (1946)
- Universal Declaration of Human Rights, *adopted* 10 December 1948 (U.N. Doc. A/810)
- European Convention for the Protection of Human Rights and Fundamental Freedoms, *opened for signature* 4 November 1950 (213 UNTS 221)
- United Nations Convention Relating to the Status of Refugees, *done* at Geneva on 28 July 1951 (189 UNTS 137)
- United Nations Protocol Relating to the Status of Refugees, *done* 31 January 1967 (606 UNTS 267)
- Organisation on African Unity (OAU) Convention Governing the Specific Aspects of Refugee Problems in Africa, *adopted* 10 September 1969 (UNTS no.14691)
- Cartagena Declaration on Refugees, *adopted* 19–22 November 1984
- Treaty on European Union (1992)

League of Nations
Official Records:

- *Monthly Summary of the League of Nations* (1921–40)
- *League of Nations Treaty Series* (1920–46)
- *Official Journal* (1922–39)

Reports by the High Commissioner for Refugees, the High Commissioner for Refugees Coming from Germany, and other League of Nations bodies:

- 'Conference on the Question of Russian Refugees: Resolutions Adopted by the Conference on August 24th, 1921', 1921 [L.N.1921.7]

- 'Armenian and Russian Refugee Problems: Report of the Fifth Committee to the Assembly', 1926 [L.N.IV.1926.12]
- 'Questions Concerning Armenian and Russian Refugees: Resolution Adopted by the Assembly', 1926 [L.N.IV.1926.18]
- 'Measures in Favour of Armenian and Russian Refugees: Report of the Fifth Committee to the Assembly', 1927 [L.N.IV.1927.13]
- 'Russian, Armenian, Assyrian, Assyro-Chaldean and Turkish Refugees: Report to the Ninth Ordinary Session of the Assembly', 1928 [L.N.VIII.1928.6]
- 'Russian, Armenian, Assyrian, Assyro-Chaldean and Turkish Refugees: Report of the Sixth Committee to the Assembly', 1929 [L.N.VII.1929.4]
- 'Russian, Armenian, Assyrian, Assyro-Chaldean and Turkish Refugees: Report to the Tenth Assembly', 1929 [L.N.VII.1929.2]
- 'Russian, Armenian, Assyrian, Assyro-Chaldean and Turkish Refugees: Report by the Secretary-General on the Future Organisation of Refugee Work', 1930 [L.N.XIII.1930.2]
- 'Report of the Intergovernmental Advisory Commission for Refugees on the Work of its Fifth Session', 1933 [L.N.V.1933.1]
- Committee on International Assistance to Refugees: 'Report by the Committee Submitted to the Council of the League of Nations', 1936 [L.N.XII.B.1936.1]
- 'International Assistance to Refugees, Report Submitted by the Sixth Committee to the Assembly', 1936 [L.N.XII.B.1936.12]
- 'Refugees Coming from Germany: Report Submitted to the Seventeenth Ordinary Session of the Assembly by the High Commissioner, Sir Neill Malcolm', 1936 [L.N.1936.12.B.6]
- 'Refugees Coming from Germany: Report Submitted to the Eighteenth Ordinary Session of the Assembly by the High Commissioner, Sir Neill Malcolm', 1937 [L.N.1937.12.B.2]
- 'International Assistance to Refugees: Report by Sir Herbert Emerson', 1939 [L.N.1939.12.B.1]

International Refugee Organization (IRO)

IRO Preparatory Commission documents, 1947
IRO General Council 1st–9th Sessions, 1948–52

UNHCR

- UNHCR EXCOM, 'Non-refoulement', Conclusion No. 6 (XXVIII), 1977
- 'Refugee Protection and International Migration', June 2006
- 'Addressing Mixed Migratory Movements: A 10-Point Plan of Action', June 2006
- '2005 Global Refugee Trends: Statistical Overview of Populations of Refugees, Asylum-seekers, Internally Displaced Persons, Stateless Persons, and Other Persons of Concern to UNHCR' (Geneva: UNHCR, 2006)

- 'Observations on the Communication from the European Commission to the Council and the European Parliament on Regional Protection Programmes'
- 'Basic Facts: Who Is a refugee?', http://www.unhcr.ch/cgi-bin/texis/vtx/basics

European Commission

- 'Communication on Integrating Migration Issues in the European Union's Relations with Third Countries', COM(2002) 703 final
- 'Communication on Towards More Accessible, Equitable and Managed Asylum Systems', COM(2003) 315 final
- 'Communication on the Managed Entry in the EU of Persons in Need of International Protection and Enhancement of the Protection Capacity of the Regions of Origin: Improving Access to Durable Solutions', COM(2004) 410 final
- 'Communication on Regional Protection Programmes', COM(2005) 388 final
- 'Communication on the Global Approach to Migration One Year On: Towards a Comprehensive European Migration Policy', COM(2006) 735 final

European Union

- Presidency Conclusions, European Council, Tampere, 15–16 October 1999
- Presidency Conclusions, European Council, Laeken, 14–15 December 2001
- Presidency Conclusions, European Council, Seville, 21–2 June 2002
- Presidency Conclusions, European Council, Thessaloniki, 19–20 June 2003
- Presidency Conclusions: 'The Hague Programme', European Council, Brussels, 4–5 November 2004
- Presidency Conclusions: 'The Global Approach to Migration: Priority Actions Focusing on Africa and the Mediterranean', European Council, Brussels, 15–16 December 2005

Secondary sources

Adelman, Howard, 'Modernity, Globalization, Refugees and Displacement', in Alastair Ager (ed.), *Refugees: Perspectives on the Experience of Forced Migration* (London and New York: Continuum, 1999), 83–110

Agamben, Giorgio, *Homo Sacer: Sovereign Power and Bare Life*, translation (Stanford University Press, 1998)

Albert, Mathias, Jakobson, David and Lapid, Yosef (eds.), *Identities, Borders, Orders: Rethinking International Relations Theory* (Minneapolis: University of Minnesota Press, 2001)

Aleinikoff, T. A., 'The Meaning of "Persecution" in United States Asylum Law', *International Journal of Refugee Law* 3, 1 (1991), 25–56

'State-centred Refugee Law: From Resettlement to Containment', in E. V. Daniel and J. R. Knudsen (eds.), *Mistrusting Refugees* (Berkeley: University of California Press, 1995), 257–78

Alston, Philip, Bustelo, Mara R. and Heenan, James, *The EU and Human Rights* (Oxford University Press, 1999)

Anderson, Benedict, *Imagined Communities: Reflections on the Origin and Spread of Nationalism* (London and New York: Verso, 1983)

Angell, Norman and Buxton, Dorothy Frances, *You and the Refugee: The Morals and Economics of the Problem* (Harmondsworth: Penguin Books, 1939)

Arboleda, Eduardo, 'The Cartagena Declaration of 1984 and Its Similarities to the 1969 OAU Convention – A Comparative Perspective', *International Journal of Refugee Law*, special issue (1995), 87–101

Arendt, Hannah, *The Origins of Totalitarianism* (New York: Harcourt, Brace and World, 1966)

'We Refugees', *Menorah Studies* 31 (1943), 69–77

Bauböck, Rainer, *Transnational Citizenship: Membership and Rights in International Migration* (Aldershot and Brookfield, Vt.: Edward Elgar, 1994)

Beck, Robert J., 'Britain and the 1933 Refugee Convention: National or State Sovereignty?', *International Journal of Refugee Law* 11, 4 (1999), 597–624

Bennett, Jon, 'Internal Displacement in Context: The Emergence of a New Politics', in Wendy Davies (ed.), *Rights Have No Borders: Worldwide Internal Displacement* (Geneva and Oslo: Global IDP Survey/Norwegian Refugee Council, 1998), 15–29

Bentwich, Norman, *The Refugees from Germany: April 1933 to December 1935* (London: Allen & Unwin, 1936)

Berlin, Isaiah, *The Crooked Timber of Humanity: Chapters in the History of Ideas* (London: John Murray, 1990)

Beyani, Chaloka, *Human Rights Standards and the Free Movement of People Within States* (Oxford University Press, 2000)

'State Responsibility for the Prevention and Resolution of Forced Population Displacements in International Law', *International Journal of Refugee Law* (special issue) 1995, 130–47

Bhabha, Jacqueline, 'Embodied Rights: Gender Persecution, State Sovereignty and Refugees', *Public Culture* 9, 1 (1996), 3–32

Boswell, Christina, 'The Conflict between Refugee Rights and National Interests: Background and Policy Strategies', *Refugee Survey Quarterly* 18, 2 (1999), 64–84

The Ethics of Refugee Policy (Aldershot: Ashgate, 2005)

'European Values and the Asylum Crisis', *International Affairs* 76, 3 (2000), 537–57

'The "External Dimension" of EU Immigration and Asylum Policy', *International Affairs* 79, 3 (2003), 619–38

Brown, Chris, 'Human Rights and Human Dignity: An Analysis of the "Human-Rights Culture" and its Critics', paper presented at the Universal Human Rights Conference, University of Otago, 3–6 July 1998

'World Society and the English School: An "International Society" Perspective on World Society', *European Journal of International Relations* 7, 4 (2001), 423–41

Brubaker, William Rogers, *Citizenship and Nationhood in France and Germany* (Cambridge, Mass.: Harvard University Press, 1992)

Immigration and the Politics of Citizenship in Europe and North America (Lanham and London: University Press of America, 1989)

Bull, Hedley, *The Anarchical Society: A Study of Order in World Politics*, 2nd edn (Basingstoke: Macmillan Press, 1995)

'The Grotian Conception of International Society', in Herbert Butterfield and Martin Wight (eds.), *Diplomatic Investigations: Essays in the Theory of International Politics* (London: Allen & Unwin, 1966), 51–73

and Watson, Adam, *The Expansion of International Society* (Oxford: Clarendon Press, 1984)

Buzan, Barry, *From International to World Society?: English School Theory and the Social Structure of Globalisation* (Cambridge University Press, 2004)

People, States and Fear: An Agenda for International Security Studies in the Post-Cold War Era, 2nd edn (Hemel Hempstead: Harvester Wheatsheaf, 1991)

Wæver, Ole and de Wilde, Jaap, *Security: A New Framework for Analysis* (Boulder, Colo. and London: Lynne Rienner Publishers, 1998)

Campbell, David, *Writing Security: United States Foreign Policy and the Politics of Identity* (Minneapolis: University of Minnesota Press, 1992)

Camus-Jacques, Genevieve, 'Refugee Women: The Forgotten Majority', in Gil Loescher and Laila Monahan (eds.), *Refugees and International Relations* (Oxford: Clarendon Press, 1989), 141–57

Caney, Simon, George, David and Jones, Peter (eds.), *National Rights, International Obligations* (Boulder, Colo.: Westview Press, 1996)

Carens, Joseph H., 'Realistic and Idealistic Approaches to the Ethics of Migration', *International Migration Review* 30, 1 (1996), 156–70

Castel, Jacqueline R., 'Rape, Sexual Assault and the Meaning of Persecution', *International Journal of Refugee Law* 4 (1992), 39–56

Cederman, Lars-Erik, 'Exclusion Versus Dilution: Real or Imagined Trade-off?', in Lars-Erik Cederman (ed.), *Constructing Europe's Identity: The External Dimension* (Boulder, Colo.: Lynne Rienner Publishers, 2001), 233–62

Ceyhan, Ayse and Tsoukala, Anastassia, 'The Securitization of Migration in Western Societies: Ambivalent Discourses and Politics', *Alternatives* 27 supplement (2002), 21–39

Checkel, Jeffrey T., 'The Constructivist Turn in International Relations Theory', *World Politics* 50, 2 (1998), 324–48

Chimni, B. S., 'The Geopolitics of Refugee Studies: A View from the South', *Journal of Refugee Studies* 11, 4 (1998), 350–74

Christensen, Arne Piel and Kjaerum, Morten, 'Refugees and Our Role in the European House', *International Journal of Refugee Law* 2 (1990), 323–33

Cobban, Alfred, *The Nation State and National Self-Determination* (London: Collins, 1969)

Cohen, Roberta and Deng, Francis M. (eds.), *The Forsaken People: Case Studies of the Internally Displaced* (Washington D.C.: Brookings Institution Press, 1998) (eds.), *Masses in Flight: The Global Crisis of Internal Displacement* (Washington D.C.: Brookings Institution Press, 1998)

Cole, Tim, 'Constructing the "Jew", Writing the Holocaust: Hungary 1920–45', *Patterns of Prejudice* 33, 3 (1999), 19–27

Collingwood, R. G., *The New Leviathan or Man, Society, Civilization and Barbarism* (Oxford: Clarendon Press, 1947)

Colombey, Jean (ed.), *Collection of International Instruments and Other Legal Texts Concerning Refugees and Displaced Persons* (Geneva: Division of International Protection of the Office of the United Nations High Commissioner for Refugees, 1995)

Colson, Elizabeth, 'Forced Migration and the Anthropological Response', *Journal of Refugee Studies* 16, 1 (2003), 1–18

Connolly, William E., *The Terms of Political Discourse*, 2nd edn (Princeton University Press, 1983)

Crisp, Jeff, *Policy Challenges of the New Diasporas: Migrant Networks and Their Impact on Asylum Flows and Regimes*, New Issues in Refugee Research, Working Paper No. 7 (Geneva: UNHCR, 1999)

'Refugee Protection in Regions of Origin: Potential and Challenges', http://www.migrationinformation.org/Feature/displau.cfm?id=182 (December 2003)

Crowley, John, 'Locating Europe', in Kees Groenendijk, Elspeth Guild and Paul Minderhoud (eds.), *In Search of Europe's Borders* (The Hague: Kluwer Law International, 2003), 27–44

Darst, Robert, 'Guaranteed Human Beings for Sale: The Collaborative Relocation of Jews from Axis Europe, 1933–45', *Journal of Human Rights* 1, 2 (2002), 207–30

Deng, Francis M., 'Flocks Without Shepherds: The International Dilemma of Internal Displacement', in Wendy Davies (ed.), *Rights Have No Borders: Worldwide Internal Displacement* (Geneva and Oslo: Global IDP Survey/ Norwegian Refugee Council, 1998), 1–13

'In the Vacuum of Sovereignty: The International Challenge of Internal Displacement', *Forced Migration Review* 17 (2003), 56

Diez, Thomas and Whitman, Richard, 'Analysing European Integration: Reflecting on the English School – Scenarios for an Encounter', *Journal of Common Market Studies* 40, 1 (2002), 43–67

Dillon, Michael, 'The Scandal of the Refugee: Some Reflections on the "Inter" of International Relations and Continental Thought', in David Campbell and Michael J. Shapiro (eds.), *Moral Spaces: Rethinking Ethics and World Politics* (Minneapolis: University of Minnesota Press, 1999), 92–124

Dowty, Alan and Loescher, Gil, 'Refugee Flows as Grounds for International Action', *International Security* 21, 1 (1996), 43–71

Dulles, Eleanor Lansing, *Berlin: The Wall Is not Forever* (Chapel Hill: University of North Carolina Press, 1967)

Dunne, Timothy, 'International Society. Theoretical Promises Fulfilled', *Cooperation and Conflict* 30, 2 (1995), 125–54

Inventing International Society: A History of the English School (Basingstoke: Macmillan Press, 1998)

'The Social Construction of International Society', *European Journal of International Relations* 1, 3 (1995), 367–89

Feller, Erika, Türk, Volker and Nicholson, Frances (eds.), *Refugee Protection in International Law: UNHCR's Global Consultations on International Protection* (Cambridge University Press, 2003)

Finnemore, Martha, 'Constructing Norms of Humanitarian Intervention', in Peter J. Katzenstein (ed.), *The Culture of National Security: Norms and Identity in World Politics* (New York: Columbia University Press, 1996), 153–85

Fitzpatrick, Joan, 'Temporary Protection of Refugees: Elements of a Formalized Regime', *American Journal of International Law* 94, 2 (2002), 279–306

Flemming, Thomas, *The Berlin Wall: Division of a City* (Berlin: be.bra-verlag, 2000)

Forsythe, David P., *Human Rights in International Relations* (Cambridge University Press, 2000)

Fox, John P., 'German and European Jewish Refugees, 1933–45: Reflections on the Jewish Condition under Hitler and the Western World's Response to Their Expulsion and Flight', in Anna Bramwell (ed.), *Refugees in the Age of Total War* (London: Unwin Hyman, 1988), 69–85

Frelick, Bill, 'Displacement Without End: Internally Displaced Who Can't Go Home', *Forced Migration Review* 17 (2003), 10–12

'Down the Rabbit Hole: The Strange Logic of Internal Flight Alternatives', *World Refugee Survey 1999: An Assessment of Conditions Affecting Refugees, Asylum Seekers, and Internally Displaced Persons* (Washington D.C.: United States Committee for Refugees, 1999), 22–9

'Preventing Refugee Flows: Protection or Peril?', *World Refugee Survey 1993* (Washington D.C.: United States Committee for Refugees, 1993), 5–13

Frost, Mervyn, 'Migrants, Civil Society and Sovereign States: Investigating an Ethical Hierarchy', *Political Studies* 46 (1998), 871–85

Garton-Ash, Timothy, *We the People: The Revolution of '89 Witnessed in Warsaw, Budapest, Berlin and Prague*, 2nd edn (London: Penguin, 1999)

Geddes, Andrew, 'Europe's Border Relationships and International Migration Relations', *Journal of Common Market Studies* 43, 4 (2005), 787–806

Gellner, Ernest, *Nations and Nationalism* (Oxford: Blackwell, 1983)

Gibney, Mark, *Strangers or Friends: Principles for a New Alien Admission Policy* (Westport, Conn.: Greenwood Press, 1986)

Gibney, Matthew J., *The Ethics and Politics of Asylum: Liberal Democracy and the Response to Refugees* (Cambridge University Press, 2004)

Goodwin, Robert E., 'What Is so Special about Our Fellow Countrymen?', *Ethics* 98 (1988), 663–86

Goodwin-Gill, Guy, *International Law and the Movement of Persons Between States* (Oxford University Press, 1978)

The Refugee in International Law, 2nd edn (Oxford: Clarendon Press, 1996)

Gordenker, Leon, *Refugees in International Politics* (Beckenham: Croom Helm, 1987)

Gowlland-Debbas, Vera (ed.), *The Problem of Refugees in the Light of Contemporary International Law Issues* (The Hague, Boston and Cambridge, Mass.: M. Nijhoff, 1996)

Grahl-Madsen, Atle, *The Status of Refugees in International Law, volume I: Refugee Character, volume II: Asylum, Entry and Sojourn* (Leiden: Sijthoff, 1966 and 1972)

Greatbach, Jacqueline, 'The Gender Difference: Feminist Critiques of Refugee Discourse', *International Journal of Refugee Law* 1 (1989), 518–27

Gwynn, Robin D., *Huguenot Heritage: The History and Contribution of the Huguenots in Britain* (London: Routledge & Kegan Paul, 1985)

Haddad, Emma, 'The Refugee: The Individual Between Sovereigns', *Global Society* 17, 3 (2003), 297–322

'Refugee Protection: A Clash of Values', *International Journal of Human Rights* 7, 3 (2003), 1–26

Hammar, Tomas, *Democracy and the Nation State: Aliens, Denizens and Citizens in a World of International Migration* (Aldershot: Avebury; Brookfield, Vt.: Gower, 1990)

Harrell-Bond, B. E. and Voutira, E., 'Anthropology and the Study of Refugees', *Anthropology Today* 8, 4 (1992), 6–10

and Leopold, Mark, 'Counting the Refugees: Gifts, Givers, Patrons and Clients', *Journal of Refugee Studies* 5, 3/4 (1992), 205–25

Hassner, Pierre, 'Refugees: A Special Case for Cosmopolitan Citizenship?', in Danièle Archibugi, David Held and Martin Köhler (eds.), *Re-imagining Political Community: Studies in Cosmopolitan Democracy* (Cambridge: Polity Press, 1998), 273–86

Hathaway, James C., *The Law of Refugee Status* (Toronto: Butterworths, 1991)

(ed.), *Reconceiving International Refugee Law* (Cambridge, Mass.: Kluwer Law International, 1997)

Hein, Jeremy, 'Refugees, Immigrants and the State', *Annual Review of Sociology* 19 (1993), 43–59

Hinsley, F. H., *Sovereignty*, 2nd edn (Cambridge University Press, 1986)

Hirschfeld, Gerhard (ed.), *Exile in Britain: Refugees from Hitler's Germany* (New Jersey: Berg Publishers, 1984)

Hirschman, Albert, 'Exit, Voice, and the Fate of the German Democratic Republic: An Essay in Conceptual History', *World Politics* 45, 2 (1993), 173–202

Hobsbawm, Eric J., *Nations and Nationalism since 1780: Programme, Myth, Reality*, 2nd edn (Cambridge University Press, 1992)

Hoffmann, Stanley, *Duties Beyond Borders: On the Limits and Possibilities of Ethical International Politics* (New York: Syracuse University Press, 1981)

Holborn, Louise W., *The International Refugee Organization. A Specialized Agency of the United Nations: Its History and Its Work, 1946–1952* (Oxford University Press, 1956)

Huysmans, Jef, 'Defining Social Constructivism in Security Studies: The Normative Dilemma of Writing Security', *Alternatives* 27 supplement (2002), 41–62

'The European Union and the Securitization of Migration', *Journal of Common Market Studies* 38, 5 (2000), 751–77

'Migrants as a Security Problem: Dangers of "Securitizing" Societal Issues', in Robert Miles and Dietrich Thränhardt (eds.), *Migration and European Integration: The Dynamics of Inclusion and Exclusion* (London: Pinter Publishers, 1995), 53–72

'The Question of the Limit: Desecuritisation and the Aesthetics of Horror in Political Realism', *Millennium: Journal of International Studies* 27, 3 (1998), 569–89

Hyndman, Jennifer, *Managing Displacement: Refugees and the Politics of Humanitarianism* (Minneapolis: University of Minnesota Press, 2000)

Indra, Doreen M., 'Gender: A Key Dimension of the Refugee Experience', *Refuge* 6 (1987), 3–4

Institute for Public Policy Research, *Asylum in the UK: An IPPR Fact File* (London: IPPR, 2003)

International Commission on Intervention and State Sovereignty, *The Responsibility to Protect* (Ottawa: International Development Research Centre, 2001)

International Committee of Jurists, *The Berlin Wall: A Defiance of Human Rights* (Geneva: 1962)

International Refugee Organization, *The Facts about Refugees* (Geneva: 1948)
Migration from Europe: A Report of Experience (Geneva: 1951)
SOS: A Call from 100,000 of Your Neighbours in Distress (Geneva: 1950)

Jackson, Robert, *The Global Covenant: Human Conduct in a World of States* (Oxford University Press, 2000)
Quasi-States: Sovereignty, International Relations and the Third World (Cambridge University Press, 1990)
(ed.), *Sovereignty at the Millennium* (Oxford: Political Studies Association/ Blackwell Publishers, 1999)

Jackson-Preece, Jennifer, 'Ethnic Cleansing as an Instrument of Nation-State Creation: Changing State Practices and Evolving Legal Norms', *Human Rights Quarterly* 20 (1998), 817–42
'Ethnocultural Diversity as a Security Dilemma', paper presented at the International Ethics of Security Conference, University of British Columbia, Vancouver, 5–7 April 2001
'Minority Rights in Europe: From Westphalia to Helsinki', *Review of International Studies* 23 (1997), 75–92
National Minorities and the European Nation-States System (Oxford: Clarendon Press, 1998)

Janowsky, Oscar I. and Fagen, Melvin M., *International Aspects of German Racial Policies* (Oxford University Press, 1937)

Jepperson, Ronald L., Wendt, Alexander and Katzenstein, Peter J., 'Norms, Identity, and Culture in National Security', in Peter J. Katzenstein (ed.), *The Culture of National Security: Norms and Identity in World Politics* (New York: Columbia University Press, 1996), 33–75

Johnson, T. F., *International Tramps. From Chaos to Permanent World Peace* (London: Hutchinson & Co., 1938)

Joly, Danièle, 'Convergence towards a Single Asylum Regime: A Global Shift of Paradigm', *International Journal of Human Rights* 5, 4 (2001), 1–17

(ed.), *Global Changes in Asylum Regimes* (Basingstoke: Palgrave Macmillan, 2002) 'Odyssean and Rubicon Refugees: Toward a Typology of Refugees in the Land of Exile', *International Migration* 40, 6 (2002), 3–22

Jones, Peter, 'Individuals, Communities and Human Rights', *Review of International Studies* 26 (2000), 199–215

Rights (Basingstoke: Macmillan Press, 1994)

Joppke, Christian, 'How Immigration Is Changing Citizenship: A Comparative View', *Ethnic and Racial Studies* 22, 4 (1999), 629–52

Immigration and the Nation-State: The United States, Germany and Great Britain (Oxford University Press, 1999)

Kapp, Yvonne and Mynatt, Margaret, *British Policy and the Refugees, 1933–1941* (London: Frank Cass, 1997)

Karatani, Rieko, 'How History Separated Refugee and Migrant Regimes: In Search of Their Institutional Origins', *International Journal of Refugee Law* 17, 3 (2005), 517–41

Kee, Robert, *Refugee World* (Oxford University Press, 1961)

Keeton, George W., *National Sovereignty and International Order: An Essay upon the International Community and International Order* (London: Peace Book Company, 1939)

Kibraeb, Gaim, 'Revisiting the Debate on People, Place, Identity and Displacement', *Journal of Refugee Studies* 12, 4 (1999), 384–410 and responses 411–28

Kjaerum, Morten, 'Temporary Protection in Europe in the 1990s', *International Journal of Refugee Law* 6, 3 (1994), 444–56

Klusmeyer, Douglas B. and Aleinikoff, Thomas Alexander, *From Migrants to Citizens: Membership in a Changing World* (Washington, D.C.: Carnegie, 2000)

Knudsen, Tonny Brems, 'The English School of International Relations and the International Society Approach', in Kerstin Imbusch and Klaus Segbers (eds.), *International Relations Online* (Free University of Berlin, 2002), 1–20

Kohn, Hans, *The Idea of Nationalism: A Study in Its Origins and Background* (New York: The Macmillan Company, 1946)

Korn, David A., *Exodus Within Borders: An Introduction to the Crisis of Internal Displacement* (Washington D.C.: Brookings Institution Press, 1998)

Koser, Khalid, 'New Approaches to Asylum?', *International Migration* 39, 6 (2001), 85–99

and Van Hear, Nicholas, 'Asylum Migration and Implications for Countries of Origin', United Nations University, World Institute for Development Economics Research Discussion Paper No. 2003/20

Kostakopoulou, Dora, 'The "Protective Union": Change and Continuity in Migration Law and Policy in Post-Amsterdam Europe', *Journal of Common Market Studies* 38, 3 (2000), 497–518

Krasner, Stephen D., *Sovereignty: Organized Hypocrisy* (Princeton University Press, 1999)

Kristeva, Julia, *Strangers to Ourselves* (New York: Columbia University Press, 1991)

Kubálakova, Vendulka, Onuf, Nicholas and Kowert, Paul, *International Relations in a Constructed World* (New York: M. E. Sharpe, 1998)

Kuhlman, Tom, 'Towards a Definition of Refugees', Refugee Studies Centre Documentation Centre, University of Oxford (1991)

Kulischer, Eugene M., *Europe on the Move: War and Population Changes, 1917–47* (New York: Columbia University Press, 1948)

Kunz, Egon F., 'Exile and Resettlement: Refugee Theory', *International Migration Review* 15, 1 (1981), 42–51

'The Refugee in Flight: Kinetic Models and Forms of Displacement', *International Migration Review* 7, 2 (1973), 125–46

Kushner, Tony and Knox, Katherine, *Refugees in an Age of Genocide: Global, National and Local Perspectives during the Twentieth Century* (London: Frank Cass, 1999)

Lakoff, George, *Women, Fire and Dangerous Things: What Categories Reveal about the Mind* (University of Chicago Press, 1987)

Lammers, Ellen, *Refugees, Gender and Human Security: A Theoretical Introduction and Annotated Bibliography* (Utrecht: International Books, 1999)

Landgren, Karin, 'Safety Zones and International Protection: A Dark Grey Area', *International Journal of Refugee Law* 8, 3 (1995), 416–32

Lavenex, Sandra, *The Europeanisation of Refugee Policies: Between Human Rights and Internal Security* (Aldershot: Ashgate, 2001)

'The Europeanization of Refugee Policies: Normative Challenges and Institutional Legacies', *Journal of Common Market Studies* 39, 5 (2001), 851–74

'Shifting Up and Out: The Foreign Policy of European Immigration Control', *West European Politics* 29, 2 (2006), 329–50

and Uçarer, Emek M., 'The External Dimension of Europeanization: The Case of Immigration Policies', *Cooperation and Conflict* 39, 4 (2004), 417–43

League of Nations Union, *The Covenant Explained for Speakers and Study Circles* (London: 1919)

Lee, Luke T., 'Internally Displaced Persons and Refugees: Toward a Legal Synthesis?', *Journal of Refugee Studies* 9, 1 (1996), 27–42

Loescher, Gil, *Beyond Charity: International Cooperation and the Global Refugee Crisis* (Oxford University Press, 1993)

'Introduction: Refugee Issues in International Relations', in Gil Loescher and Laila Monahan (eds.), *Refugees and International Relations* (Oxford University Press, 1989), 1–33

Refugee Movements and International Security, Adelphi Paper 268, International Institute for Strategic Studies (London: Brassey's, 1992)

'Refugees: A Global Human Rights and Security Crisis', in Tim Dunne and Nicholas J. Wheeler (eds.), *Human Rights in Global Politics* (Cambridge University Press, 1999), 233–58

The UNHCR in World Politics: A Perilous Path (Oxford University Press, 2001)

Lohrmann, Reinhard, 'Migrants, Refugees and Insecurity. Current Threats to Peace?', *International Migration*, 38, 4 (2000), 3–22

London, Louise, 'Whitehall and the Refugees: the 1930s and the 1990s', *Patterns of Prejudice* 34, 3 (2000), 17–26

Luoma-aho, Mika, 'Carl Schmitt and the Transformation of the Political Subject', *The European Legacy* 5, 5 (2002), 703–16

Macartney, C. A., *National States and National Minorities* (Oxford University Press, 1934)

MacIver, R. M., *The Modern State* (Oxford University Press, 1926)

Malkki, Liisa H., 'Citizens of Humanity: Internationalism and the Imagined Community of Nations', *Diaspora* 3, 1 (1994), 41–68

'National Geographic: The Rooting of Peoples and the Territorialization of National Identity Among Scholars and Refugees', *Cultural Anthropology* 7, 1 (1992), 24–44

Purity and Exile: Violence, Memory, and National Cosmology among Hutu Refugees in Tanzania (University of Chicago Press, 1995)

'Refugees and Exile: From "Refugee Studies" to the National Order of Things', *Annual Review of Anthropology* 24 (1995), 495–523

'Speechless Emissaries: Refugees, Humanitarianism, and Dehistoricization', *Cultural Anthropology* 11, 3 (1996), 377–404

Manners, Ian, 'Normative Power Europe: A Contradiction in Terms?', *Journal of Common Market Studies* 40, 2 (2002), 235–58

Marrus, Michael R., *The Unwanted: European Refugees in the Twentieth Century* (Oxford University Press, 1985)

Martin, D., 'The Refugee Concept: On Definitions, Politics, and the Careful Use of a Scarce Resource', in H. Adelman (ed.), *Refugee Policy: Canada and the United States* (Toronto: York Lanes Press, 1991), 30–51

Martiniello, Marco (ed.), *Migration, Citizenship and Ethno-National Identities in the European Union* (Aldershot: Avebury, 1995)

Mayall, James (ed.), *The Community of States: A Study in International Political Theory* (London: Allen & Unwin, 1982)

Nationalism and International Society (Cambridge University Press, 1990)

World Politics: Progress and Its Limits (Cambridge: Polity, 2000)

Merritt, Richard L. and Merritt, Anna J., *Living with the Wall: West Berlin, 1961–1985* (Durham, N.C.: Duke University Press, 1985)

Mertus, Julie, 'The State and the Post-Cold War Refugee Regime: New Models, New Questions', *International Journal of Refugee Law* 10, 3 (1998), 321–48

Miller, David, *On Nationality* (Oxford University Press, 1995)

Miller, J. D. B., *The World of States: Connected Essays* (London: Croom Helm, 1981)

Miller, Mark J., 'International Migration in Post-Cold War International Relations', in Bimal Ghosh (ed.), *Managing Migration: Time for a New International Regime?* (Oxford University Press, 2000), 27–47

Mills, Kurt, 'Permeable Borders: Human Migration and Sovereignty', *Global Society* 10, 2 (1996), 77–106

Morgan, Roger, 'A European "Society of States" – But Only States of Mind?', *International Affairs* 76, 3 (2000), 559–74

Nadig, Aninia, 'Human Smuggling, National Security, and Refugee Protection', *Journal of Refugee Studies* 15, 1 (2002), 1–25

Nardin, Terry, *Law, Morality, and the Relations of States* (Princeton University Press, 1983)

Newland, Kathleen, 'Ethnic Conflict and Refugees', *Survival* 35, 1 (1993), 81–101

Newman, Edward, 'Human Security and Constructivism', *International Studies Perspectives* 2 (2001), 239–51

Nicholson, Frances and Twomey, Patrick M. (eds.), *Refugee Rights and Realities: Evolving International Concepts and Regimes* (Cambridge University Press, 1999)

Norwood, Frederick A., *Strangers and Exiles: A History of Religious Refugees*, vol. I (Nashville and New York: Abingdon Press, 1969)

Nyers, Peter, 'Emergency or Emerging Identities? Refugees and Transformations in World Order', *Millennium: Journal of International Studies* 28, 1 (1999), 1–26

Ogata, Sadako, *The Turbulent Decade: Confronting the Refugee Crises of the 1990s* (New York: W. W. Norton & Company, 2005)

Osiander, Andreas, *The States System of Europe, 1640–1990* (Oxford University Press, 1994)

Phuong, Catherine, 'The Concept of "Effective Protection" in the Context of Irregular Secondary Movements and Protection in Regions of Origin', *Global Migration Perspectives* 26 (April 2005), http://www.gcim.org/en/ir_gmp.html

   'Internally Displaced Persons and Refugees: Conceptual Differences and Similarities', *Netherlands Quarterly of Human Rights* 18, 2 (2000), 215–29

Plender, Richard, *International Migration Law* (Leiden: A. W. Sijthoff, 1972)

Proudfoot, Malcolm J., *European Refugees 1939–1952: A Study in Forced Population Movement* (London: Faber, 1957)

Rae, Heather, *State Identities and the Homogenisation of Peoples* (Cambridge University Press, 2002)

Rajaram, Prem Kumar, 'Exile and Desire: Refugees, Aesthetics and the Territorial Borders of International Relations', unpublished Ph.D thesis, London School of Economics (2002)

   'Humanitarianism and Representations of the Refugee', *Journal of Refugee Studies* 15, 3 (2002), 247–64

Reus-Smit, Christian, 'Imagining Society: Constructivism and the English School', *British Journal of Politics and International Relations* 4, 3 (2002), 487–509

Richmond, Anthony H., 'Social Theories of International Migration: The Case of Refugees', *Current Sociology* 36, 2 (1988), 7–25

Roberts, Adam, 'More Refugees, Less Asylum: A Regime in Transformation', *Journal of Refugee Studies* 11, 4 (1998), 375–95

Roth, Brad R., *Governmental Illegitimacy in International Law* (Oxford University Press, 2000)

Roucek, Joseph, 'Minorities: A Basis of the Refugee Problem', *Annals of the American Academy of Political and Social Science* 203 (1939), 1–17

Rubenstein, Maître J. L., 'The Refugee Problem', *International Affairs* 15, 5 (1936), 716–34

Rudge, Philip, 'Europe in the 1990s: The Berlin Walls of the Mind', *World Refugee Survey – 1989 in Review* (Washington D.C.: United States Committee for Refugees, 1989), 20–4

'Reconciling State Interests with International Responsibilities: Asylum in North America and Western Europe', *International Journal of Refugee Law* 10, 1/2 (1998), 7–20

Ruggie, John Gerard, *Constructing the World Polity: Essays on International Institutionalisation* (London and New York: Routledge, 1998)

Rystad, Göran, *The Uprooted: Forced Migration as an International Problem in the Post-War Era* (Lund University Press, 1990)

Said, Edward W., *Reflections on Exile and Other Literary and Cultural Essays* (London: Granta, 2001)

Salomon, Kim, *Refugees in the Cold War* (Lund University Press, 1991)

Sassen, Saskia, *Guests and Aliens* (New York: The New York Press, 1999)

Losing Control? Sovereignty in an Age of Globalization (New York: Columbia University Press, 1996)

Schechtman, Joseph B., *European Population Transfers 1939–1945* (Oxford University Press, 1946)

Seton-Watson, Hugh, *Nations and States: An Enquiry into the Origins of Nations and the Politics of Nationalism* (London: Methuen, 1977)

Shacknove, Andrew E., 'From Asylum to Containment', *International Journal of Refugee Law* 5, 4 (1993), 516–33

'Who Is a Refugee?', *Ethics* 95 (1985), 274–84

Shore, Cris, 'Inventing the "People's Europe": Critical Approaches to European Community "Cultural Policy"', *Man* 28, 4 (1993), 779–800

Sieghart, Paul, *The Lawful Rights of Mankind: An Introduction to the International Legal Code of Human Rights* (Oxford University Press, 1985)

Simpson, Sir John Hope, *The Refugee Problem: Report of a Survey* (Oxford University Press and the Royal Institute of International Affairs, 1939)

Singer, Peter and Renata, 'The Ethics of Refugee Policy', in Mark Gibney (ed.), *Open Borders? Closed Societies? The Ethical and Political Issues* (New York and London: Greenwood, 1989), 111–30

Sjöberg, Tommie, *The Powers and the Persecuted: The Refugee Problem and the Intergovernmental Committee on Refugees (IGCR), 1938–1947* (Lund University Press, 1991)

Skran, Claudena, *Refugees in Inter-war Europe: The Emergence of a Regime* (Oxford: Clarendon Press, 1995)

Smith, Anthony D., *National Identity* (London: Penguin Books, 1991)

Nationalism and Modernism: A Critical Survey of Recent Theories of Nations and Nationalism (New York: Routledge, 1998)

Theories of Nationalism (New York: Holmes and Meier, 1983)

Smith, Steve, 'New Approaches to International Relations', in John Baylis and Steve Smith (eds.), *The Globalization of World Politics: An Introduction to International Relations* (Oxford University Press, 1997), 165–190

Soguk, Nevzat, *States and Strangers: Refugees and Displacements of Statecraft* (Minneapolis: University of Minnesota Press, 1999)

Sørensen, Jens Magleby, *The Exclusive European Citizenship: The Case for Refugees and Immigrants in the European Union* (Aldershot: Avebury, 1996)

Soysal, Yasemin, *Limits of Citizenship: Migrants and Postnational Membership in Europe* (University of Chicago Press, 1994)

Steinbock, Daniel J., 'The Refugee Definition as Law: Issues of Interpretation', in Frances Nicholson and Patrick M. Twomey (eds.), *Refugee Rights and Realities: Evolving International Concepts and Regimes* (Cambridge University Press, 1999), 13–36

Stevens, Austin, *The Dispossessed* (London: Barrie & Jenkins, 1975)

Stoessinger, John G., *The Refugee and the World Community* (Minneapolis: University of Minnesota Press, 1956)

Sutkloff, Marie, *The Life Story of a Russian Exile. The Remarkable Experience of a Young Girl: Being an Account of Her Peasant Childhood in Prison, Her Exile to Siberia and Escape from There*, translated by Gregory Yarros (London: William Heinemann, 1915)

Sztucki, Jerzyv, 'Who Is a Refugee? The Convention Definition: Universal or Obsolete?', in Francis Nicholson and Patrick M. Twomey (eds.), *Refugee Rights and Realities: Evolving International Concepts and Regimes* (Cambridge University Press, 1999), 55–80

Tabori, Paul, *The Anatomy of Exile: A Semantic and Historical Study* (London: Harrap and Co., 1972)

Thompson, Dorothy, *Refugees: Anarchy or Organization?* (New York: Random House, 1938)

Tuitt, Patricia, *False Images: The Law's Construction of the Refugee* (London: Pluto Press, 1996)

'Rethinking the Refugee Concept', in Frances Nicholson and Patrick M. Twomey (eds.), *Refugee Rights and Realities: Evolving International Concepts and Regimes* (Cambridge University Press, 1999), 106–18

Uçarer, Emek M., 'Managing Asylum and European Integration: Expanding Spheres of Exclusion?', *International Studies Perspectives* 2 (2001), 288–304

United Nations Department of Public Information, *Magna Carta for Refugees* (New York, 1951)

What the United Nations Is Doing for Refugees and Displaced Persons (New York: 1948)

United Nations, Office of the United Nations High Commissioner for Refugees, *The State of the World's Refugees, 1995: In Search of Solutions* (Oxford University Press, 1995)

The State of the World's Refugees, 1997–8: A Humanitarian Agenda (Oxford University Press, 1997)

The State of the World's Refugees, 2000: Fifty Years of Humanitarian Action (Oxford University Press, 2000)

The State of the World's Refugees: Human Displacement in the New Millennium (Oxford University Press, 2006)

United States Office of Public Affairs, Department of State, *The IRO: Background Summary* (March 1947)

Van Selm-Thorburn, Joanne, *Refugee Protection in Europe: Lessons of the Yugoslav Crisis* (The Hague: Martinus Nijhoff, 1998)

Vernant, Jacques, *The Refugee in the Post-War World* (London: Allen & Unwin, 1953)

Vincent, R. J., *Human Rights and International Relations* (Cambridge University Press, 1986)

Wæver, Ole, 'European Security Identities', *Journal of Common Market Studies* 34 (1996), 103–32

Buzan, Barry, Kelstrup, Morten and Lemaitre, Pierre, *Identity, Migration and the New Security Agenda in Europe* (London: Pinter Publishers, 1993)

Walker, R. B. J., *Inside / Outside: International Relations as Political Theory* (Cambridge University Press, 1993)

Wallace, Rebecca M., *Refugees and Asylum: A Community Perspective* (London: Butterworths, 1996)

Walzer, M., *Spheres of Justice* (New York: Basic Books, 1983)

Ward, Ian, 'Identifying the European Other', *International Journal of Refugee Law* 14, 2/3 (2002), 219–37

Warner, Daniel, 'The Refugee State and State Protection', in Frances Nicholson and Patrick M. Twomey (eds.), *Refugee Rights and Realities: Evolving International Concepts and Regimes* (Cambridge University Press, 1999), 253–68

'Voluntary Repatriation and the Meaning of Return to Home: A Critique of Liberal Mathematics', *Journal of Refugee Studies* 7, 2/3 (1994), 160–74

'We Are All Refugees', *International Journal of Refugee Law* 4, 3 (1992), 365–72

Watson, Adam, *The Evolution of International Society: A Comparative Historical Analysis* (London: Routledge, 1922)

Weiner, Myron, 'Bad Neighbors, Bad Neighborhoods: An Inquiry into the Causes of Refugee Flows, 1969–1992', in Rainer Münz and Myron Weiner (eds.), *Migrants, Refugees, and Foreign Policy: US and German Policies toward Countries of Origin* (Providence and Oxford: Berghahn Books, 1997), 183–229

'Ethics, National Sovereignty and the Control of Immigration', *International Migration Review* 30, 1 (1996), 171–97

The Global Migration Crisis: Challenges to States and to Human Rights (New York: HarperCollins Publishers, 1995)

(ed.), *International Migration and Security* (Boulder, Colo.: Westview Press, 1993)

'Security, Stability, and International Migration', in Sean M. Lynn-Jones and Steven E. Miller (eds.), *Global Dangers: Changing Dimensions of International Security* (Massachusetts: The MIT Press, 1995), 183–218

Weis, Paul, 'The Convention of the Organisation of African Unity Governing the Specific Aspects of Refugee Problems in Africa', *Human Rights Journal* 3, 3 (1970), 3–70

The Refugee Convention, 1951: The Travaux Préparatoires Analysed, with a Commentary by Dr Paul Weis (Cambridge University Press, 1995)

Weiss, Thomas G. and Pasic, Amir, 'Reinventing UNHCR: Enterprising Humanitarians in the Former Yugoslavia, 1991–1995', *Global Governance* 3 (1997), 41–57

Wendt, Alexander, 'Anarchy Is What States Make of It', *International Organisation* 46, 2 (1992), 391–425

'Collective Identity Formation and the International State', *American Political Science Review* 88, 2 (1994), 384–96

Social Theory of International Politics (Cambridge University Press, 1999)

Westin, Charles, 'Regional Analysis of Refugee Movements: Origins and Response', in Alastair Ager (ed.), *Refugees: Perspectives on the Experience of Forced Migration* (London and New York: Continuum, 1999), 24–45

Wheeler, Nicholas J., *Saving Strangers: Humanitarian Intervention in International Society* (Oxford University Press, 2000)

and Dunne, Timothy, 'Hedley Bull's Pluralism of the Intellect and Solidarism of the Will', *International Affairs* 72, 1 (1996), 91–107

White, Alan R., *Rights* (Oxford: Clarendon Press, 1984)

Wight, Martin, *International Theory: The Three Traditions* (Leicester University Press, 1991)

Systems of States (Leicester University Press, 1977)

'Western Values in International Relations', in Herbert Butterfield and Martin Wight (eds.), *Diplomatic Investigations: Essays in the Theory of International Politics* (London: Allen & Unwin, 1966), 89–131

Woodbridge, George, *UNRRA: The History of the United Nations Relief and Rehabilitation Administration* (New York: Columbia University Press, 1950)

Wyman, Mark, *Displaced Persons: Europe's Displaced Persons, 1945–1951* (Ithaca, New York: Cornell University Press, 1998)

Xenos, Nicholas, 'Refugees: The Modern Political Condition', in Michael J. Shapiro and Alker Hayward (eds.), *Challenging Boundaries: Global Flows, Territorial Identities* (Minneapolis: University of Minnesota Press, 1996), 233–46

Zehfuss, Maja, *Constructivism in International Relations: The Politics of Reality* (Cambridge University Press, 2002)

Zetter, Roger, 'Labelling Refugees: Forming and Transforming a Bureaucratic Identity', *Journal of Refugee Studies* 4, 1 (1991), 39–62

'Refugees and Refugee Studies – A Label and an Agenda', *Journal of Refugee Studies* 1, 1 (1988), 1–6

Zolberg, Aristide R., 'The Formation of New States as a Refugee-generating Process', *Annals of the American Academy of Political and Social Science* 467 (1983), 24–38

Zolberg, Aristide R., Suhrke, Astri and Aguayo, Sergio, *Escape from Violence: Conflict and the Refugee Crisis in the Developing World* (Oxford University Press, 1989)

Index

CAMBRIDGE STUDIES IN INTERNATIONAL RELATIONS